C A L L B A C K

GET THE CALLBACK

The Art of Auditioning for Musical Theatre

Second Edition

Jonathan Flom

ROWMAN & LITTLEFIELD
Lanham • Boulder • New York • London

Published by Rowman & Littlefield
A wholly owned subsidiary of The Rowman & Littlefield Publishing Group, Inc.
4501 Forbes Boulevard, Suite 200, Lanham, Maryland 20706
www.rowman.com

Unit A, Whitacre Mews, 26-34 Stannary Street, London SE11 4AB

British Library Cataloguing in Publication Information Available

Library of Congress Cataloging-in-Publication Data

Names: Flom, Jonathan, 1977– author.
Title: Get the callback : the art of auditioning for musical theatre / Jonathan Flom.
Description: Second edition. | Lanham : Rowman & Littlefield, [2016] | Includes bibliographical references and index.
Identifiers: LCCN 2015050297 (print) | LCCN 2015051275 (ebook) | ISBN 9781442266599 (cloth : alk. paper) | ISBN 9781442266605 (pbk. : alk. paper) | ISBN 9781442266612 (electronic)
Subjects: LCSH: Musicals–Auditions. | Acting–Auditions.
Classification: LCC MT956 .F56 2016 (print) | LCC MT956 (ebook) | DDC 792.602/8–dc23 LC record available at http://lccn.loc.gov/2015050297

♾™ The paper used in this publication meets the minimum requirements of American National Standard for Information Sciences—Permanence of Paper for Printed Library Materials, ANSI/NISO Z39.48-1992.

Printed in the United States of America

CONTENTS

Foreword by Joy Dewing, CSA   vii

Acknowledgments   ix

Introduction   xi

1   Before the Audition   1

2   A Detailed Guide to Building the Actor's Repertoire Book   19

3   Walking through the Audition   49

4   Callbacks   79

5   Job Offers   97

6   Headshots, Résumés, and Cover Letters   107

7   Auditioning for Colleges   139

Conclusion: Some Dos and Don'ts   159

Appendix A: Repertoire Genre Lists   163

Appendix B: Sample Repertoire by Actor Type   171

Appendix C: Recommended Reading   179

Glossary   181

Index   185

About the Author   193

FOREWORD

Throughout your career as a performer, you will never experience a shortage of advice about how to audition successfully. In New York City and beyond, there are classes, workshops, books, podcasts, blogs, and social media accounts that will tell you what to do in the audition studio and how to do it. The book you're holding in your hands right now would be mere kindling in a massive bonfire of audition books, if you became understandably overwhelmed with the glut of audition advice and decided to torch them all. Except for one thing—Jonathan Flom works from the unique perspective of an academic who is *also* an artist, creator, collaborator, and sponge. He works hard to stay not just relevant but ahead of the trends that shift so quickly and unpredictably in this industry. I've never known anyone to ask so many questions, pick so many brains, investigate deeper, or explore further. He isn't interested in packaging his students into little molded plastic boxes and shipping them off to New York City in LaDucas and jewel-toned dresses to stand in line with carbon copies of themselves. He is interested in discovering the person inside the performer, and bringing their humanity to life in the audition room. How refreshing!

In the previous edition of this book, readers collected a lot of great advice that was absolutely on point *for its time*. But things change rapidly in the theatre business, and we are moving away from the technicalities of auditions and toward authenticity, individuality, and personality. Jonathan could have easily sat back and continued to sell his book as it was; but instead, he

picked it apart with a fine-toothed comb and updated the outdated information, redirected the focus toward the heart and soul of auditioning, and
softened the more technical aspects of it. The result, I hope, is that actors
who incorporate Jonathan's advice will walk into my audition room with
confidence, openness, and a well-developed (and constantly evolving) sense
of themselves as both performers and as *human beings* with a story to tell.

If you've picked up this book, you've taken an important step: You've acknowledged that there is room for improvement in your auditions and you
are seeking guidance on how to move forward. Whether you're starting out
or you're a seasoned auditioner, take a moment to respect yourself for being wherever you are *right now* in your career. You don't know everything;
but guess what? It's not your job to know everything. It's your job to know
YOU and to be the foremost authority on what YOU bring to the process.
You have no control over what "They" think or do or say behind the table.
You have no control over whether you are "right" for the project or not.
But whether you realize it or not, you have immense power in the audition
room. A prepared, open-hearted, passionate, skilled, intelligent actor with
the right tools can light up a room and make my heart beat a little faster.
Really, you can't imagine how thrilling it is to be on the other side of the
table when everything comes together and you have the right actor at the
right time and place with the right material.

In order to create this kind of magic, you're going to need a little guidance. Just as Dorothy and friends had what they needed all along, you have
everything you need within you to get that callback. You just need to unlock
it; and the keys to that lock are in these pages. What you do with them is
up to you.

Joy Dewing
casting director
Joy Dewing Casting

*Joy Dewing, CSA, is a casting director in New York City who handles
casting for Broadway, Off Broadway, regional theatre, dance companies,
and multiple national tours. She serves on the board of directors for the
Casting Society of America and cochairs the Diversity Committee. Joy and
her associates travel to the nation's top universities and training programs
to discover the next generation of our industry's most talented performers.
www.joydewingcasting.com.*

ACKNOWLEDGMENTS

This first edition of this book was a joyous project for me because I love the theatre and I love the audition process. The second edition was even more exhilarating because I can look back on what I wrote and marvel at how much I've learned since I first created this guide. However, neither version would have been possible without the continuing support of my friends, mentors, and family, not to mention the producers who have hired me, the actors I have hired (and not hired), my students, and my friends in the casting business, who have instilled in me the knowledge and experiences I have set forth in these pages. It is my privilege to thank the following people specifically for their contributions:

First Edition:

- Mark Olsen and Lori Sessions for their suggestions and encouragement
- Ed Linderman for teaching me the joy of auditioning
- Cary Libkin for taking a young director under his wing years ago
- Penn State School of Theatre faculty for all the training and the constant support
- Mary Saunders and Mollye Otis for tips from the voice experts
- Tom Albert, Susan Russell, and Todd Courson for helping to shepherd the book to publishers

- Melissa Carlile-Price, Morgan Faulkner, and Shaina Taub for their stories
- Julie Foster, Michele Dunleavy, Kimberlee Johnson, Zachary Durand, Tom Albert, Carolyn Coulson-Grigsby, and Sharon Durand for being readers
- My Shenandoah Conservatory students for being my guinea pigs
- Renée Camus for making this project a reality

Second Edition:

- Joy Dewing for her casting wisdom and professional support and encouragement
- Alex Brightman for his professional audition insight
- VP Boyle for helping me understand the irreverent "Zen" of auditioning
- Sheri Sanders for showing my students and me how to truly Rock the Audition
- Lynne Kurdziel Formato for her beautiful contribution to my dance audition advice
- Stephen Ryan at Rowman & Littlefield for continuing to support my projects
- Matthew Edwards for teaching me how the voice works (and for being the Simon to my Garfunkel . . . or the Garfunkel to my Simon? I can never tell who's who)
- Jenna Pinchbeck for contributing photos and headshot wisdom (www .jennapphotography.com)
- Joey Chancey for his fantastic advice from the musical director's chair
- Christopher Castanho, Emily Lynne, Lauren Monteleone, Maranda Rossi, Doug Shapiro, and Tamara Young for sharing the contents of their audition books for readers' consumption
- My global colleagues at Baardar, Balettakademien, Det Danske Musicalakademi, Shu-Te, MTS, and WAAPA, for welcoming me like a rock star and letting me work with your students
- Hopscotch Coffee Roasters for the daily fuel and workspace
- My family for their unending support and love

INTRODUCTION

When I first set out to write *Get the Callback* in 2007, I was teaching at a small state college in northeastern Vermont, far removed from what I would consider civilization. I had a great deal of time on my hands, few distractions, and the energy of a freshly minted MFA director who wanted to make his mark on the world of theatre education. In addition to my graduate training, I had professional experience directing theatre and coaching auditions in New York as well as Chicago, so I thought I knew a lot. I certainly had no shortage of opinions, many of which seemed to be widely supported by my colleagues, as the success of the first edition would indicate.

However, in the rather short interim since I was able to give my proud parents a copy of their son's first book, I have been restlessly itching for a redo. As I went back into this manuscript, I realized several things about the original work and about myself.

For starters, much of the advice set forth in the first edition is dryly academic and aimed toward the young, novice performer who needs to know the very basics of how auditions work. I don't think there's anything inherently wrong with that in and of itself, but when I tried to assign this book as a text for my junior-level students in the pre-professional training program at Shenandoah Conservatory a couple of years later, their general response was something like, "Yeah, we know all this." So I fell short of my goal to make this a book for professionals as well as young artists.

Second, we must acknowledge that this business changes daily. What's trendy now is overdone tomorrow. What's irritating today may very well be a welcome throwback next week. Therefore, for me to endeavor to suggest specific repertoire is a disservice to my readers if I don't offer a fresh update from time to time. Over the last few years, I've questioned some students' audition material choices only to be told that they got the ideas from *my book*! So clearly, it was time to revisit what I recommend as repertoire. (Perhaps some day I'll get a digital resource together to continuously update this section of the book.)

Third, the dry, technical approach to auditioning, including the formal slate, is really passé now. I have grown increasingly concerned that if my book continued to circulate, I would be responsible for misleading young actors into inauthentic auditions because they followed the step-by-step method I laid out. So it was definitely time to offer some new advice.

Finally, after running a major musical theatre program for over eight years, continuing to expand my network of agent and casting director contacts in the big cities, and getting myself into professional audition rooms as much as I possibly can, I realize just how much new information I have learned since this book first hit the shelves only six short years ago. I've been a virtual sponge, soaking up new knowledge everywhere I can, from Broadway directors, producers, and casting directors, to entrepreneurs and business people. The person writing this new introduction is not the same person who wrote the previous one.

All that is to say that I am grateful for all of the people who have continued to teach and inspire me; I'm grateful that I have been open to receive new ideas and information freely; and I'm grateful for the opportunity to offer the new, more insightful edition of *Get the Callback* that you now hold in your hands (or on your eReader!).

This edition of the book is truly delivered from the perspective of how professional musical theatre auditions work. If you are a high school student or you are teaching high school students, I urge you to hold to the same standards of professional preparation. The bar has been raised so high for admissions to competitive college programs that in most cases knowing how to conduct oneself like a professional actor will often make the difference between one performer being accepted and another equally talented young person being denied.

This book also comes with the added punch of my recent years of exploring the business of branding and marketing and how those entrepreneurial approaches can enhance an actor's auditions. You'll hear me mention brand (and of course, plug my other book, *Act Like It's Your Business*) and authenticity throughout the course of the chapters with great frequency. Having a strong sense of self is a key factor in an actor's effort to be memorable and successful in the audition room.

And speaking of success in the audition room, let's talk about the catchy title of this book for a moment. I still love the idea of the callback being a more realistic, tangible goal than getting a job; however, I have come to realize that auditions can be immensely successful without an actor receiving a callback at the end of the day. Preparing as much as possible and delivering an earnest, sincere performance in the audition room is completely within your control. Receiving an invitation to a second or third audition is not. So another major mind shift in this edition of the book will be focusing on what is in your control and letting go of what isn't. Hopefully you will find it empowering to turn your attention to those factors that you can own and to release the burden of trying to "get it right" or show them what "they want to see." Getting a callback is great. Getting a job is even better. But let's begin by focusing on having a good time in auditions and delivering our best, most authentic selves.

As you work through this book, you may find that some of the information is new to you. Some of it may be review of things you already know and hold to be true, while other parts may be contrary to what you have experienced or been taught. Just remember that art is subjective. While I would like to tell you that everything I write is fact—I am a *professor*, therefore, I am an authority—obviously, that is not the case. (I mean, I just admitted to you that I was creating a second edition because I felt the need to correct so much of the last version of this book.) I encourage you to read the chapters with an open heart and an open mind and look for what is useful and applicable to you. At the end of the day, auditioning for theatre should be a deeply personal experience, and in order to get really good at it, you'll have to be sensitive to what works for *you* and what doesn't, and you must be able to adapt and grow in order to reach your maximum potential.

Whatever you do, remember to *have fun*! This business is hard work, and if you don't love it, it can really eat you alive. Try to find the daily joy in auditioning so that it doesn't suck your soul—it is possible, believe me. You just have to remind yourself sometimes why you began doing this and what first drew you to performing. Feel free to contact me if you have questions or find yourself stuck. Cheers, merde, and break a leg.

❶

BEFORE THE AUDITION

HOLDING THE BABY

You probably know that a director's job begins long before the first day of casting. By the time the notices are posted, the director has spent months, sometimes years, of her life preparing for the moment when she will start meeting actors. I always equate the casting of actors in a show with the idea of babysitting a newborn child. The play is the director's baby. She has invested time and passion and love into helping the little project develop. Often, there are also producers who are investing large sums of money as well. When audition time arrives, the director must decide whom she trusts to "hold the baby." Are you trustworthy and reliable? Will you help foster the child's development and ensure success?

Choosing actors is an equal mix of excitement and angst: the director may find the perfect person, or she may have to settle for something other than her vision. An actor should be sensitive to the director's position in regards to the audition process. Realize that no director in his or her right mind hopes that you will come into the room and fail. We are all hoping that you walk in and blow us all away! We want you to be exactly what we envisioned; better yet, we want you to show us that you can be much better than we imagined. Unfortunately with the success of television singing shows such as *American Idol*, *The X Factor*, and *The Voice*, the general populous has come to believe that the audition process involves a certain entertainment factor that accompanies flop auditions. Part of those shows' ratings depends on humiliating terrible singers publicly, and so people think that's what happens in all auditions. The reality is theatre and film/television producers have spent a great deal of money on renting a studio, hiring an accompanist, and staffing the whole process; your failure helps them not one iota. The creative team relies on your ability to soar and be successful in the audition room. The director may be more nervous than you, in fact. You may not need the job, but she *needs* to cast the show.

All that said, you must prove that you are worthy of holding the baby. The only surefire way to do that is to prepare. Prepare for anything and everything. When you walk in the door, you must communicate to the production team that you are not only talented enough for the role but you are also tenacious, enthusiastic, professional, and above all authentic. Composer Ed Linderman instructs students to "convince the people behind the table that putting you in their show will make them look good." I cannot think of better advice to offer an actor. It's completely unselfish. And it's the absolute opposite of the typical "I need a job" mentality with which most actors regard auditions.

Obviously, training is of the utmost importance for survival in the theatre. A performing artist, in particular a musical theatre performer, must be a well-trained actor, singer, and dancer to compete in today's market. And while this book is in no way intended to be a book on acting, singing, or dance technique, I can offer some sound advice that will enhance your overall audition presentation package: your "you" show.

First of all, *act everything*. Do not for a moment think that acting is for the monologue and reading auditions, and leave your vocal and dance skills to handle everything else. We want to see you invest fully in the character you are portraying whether the story you are telling is through dance, spoken word, or sung lyrics. This is, after all, what good musical theatre is about. Assuming you are taking scene study classes in high school, college, or in a city somewhere, you should be sure to apply everything you are learning about acting and being truthful to every song you sing and every piece of choreographed movement you execute. Furthermore, to that end, I highly recommend *A Practical Handbook for the Actor* by Melissa Bruder et al. (Vintage, 1986). It lays out in simple and concise terms a vocabulary and a technique for actors at any level.

Second, continued vocal training and coaching is of the utmost importance all the way through one's career. Once you learn a technique for breath, posture, and healthy voice function (and you must), you need to practice regularly under guidance. Performing in shows and auditioning is not enough, since no one will be attending to your vocal needs and issues directly, apart from the musical director, who is only concerned about how you sing the particular score on which you are working. You need to invest time and money in someone who will help you continue to grow and develop as a singer, and who will hopefully help you learn to infuse acting into your song presentation. Not to mention that having a vocal coach to play piano for you eliminates the trap of original cast recordings. But we will discuss that in more detail soon.

Finally, take dance classes. Take any dance class you can. Musical theatre was once known for its integration of traditional ballet technique in the age of Agnes de Mille, and classical ballet has seen a recent resurgence in the hands of Warren Carlyle and Joshua Bergasse, among others. Later, Jerome Robbins became the predominant Broadway choreographer, employing more jazz dance style, which is continued in the work of Susan Stroman and Andy Blankenbuehler. Bob Fosse created a unique, isolation/movement–based dance technique that infiltrated the ranks of Broadway shows in the 1970s, and we continue seeing his work recreated on the professional stage to this day. Tap has always been part of the musical theatre vocabulary, from Gower Champion to Randy Skinner. And now, more and more frequently, shows are infusing blends of modern, urban, and cultural dance styles into their productions. The bottom line is this: the more you know, the better off you will be. You may not consider yourself a great dancer, but I promise you that if you want a career in musical theatre, having a solid (and constantly growing) set of dance fundamentals will be invaluable to you along your path. So take a social dance class. Learn some modern. Why not go to the local town hall on swing or salsa dance lesson night? Do video research on the history and chronology of Broadway choreographers and their work (*everything* is available on YouTube!). And again, act the heck out of every piece of choreography you are asked to execute.

The Idol Truth

I think the popularity of reality "talent" shows such as *American Idol* has created a vast misperception as to the nature and purpose of auditioning. People's (a cappella) auditions are put on display for judgment and mockery by the three stern judges. Ratings are particularly high when a tone-deaf ignoramus is humiliated for public enjoyment. However, I assure you this is not what you should expect to encounter in the real world of auditions, professional or amateur.

This is not to say you won't have frustrating or uncomfortable experiences along the way, but by and large, auditions are a means to an end. A director or artistic team wishes to find the ideal cast for their project, and when you walk in the room they hope you will wow them.

You will almost always find that piano accompaniment will be provided (unless otherwise stated in the casting ad), so you should not prepare to sing a cappella. Once I actually had a young girl show up at an audition and sing unaccompanied with her iPod playing in her ears. This is not the best choice by far! Even for community, high school, and other amateur auditions, you should do your best to follow the guidelines set out in this book and look professional.

INVESTING IN YOUR CAREER

As I mentioned before, and as you'll hear over and over again, a career in the arts is an investment. You cannot hope to be successful if you are unwilling to spend the time and money it takes to compete. Assuming you have already committed to classes in acting, singing, and dancing, your next move is to get yourself a fantastic headshot. The headshot can range in price from as low as $250 to upward of $1,000. While the amount of money you spend on photos is not necessarily in direct proportion to the quality of the shots, it is nonetheless too important a factor in your career to leave in the hands of an amateur photographer.

I cannot tell you the number of times a student has asked me to look at her new "headshots"—pictures that her father took in the backyard—and advise which one she should use. My answer is always "None." A photographer requires a very specific understanding of the theatre industry to shoot actors' headshots. While you may look extremely pretty or handsome in the pictures your cousin took with her new digital camera, chances are your pictures will not even come close to being in the same class as the myriad others that come across a director's desk during the casting process. And, chances are, your unprofessional shots will wind up in the express lane to the "round file."

Now being completely realistic, it is silly to imagine a high school student auditioning for colleges spending the kind of money that a seasoned professional would spend on photos, especially considering that the younger you are, the more you will change, and the more frequently you will need to get new headshots. However, an actor at any level with professional aspirations should get herself at least a minimally passable headshot. Although some colleges and community theatre auditions will not require it, it is another way of giving you a professional edge and showing that you are serious and committed to your career as a performer. In a later chapter, I will go more in depth on what to look for in a headshot. But for now, let us agree that it is a necessary and logical expense. Along with the headshot, of course, comes the résumé. I will discuss the art of crafting a polished résumé in a later chapter as well.

Finally, you'll need your materials for a repertoire book, which I will discuss in detail in the next chapter. And I think every serious actor should also have a journal or a blank book. This way, you can keep track of every director, casting director, choreographer, and producer you audition for. You should make a note of every project you go in for: who was behind the table, what you sang or what monologue you performed, and any reaction you received from them, including whether or not they called you back. This way, when you go in for those artists again, you will know what works or what doesn't work. It will show signs of a savvy, professional performer.

FINDING THE WORDS TO SAY

One of the most common questions I am asked by students of all ages is how and where to find good material. As far as finding monologues is concerned, I will offer first this single suggestion: *Get rid of the monologue books.* The best thing you can do as an aspiring actor is to be reading and seeing plays constantly. This is where you will find your sources for audition pieces. Go to the theatre and bring a scratch pad with you. Sit in a bookstore with a great drama section and read, read, read. Even if you consider yourself "just" a musical theatre performer, you will need monologues ready at the helm at all times. Believe it or not, some musical theatre auditions call for monologues as well as songs.

Monologue books are generally filled with contentless performance pieces. The characters are not fully developed. More often than not, the speeches are either designed to bring the house down with laughter or to extract painful tears from the listener as the character talks about his dead best friend, sibling, or parent. And generally, these pieces fail on either front: The comedic ones are almost never funny, and the only thing painful about the sad ones is that they seem to go on forever.

If you are serious about being an actor, you need to search out plays that contain roles that are appropriate to your specific age and type. You need to find plays that speak to you somehow, so that you can fully invest in an understanding of the character and his world. You should be able to discuss in detail the needs and actions of any character whom you are portraying, and the only way this is possible is if the monologue is part of a fully developed play that you have read and comprehended.

Admittedly, some directors do not consider monologue book pieces to be as great a pet peeve as I do. Doing one will not necessarily keep you from being cast. However, coming in with an appropriate piece from a real play will only enhance your appearance of being a professional and increase the odds of the director wanting to work with you. *It will give you an edge.*

If you feel you must use a monologue book as a source of age-appropriate character material, be sure the speech is from an actual play, and read the play before performing the piece. Avoid using monologues from musicals, especially turning song lyrics or poetry into spoken dialogue. And for goodness sake, do not write your own monologue!

You may have noticed that all my talk of monologues has stipulated that they be from plays. I am being very specific about that. Other common sources of monologues for young actors include films, television episodes, and Internet websites. Again, there are some directors who won't care what the material is, so long as you perform it well; however, many theatre practitioners are very particular about actors choosing material from dramatic literature. So in order to avoid unpleasant reactions, why not just find all your source material in plays? There are certainly enough out there to give you limitless options.

The Internet often leads you to more contentless pieces written as performance art, similar to the monologue book. And the danger in film and television monologues is that you will be performing a piece indelibly connected with the specific actor who originated the role on film. You'll either be imitating her or not living up to how she delivered the speech. Either way, I feel it's not a risk worth taking. As Broadway audition coach VP Boyle says, those kinds of pieces have a "price tag." You need to determine whether the material is worth the price tag that accompanies it.

When it comes to finding music, I offer similar counsel. Shy away from anthologies and collections of *Great Songs for Musical Theatre Whatevers* as your primary sources. Go see musicals, read libretti (musical theatre scripts), find characters for which you are castable and sing their songs. The anthologies in and of themselves are not as bad as monologue books—in fact, they can be quite helpful tools for finding published sheet music. Here's the trap, though: Too often, actors rely on the books alone to be their sources of material. They do not understand what the play is about or who the character is (e.g., the 17-year-old girl who sings "Broadway Baby," a song from *Follies* written for a woman in her 70s). Like the bad monologues, these audition songs become contentless, and thus they are poor choices.

In conjunction with the dangers of the anthology, let me also warn you about the trap of original cast recordings. Many performers rely on the cast album to learn their music for auditions. I can offer you several reasons why this is a bad idea. First of all, you are not learning the song; rather, you are learning a particular actor's version of that song. Even if that actor sings the piece note perfect (which is not usually the case), he still has his own nuances and interpretations. We can assume he has made his own character choices, which will then inform his delivery of the song. You are much more likely to sing the song as you learned it, through that particular artist's style, as opposed to the literal way it is notated on the page (I have yet to hear a song from Stephen Schwartz's *Wicked* in an audition—all I've heard are imitations of Idina Menzel and Kristin Chenoweth). Furthermore, you will often find that the keys are changed from the original score when they are published in vocal selection and anthology books. All too often, actors learn a song along with a CD only to discover *in the audition room* that their vocal selections book is written in a key way too high or way too low for them. Embarrassing, I assure you.

This all relates back to my insistence that a career in the arts involves expenditures galore. You must be willing to pay a coach or an accompanist to sit down and play through all of your music with you (unless you play piano yourself, another very valuable skill). You can then employ your sight-reading skills and your recording device of choice to make this process much easier and more efficient. Experience tells me that this is the only truly reliable way to learn music and avoid humiliation of the sort I just mentioned.

As long as you are willing to learn your music directly from the written page, I will retract my admonition to avoid cast recordings, and I will instead suggest them as another valuable way of finding material. When I am discovering new musicals, I like to sit down with the libretto and the cast recording and listen to the songs as I come to them in my reading. However, once I am committed to directing or performing in a project, I cease listening to the recording to avoid its influencing my own personal artistic choices. This is the path I recommend to you.

Whether you are just beginning to collect repertoire material or you have a six-inch-thick binder full of music, I would suggest that you consider creating two compilations: Let us call them your "A" book and your "B" book. The "A" book is the one that goes everywhere with you (a performer should never be without music; you never know when a performance opportunity may arise). This is the book that is not too heavy to schlep around in a backpack or briefcase. It contains a variety of songs from varying genres, decades, and styles. Most important, *you must know every song in this book by rote and be ready to sing any of them.*

If you have songs in your book that you once copied and intended to learn, take them out until you've learned them. If you have songs that you hate to sing or that you are not comfortable performing, take them out. I cannot tell you how often an actor will come in to audition, give her music to the accompanist, and do the song she prepared. The director will take an interest in her, but the song she chose just isn't bringing out what he needs to see, so he asks if she has something else. Guess what the accompanist does? He thumbs through that actor's rep book and calls out some titles to the director (after all, the accompanist very likely knows what kind of song the director would prefer to hear). If the actor is not able to sing something in that book, it's egg on her face. So, while it is wise to have a widely varied book covering every imaginable style of song, it is counterproductive to you unless you can sing any of the songs at the drop of a hat. *I would prefer you only had five choices: a contemporary ballad and an up-tempo, a standard ballad and an up-tempo, and a pop/rock song—that you know perfectly.*

The purpose of the "B" book is to house all of that other music you have amassed that doesn't need to be carted along with you everywhere. This includes songs you are learning or plan to learn, songs that are not performance-ready aces for you, and songs you are tired or bored with. The "B" book is the one you take to your voice lessons and coaching sessions. This is your private work-in-progress book. No accompanist in an audition situation should ever get his hands on this binder.

In addition, you should be prepared to sing from shows you've done; if you aren't comfortable singing a role you've done in your career, consider removing it from your résumé. Anything listed on there must be considered fair game at an audition. We will often see a role you've played as useful to what we are casting at the moment and ask you to perform something from it.

In the chapter that follows, I will go into much greater detail on building and maintaining a working repertoire book.

FINDING THE CHANCE TO SAY THE WORDS YOU'VE FOUND

When I first moved to New York, the Internet was up and running, but most theatre jobs were still only posted in print. You had to turn to *Back Stage* or *Show Business* to find audition notices. Now, however, theatre has gone techno, and most openings for performers can be accessed on the web. Furthermore, with the vast accessibility of the Internet, theatres all over the country are inclined to post audition information online, so you can hear about casting calls from the MUNY in St. Louis just as easily as you can be informed about Broadway cattle calls. Some websites you may find helpful include

www.actorsequity.org
www.backstage.com
www.playbill.com
www.performink.com (Chicago)
www.tcg.org (ArtSearch)
www.upta.org

And those are just for starters. I'm certain that by the time this book is published there will be at least a dozen other online sources for gigs. Use Google—it's your friend!

Wherever you find your casting call ads or your college audition requirements, it is incumbent upon you as a professional to read carefully. If it's a show, what role(s) are they casting? If it's a season, what shows? How do you get an audition? Do you show up, sign up, or submit a headshot and résumé by e-mail? What are they asking to hear at auditions? Do they want one song, two songs, song cuttings, etcetera? There is a great deal of information contained in a casting ad, and you need to understand, interpret, and read between the lines. Misinterpreting a call or arriving underprepared will make you look very unprofessional and take away your edge.

My first job when I moved to New York was editing and typing casting call ads for *Back Stage*. It was my job to put every advertisement into the standard format and to make sure the theatres were all, at the very least, legitimate. (As a smart actor, you should realize that a casting call for some Podunk theatre in a burned-out warehouse in Brooklyn is going to read as legit and professional as an Off-Broadway Equity casting. There are a lot of scams and scummy theatres out there, and you should rely on word of mouth and the Internet to stay informed.) Let's take a look at a hypothetical example and see what we can glean:

The Last Five Years, Pawtucket Players

Fri. June 29 & Sat. June 30 from 12 p.m. to 3 p.m. at Pawtucket High Auditorium, 5 Main St.

The Pawtucket Players, a 30-year-old regional theatre in historic Pawtucket, RI, are casting for a summer production of Jason Robert Brown's

The Last Five Years. Bill Jones, dir.; Sadie Hawkings, mus. dir. Rehearsals begin July 1. Performances will run from July 22 through August 13. Auditions will be held Friday, June 29, and Saturday, June 30, from 12 p.m. to 3 p.m. at the Pawtucket High School auditorium. Bring pix and résumé and prepare two contrasting 16-bar cuttings from contemporary musical theatre. Both roles are paid ($350/wk.), plus housing included. For more information, visit www.pawplayers.net. **Equity Guest Artist Contract Available**.

Seeking: **Jamie**—male; 26–30; confident Jewish man, on his way up; charming; pop-rock bari-tenor voice range. **Cathy**—female; 23–28; sweet gentile girl, very vulnerable but with the ability to display inner strength when tested; belter. **EQUITY/NON-EQUITY PERFORMERS**.

And there you have it, a casting call for young men and women—simple and concise. So let's break it down.

The Show: "*The Last Five Years* by Jason Robert Brown"

Before you even consider going to this call, you'd better learn a little about the play. I find that Spotify is a useful website for the thrifty actor because it allows you to listen to most recordings in full. You'll hear that this is a very contemporary, very poppy, and very complex score. I would also try to find the libretto (or at least portions of it) online to get a sense of who these characters are—again, Google is your friend.

The Theatre: "Pawtucket Players"

According to the ad, this is an established (30 years) theatre. Visit their website, look at pictures, read reviews, and see who else has worked there. You should get an idea if this is the type of place you'd like to work before you go to the auditions.

The Staff: "Bill Jones, dir.; Sadie Hawkings, mus. dir."

This information can be helpful, particularly if you know or have some connections to the names listed. If you studied with Sadie's best pal when you were in college, make sure that name is prominently displayed on your résumé. Also, if you know people who have worked with Bill Jones, see what you can find out about him. Perhaps your friend has done several shows with Mr. Jones and tells you that the man *hates* Andrew Lloyd Webber's musicals. This would be a good indication that "Think of Me" from *The Phantom of the Opera* might not be your best audition selection this time around.

The Commitment: "Rehearsals begin July 1; Performances run from July 22 through August 13"

Are you available during this time span? If you're likely to have *any* conflicts during those six weeks, you'll want to mention them at the audition so that there are no surprises later on. I like actors to be up front with me about any unavailable times and dates at the initial audition. Having other commitments will not preclude you from being cast; rather, it will allow me to consider if I can feasibly use you in a particular role knowing that you won't be around for certain rehearsals. I once did a production of *Cabaret*, and my first choice for the role of the Emcee was going to miss an entire week of rehearsals. This was a college production, so we were on a generous schedule, and I decided that this actor was worth the risk incurred with losing him for five rehearsals. It also gave his understudy the chance to get some work in and to hone his chops a bit. The actor I cast was very successful as the Emcee, and the time missed did not affect his work.

In some cases, it might not work out that well for an actor with other obligations, but it's always better to be up front with a director. You risk burning a bridge if you take the approach of "I'll just audition now, get the job, and spring this bit on him later." Too many actors have done that to me, and I'll never cast them again.

The Compensation: "$350/week plus housing"

Often negotiating is a possibility. More on that later. It is best, however, to assume for the time being that their price is final. Is this enough for you to take that six-week commitment? If the producers are up front with you about how much they're offering, it's only fair that you will take this factor into consideration *before* you go in. If you absolutely can't work for that amount, *don't audition*. Sometimes there will be no pay at all—especially for small theatres and community organizations, where actors just work for the exposure and the résumé credits. If you can't work for free, then *don't audition*. Many people will tell you that you should audition for everything, even if you can't or won't take the job. I must strongly advise against this theory. Remember, the director is trying in earnest to cast her production. Your coming in for exposure or for practice and subsequently rejecting a job offer may be seen by that director as a waste of her valuable time. You may burn a bridge this way as well.

The Audition: "Friday, June 29, and Saturday, June 30, from 12 p.m. to 3 p.m. at the Pawtucket High School auditorium"

There is no indication on this call that you need an appointment, so just show up. Often, you will need to submit a picture and résumé in advance to schedule an audition time. For those calls, you'll need to draft a cover letter—we'll discuss cover letters in a later chapter. For this audition, however, simply get there and plan to arrive early. I'm a firm believer in "the earlier, the better." If you show up at 11:30 a.m. on Friday to sign up, it tells me that you're eager to work and that you're punctual. It also allows you to set the bar against which every actor who follows you will have to compete. Waiting until the end (while it won't keep you from being cast by any means) may show a lack of interest on your part. The role may already be well decided by the end of auditions. And quite frankly, the director's attention span may be too exhausted for you to have every advantage in your audition. Come early. If given the opportunity, go first. Trust me, it counts for something!

Variations on a Theme

Remember to read the audition notice carefully. The majority of auditions will either be open calls of the same nature as my example or auditions by appointment, for which you will need to e-mail in a headshot and résumé and await a call from the producers or the director. However, there are always other variables that may come into play depending on the nature of the particular show being cast:

1. They might be "typing out." Often at open cattle calls, if the crowd is too large to see everyone, the casting director may decide to type out before he hears people. This means they literally line people up in groups and they look at everyone and choose people to stay and audition based purely on look and type. Or they may call everyone in and dismiss anyone who has less than 10 years of tap experience. Whatever you do, don't take this personally!

2. They may have separate calls for "dancers who sing" and "actors who move." Be sure to attend the audition that is most suited to your skills—if you're not an incredible dancer, do not attend the dance audition when you have the option to do a "singers who move" audition. Typically, the

dance combination will be much faster and more complex at the dancer call.

3. They may only be seeking actors for specific roles. If you see a character breakdown, be sure to pay attention to which parts are open. Do not submit yourself for or gear your audition toward a role that has already been cast.

The Requirements: "Two contrasting 16-bar cuttings from contemporary musical theatre"

Here again, a working knowledge of the show will really be an advantage to you. Besides the fact that our fictional friend Bill Jones hates Lloyd Webber, one listen to the score of *The Last Five Years* will tell you that "Think of Me" is not appropriate for the role of Cathy. You want to try to find audition pieces that allow directors to see who you are and what you can do, while also capturing the essence of the character for which you're auditioning.

I personally have no problem with actors auditioning with music from the show itself—sometimes I even encourage it. How better to determine your appropriateness for Jamie than to hear you handle his songs from the show. Some instructors, however, disagree with this approach. They feel as though singing "Maria" for a *West Side Story* audition would somehow pigeonhole you out of consideration for the role of Riff. I think this is utter nonsense—give directors some credit for imagination! Besides, if you sing for Tony but I see you as Riff, I can always use the callback to test you in that role.

And yet, a quirk such as "no singing from the show" is just another reason that knowing who's directing can be an advantage to you as a smart actor. *Flom's directing it? Great! He'll love it if I sing "Shiksa Goddess"!*

One solution to the contentious issue of pulling material from the show they're casting is to use a song by the same composer. Look at what else Brown wrote and find music that has a similar style—that captures the *essence* of the show you're going in for. When you walk in the door, you can always ask the director if he minds hearing selections from the show, and if the response is yes, you'll have a suitable Plan B.

Note: this ad calls for 16 bars, or measures, of music. Remember, *never* go into an audition knowing *only* 16 bars or any shortened version of your song. You must be prepared to sing the entire song if they ask you to. You'd be surprised how often directors will be dazzled with your voice and want to hear more—or disappointed that you cut a song the way you did and want to hear a different, more revealing portion (e.g., "Can you jump to the bridge?" or "Let's hear how you handle the modulation in the last verse"). In these situations, you don't want to tell them you learned only your 16-bar cutting. It's unprofessional and counterproductive, not to mention embarrassing. To that end, avoid coming to auditions with an anthology of 16-bar audition cuttings. These are actually becoming very popular publications for their ease of use. Don't be lazy; learn the whole song. Nail it. Then choose *your best* 16 bars to show them at the audition. Finally on the subject of cutting, remember this simple axiom: Always leave 'em wanting more. Even if a casting call says to prepare two songs, there's no rule that says you have to sing the songs in their entirety. If you know that your song is repetitive and that you can show them everything they need to see in a verse and a chorus, then by all means *do it*. Less is more. (Make sure you don't stop mid-phrase. Your cutting must still make dramatic sense, however short.) Even generous directors who afford actors the opportunity to do a full-song audition get restless once they've seen what they need to see. Sometimes a great singer who saves the "good stuff" for the end has already lost his audience after the first uneventful two minutes. I know directors who will even cut actors off mid-song once they have either heard (or not heard) what they are looking for. If you can show them what they need (namely, your "bread-basket" notes and your acting chops) in a fraction of the time, they'll love you for it. And remember, if they want to hear more, they'll ask you to sing more: advantage, you. After all, that's what callbacks are for, and your best possible outcome at an audition is to *get a callback*.

The Open Roles: "Seeking: Jamie—male; 26–30 . . . Cathy—female; 23–28 . . ."

Pay attention to this. Some ads won't list sought roles at all (one may safely assume that all roles then would be open), but if they do list characters, you must read carefully. The descriptions given are a summary of how this director describes the characters he is casting. They may very well contain interpreted choices, and so it would behoove you to be clear on what they're looking for.

I directed a production of *Forever Plaid* some years ago, and I cast out of New York City. Although I'm generally a big advocate of cross-gender and nontraditional casting choices, I was taking a very classic approach to this production, and so my casting breakdown specified: Four men, early- to mid-20s. I was shocked at the number of women who sent me headshots and very generic cover letters. I normally keep interesting submissions even if a person is wrong for the current project—I'll look back through my files and call on them later when something more appropriate arises. However, I tossed away every female submission for *Plaid* simply because I felt they showed a lack of concern and understanding for what they were submitting. Granted, this may sound grumpy and judgmental on my part, but when you consider that I was receiving 60 to 100 envelopes each day before this audition (this was back when people submitted by snail mail!), I resented what I considered a waste of my time (ah, the young, arrogant director!). I'm sure that not all directors would react this way, but why not just avoid the possibility and save the time and the humiliation while you're at it? Concentrate on finding the shows that you are right for.

And remember, this is show *business*, not show amusement or show pastime. The people casting have a business to run, and time is money. If they perceive you as wasting their time, they are less likely to want to hire you for current or future projects. You need to treat all of your work like it's a business. People in the industry will respect you much more.

The Union Affiliations: "Equity/Non-Equity Performers"

Take this information with a grain of salt. If a call is listed as a nonunion gig, then there's generally no flexibility to allow for a rule-abiding Equity member to be cast. However, just because a show is a union production does not negate nonunion folks from consideration. Many of my friends were cast in their first Broadway productions before becoming members of Actors' Equity. In fact, now that the old points system is becoming more and more outmoded, it seems that the clearest way to gain access into the union is to be cast in your first Equity show. In a later chapter, I'll address the union issue in more detail, but for now, just be aware that it is possible to "crash" an Equity call if you don't have your card. This usually involves lining up at excruciatingly early hours and waiting all day in the hopes that they'll have time at the end to see you. But if it's worth the day to be seen by this particular director or this particular theatre, then why not go for it?

If you decide to go in for an Equity call, you'll need to arrive an hour or two before the posted sign-in time. Usually there will be a lineup, so being early is necessary for nonunion members. When they begin to sign people in, you will be put on a list and given a tentative time to return—usually late in the afternoon. If the director finishes seeing all of the Equity performers before the day is through, she may at her own discretion spend some time seeing non-Equity actors as well. Even if it's a long shot to get cast, these calls are often a good opportunity for some early exposure to big casting directors. I believe it's worth it to attend them at least once or twice in a while.

Before You Walk Out That Door . . .

So here you are: an actor. You've been taking classes; you're confident (or at least you're prepared to *act* confident); you've got a decent headshot, a growing, well-organized repertoire book, and a subscription to a trade website. You've read up on some good auditions coming up. What else must you do before you head into the studios to dazzle the director? Just a couple of things . . .

First, be prepared for *anything*. When you see someone trudging down a city street with a giant duffle bag, carrying what seems to be his whole life on his shoulder, before you assume he's homeless, consider that he's very likely an actor. An actor must dress comfortably enough to navigate the city in any weather, but at the same time, he must be prepared to look his best in an audition after running 16 blocks on his lunch break to be seen for *The Book of Mormon*. There are conflicting notions on whether or not you should "dress the role" you're going in for. I say you need to dress your *brand* (see my other book, *Act Like It's Your Business*, for a detailed branding process), but make slight adjustments depending on the show for which you are auditioning. For example, you wouldn't want to wear a suit to an audition for *Hair*, a laid-back, counterculture rock musical; but you also don't need to dress like a vagabond if you're being seen for the Homeless Woman in *A New Brain*. I generally suggest a good casual-yet-professional audition outfit that allows you to feel confident that you look great at any given audition. The bottom line is that if they need to see you in a certain look, they'll ask you to adjust your outfit at the callbacks.

At musical auditions, they may ask you to stay and dance, so you'll want to have some dance clothes to change into. You'll need your music book as well as multiple copies of your headshot/résumé. You should *always* have a hard copy of your headshot with you—even if you have already sent it digitally. You'll need water and probably a snack in case it's a long day of auditions, and many people also choose to bring a book or some work to do to pass the time.

If that hasn't all weighed you down, consider that many actors carry changes of clothing and/or shoes just in case the audition turns out that it does indeed require a different aesthetic. Or in the frequent event that while attending one audition, you'll stumble onto another prime casting opportunity at the same studio. Better to be prepared than to be caught off guard. Now, aren't you glad you spent time developing a well-varied repertoire book? (You will be after chapter 2!)

I must reiterate that it's incumbent upon you to *be prepared* in every possible way. I know this is a broad statement, and it's essentially the point of this entire book, but I will be very specific here for a moment.

An actor's job is to take care of the voice, take care of the body, and learn the lines. Before an audition, you *must* give yourself enough time to attend to your voice and body and have them in optimum readiness. For some, this might take two hours and a steaming for the sinuses; for others, some brief vocal scales and a good reach to the sky and toe-touch will do. You need to learn how your personal instrument operates and prepare accordingly to be in prime condition when you walk into the room. Attending auditions frequently is one way of conditioning the body and voice to be ready always.

A full vocal and physical warm-up is ideal, but in reality it's not always possible. At the very least, be sure you do plenty of speaking in various vocal registers throughout the hours leading up to an audition. This will get you minimally opened up. If you're in a car, sing along with the radio. If you're in a place where you have some room to move, stretch your body out before heading to the audition. Once you get in the room, you only have about 30 to 60 seconds to impress the artistic staff, so you don't have time to "warm into" your audition as you go. Be at performance level when you walk in the room so you don't shoot yourself in the foot before they get the chance to see how great you are.

Often when you arrive at the audition site, there will be a holding room where performers can stretch and vocalize, but you shouldn't bank on this. Furthermore, be sure you *arrive early* to your audition appointment. You'll want some time to focus and breathe a little before you face the creative team. They may even be running early (if it happens to be the second Monday after the third full moon of the second rain of the season with Venus rising . . .), and you don't want to keep them waiting. Technically, if you have an appointed time and the auditions are running fast, they must give you the option of waiting until your scheduled slot. But think of how they'll appreciate your willingness to move things along and to keep them ahead of schedule! It's just another way of making yourself look professional.

Remember the old theatre adage: If you're 15 minutes early, you're on time; if you're on time, you're late.

Be early. Be prepared. Be happy to perform.

SUMMARY

- No director wants actors to fail in the audition. He is hoping for you to be exactly what the role requires. He is also looking for actors who are tenacious, enthusiastic, and professional.
- Act everything. Do not simply sing pretty and dance well and save your acting choices for the monologue. Act the song and dance.
- Take classes and continue to study as often as you can.
- Do not rely on monologue books, film, or the Internet for source material. Read and see plays for age-appropriate pieces.
- Learn music from the notations on the page, not from the cast recording.
- Know every song in your "A" repertoire book by rote.
- Be sure to have at least one contemporary and one standard ballad and up-tempo song, plus pop/rock in your book that you can pull out for any audition.
- Be prepared to sing anything in your book, as well as songs from any shows listed on your résumé.
- Be sure to read and understand casting call ads thoroughly before responding or attending an audition.
- Look for appropriate audition material for the specific show you're going in for; consider songs from the same composer or genre, or songs that convey the essence of the role you are interested in.
- Never learn only 16 bars of a song. Be prepared to sing the entire piece if asked.
- Be prepared for anything at an audition!
- Always carry copies of your headshot and résumé with you to auditions.

2

A DETAILED GUIDE TO BUILDING THE ACTOR'S REPERTOIRE BOOK

The repertoire book is the most important tool in a musical theatre performer's arsenal. The contents of your book must tell a director: *first*, who you are, and *second*, what you can do. It should be diverse and varied, showcasing you at your best in a wide variety of different genres and styles. It is important to remember that no matter what stage of your career you find yourself, the rep book is an ongoing, ever-evolving project. It changes as you mature, learn new songs, learn new styles, discover exciting new material, and so forth. So whether you are just starting out and are new to this whole repertoire thing, or you are a seasoned pro with an enormous collection of songs and monologues, this section has some tips for success to create the best possible rep book, one you can bring into auditions with confidence.

I am going to walk you through a detailed process starting at the very beginning. By the end of this section, you should have a good working knowledge of how to keep your book in order for an entire career in this business. If you already have a book together and you're thinking of skipping over or skimming this section, I would advise you instead to read on. When I work with my students on repertoire, I make them pull everything out of their books and start from scratch. They inevitably find that following this method leads them to a much more organized, polished, stronger set of repertoire than they had before. So indulge me and be brave. Starting from zero again can be scary, but you'll be better off for it in the end.

STEP 1: GATHER THE NECESSARY EQUIPMENT

You will need to obtain *two* sturdy three-ring binders. The first one should be 2.5 to 3 inches thick. Any thicker would be too large and any thinner won't hold enough music. This is the "A" book you bring with you to every audition, containing only songs you could sing at the drop of a hat, which show you off well in every way. You may want the second binder to be larger, as this will house the bulk of your music that you are not toting around to every audition; this is your "B" book. The "B" book is for works in progress and material that is not audition ready and music that you feel just needs a little break from your daily rotation.

You will also need a large quantity of clear plastic *nonglare* sheets to protect your music. It is important that the package is labeled "nonglare"; otherwise, your accompanist may have a hard time seeing the notes on the page if the light in the audition room is bad. Some will argue against the plastic sheet method and instead advocate for the accordion-style layout on cardstock. I find this bulky and more complicated to deal with, so since it's my book, I'm going to tell you my way; but I will acknowledge that it's not the only way. I do, however, think everyone in the business would agree that you should *never* bring in loose, unreinforced pages. They'll blow off the piano and create havoc for the accompanist and for your audition.

Other materials you will want to have handy are tab dividers (to neatly separate your binder into individual songs), a black marker, some Post-It Notes, and a highlighter. Now you have everything you need to begin building the rep book.

STEP 2: SEARCH FOR MATERIAL

When I told you to start from scratch no matter where you are in your career, I did not mean to imply that you needed to find all new material. In fact, the best place to begin to find material is among the songs that you already know. If you have music in vocal scores, vocal selections books, or variety collections (e.g., *The Soprano's Musical Theatre Songbook*), you will need to begin by copying the music onto loose sheets. Copying the songs may seem redundant if you already own the music books, but trust me: you do not want a pianist trying to play for you out of a vocal selections book or even a bound score. The pages never stay open, and it can be the downfall of your audition. It is not the professional way to deliver your songs to the accompanist.

There is great debate over the copyright legality of photocopying music, but let me be clear about one thing: You should purchase all of your music. Whether you get it from an online site, or you pull it from a vocal selections book, it's important that the composers get paid for their work. However, it is definitely industry standard to enter an audition room with a binder full of copied music pages, as opposed to the published, bound volumes.

If you do not own any collections already, you can generally find them at any major bookstore. If you are seeking a specific musical, I would suggest checking online at www.amazon.com or www.dramabookshop.com. Just be sure when you copy music out of a book that you get the entire page copied clearly onto your paper. If the score is oversized, as many original vocal scores are, you may need to reduce the size on the copy machine; reduction to 93 percent generally works perfectly. Do be sure that none of the lyrics, notes, or dynamic markings are cut off. Sometimes when copying out of a large book you will find that the staff ends up slanted across the printed page. It's best if you try to make the music straight. And if the title of the song does not fit, be sure to write it in. Remember, you want to help the accompanist help you by making everything as clear as possible for him or her.

One other valuable source for finding sheet music is the Internet. There are websites that allow you to buy individual songs for a nominal fee and print them out right on your home computer. The best of these that I have found are www.musicnotes.com and www.sheetmusicdirect.com, which not only sell songs but also let the buyer transpose the music into different keys if the original is too high or too low. I would beware of this luxury, as some musical directors will expect to hear songs in their original key—especially classic musical theatre tunes. You want to have your songs in the right key for you, but you need to be aware of certain expectations (such as *West Side Story* and *Candide*, which are known for particular vocal ranges). Additionally, you need to be sure that the transposition makes sense and doesn't contain weird note spellings (such as $E\flat\flat$ in the key of D Major). The best way to be clear that the transposition works is to get with a pianist and have her play it through for you. You want all of your audition material fool-proof before you put it into your "A" book and allow it into the room, but occasionally, this function can be appropriate and helpful, especially for pop/rock music.

So now that you know where to look for music, let's spend some time talking about what music to look for. As I mentioned before, it is vital that you have music representing a variety of styles, eras, and genres. It is not enough anymore to rely solely on old standards by George and Ira Gershwin or Richard Rodgers and Oscar Hammerstein II to get you through every audition. Nor is it okay to assume that an entire arsenal of pop music will suffice in today's contemporary theatrical landscape. You must, as a smart musical theatre actor, be very hip to current trends, both in new musical compositions and revivals of older material. You must see and listen to a lot of musicals as well as a variety of popular music. For example, country music may not be your favorite style, but shows like *Spitfire Grill*, *Pump Boys and Dinettes*, and *Big River* are produced with enough regularity that it would help to know something about that singing style.

In the back of this book there is an appendix with a checklist of genres. You can use it for easy reference later on, but for now I'll be more detailed. Also, please realize that my suggestions all come with the caveat that you be able to perform each of these types of songs well before adding them to your repertoire—it does you no good to have an '80s rock power ballad in your book, for example, if you cannot sing it; rather, I would advise you to either find a fabulous voice teacher so you can learn how to handle those songs or avoid *Rock of Ages* auditions if that isn't your thing. And that goes for any genre that you don't feel at home performing. You should love to sing every song in your book. If you don't enjoy it, take it out. If you don't do it well, take it out. Always show your strengths and never your weaknesses in the audition room.

When I wrote the first edition of this book, there was little to no information available for actors about crafting their own personal "brands" to help them achieve greater success in the audition room. In 2013, I published my second book, *Act Like It's Your Business: Branding and Marketing Strategies for Actors*. At the risk of shameless self-promotion, I want to recommend that you read that book as part of your process when choosing repertoire. If you can strongly identify who you are as a person and as an artist, it will greatly increase the likelihood of you finding really great material that sells you well in the room.

So now let's segue (music nerd humor) into the discussion on material with the first type of music to include in a complete musical theatre audition book: "standards." Standards are also commonly referred to as "jazz standards," songs from the "American Songbook," "Tin Pan Alley," and so forth—or their later descendants: "Golden Age" or "Musical Theatre Standards." Generally speaking, when a casting notice is posted for a musical that was written in the style of those released any time prior to 1969 (*Hair* and the onset of contemporary pop-influenced musicals), they will call for either a "Standard Up-Tempo" or a "Standard Ballad." Occasionally they may be more specific and use terms such as "Golden Age Ballad/

Up-Tempo" or "Jazz Standard," which could indicate how much story and character they might be seeking, as opposed to a more stylized vocal presentation. But suffice it to say that if you have one or two solid ballads and a couple of up-tempo audition pieces from this general period, you should be well covered.

In the first edition of this book, I subdivided this section into several small bits and suggested having songs for almost every decade, but the truth is, that is overkill. In looking at both professional casting notices and college audition requirements over the past six years, I see that no one is really expecting that kind of detail, and thus you can make your binder smaller (or save room for more "flavors" of pop/rock) by narrowing down your standard offerings. Simply put, you want *at least two* contrasting songs that reflect the early 20th-century form of musical songwriting. For this category, your search should include composers and lyricists such as Harold Arlen; E. Y. Harburg; the Gershwins; Cole Porter; Kurt Weill; and Rodgers and Hart, all of whom would represent the earlier "Jazz Standard" part of the genre.

With these jazz standards, many of the stipulations that will apply to choosing songs from later musical theatre, such as age, gender, and race appropriateness, need not usually be a concern. In other words, both men and women could consider singing a tune like "Orange Colored Sky" by Milton DeLugg and Willie Stein or "It's Only a Paper Moon" by Harold Arlen, E. Y. Harburg, and Billy Rose. This style also leaves a great amount of room for vocal interpretation; hence, you will rarely find a song sounding the same in different recordings by multiple jazz artists. It is vital, however, that you first learn the music exactly as it is printed on the page before you attempt to style the song yourself. And do not simply listen to someone else's rendition of the song and think that you should (or could) sing it like him or her. I had a student in a lesson who attempted to sing some tunes by Michael Bublé. He was completely thrown when the piano accompaniment sounded nothing like the big band on the CD he had been practicing with at home. That student scrapped those song options because he couldn't separate the songs from the singer.

The other thing to note about songs from the jazz period is that they often originate without any context or character attached to them. Many of these songs were "trunk songs," written as stand-alone pieces by their composers, which later made it into a musical (or movie musical) context. They can be fairly loose in acting values and are often "vertical," meaning they don't move the plot forward or contain much action—they are more self-reflective or philosophical in nature. If you have a song in this era that you love and you sing the style well, I think it's perfectly okay to represent this type of song in your book, but I would strongly urge you to present the song with a strong personalized context and character, and also balance such a song with a contrasting piece from the slightly later Golden Age to offer you more dramatic "meat" for your actor.

The Golden Age includes the songwriters Rodgers and Hammerstein; Lerner and Loewe; Frank Loesser; Bock and Harnick; Leonard Bernstein; Jule (pronounced "Julie"!) Styne; Adler and Ross; and the list goes on and on. The Golden Age is characterized by musicals in which the book, songs, and dance were fully integrated. In other words, characters did not stop the plot to sing or dance; rather, the songs and dances carried the story further. Thus, the music of the Golden Age is mostly "horizontal" in nature. These musicals all bear striking similarity in structure. There was a formula for the placement of large production numbers, duets, comedy songs, and so forth that proved very successful with audiences of the day. That formula is still effective today, although many contemporary composers have found fortune in working against the accepted norm of the Golden Age.

With material from the Golden Age you must concern yourself with a character's age and gender when choosing songs. Thankfully, in today's industry it is normal for people of color to sing from nearly any role; however, it is not general practice for Caucasians to sing roles specifically written for Blacks, Hispanics, or Asians. There are exceptions to this rule, but those exceptions are subject to the sensibilities of a particular director. So it's important to be careful when singing race-specific material. Know for whom you are auditioning and consider how high the risk would be to play a character that goes specifically against race or gender (price tag).

This is your opportunity to really seek out roles in which you would be dynamite. Do not be afraid to use music from familiar shows, as most of the musicals of this time period are well known. You will never be able to reinvent the wheel and sing something from the Golden Age that they've never heard (if they've never heard it, there's probably a good reason!), so just find some songs that are not too cliché and perform them very well. A New York casting director friend of mine often says that she would prefer to hear "If I Loved You" from *Carousel* a million times, rather than poorly written musical theatre that doesn't tell a story or reveal character desires.

Once you have a few really solid options for standard musical theatre repertoire, it's time to turn your focus to contemporary musical theatre. The word *contemporary* is so loaded, and as I have found from looking back six years to the first edition of this book, it changes almost daily! The 2015 Broadway season included revivals of 1920s musicals, an old English Music Hall–style satire, a pop-influenced folk piece, and a rap/hip hop musical—

all of which have been critically successful! It seems like two years ago, the entire Great White Way was exploding with rock and roll music from the '70s, '80s, and '90s. So to keep up and label something as "contemporary" is really impossible.

That being said, when audition notices ask for a "Contemporary Musical Theatre" piece, they are generally speaking of music composed specifically for the stage (as opposed to popular music inserted into dramatic contexts), as part of a theatrical context (as opposed to the myriad of great songwriters who are writing for the cabaret and song-cycle circuit; i.e., Scott Alan, Jonathan Reid Gealt, Carnor and Gregor, Kooman and Dimond, etc.), sometime between the late 1960s and the present day. And to complicate matters even more, you want to be wary of pulling material from the really pop and rock-inspired musicals, such as *The Wedding Singer*, *High Fidelity*, *Rent*, *Hamilton*, and *Bloody, Bloody Andrew Jackson*, because casting calls for those kinds of shows will inevitably require *actual* radio pop/rock music (more on that in the section to come).

So what actually constitutes this contemporary musical theatre category? And are people even writing "up-tempo" tunes anymore? Broadway audition coach VP Boyle (read his book, *Audition Freedom*) would say that in fact they are not. His rep book advice is to have a contemporary ballad and a contrasting contemporary "driving dramatic" song. Driving dramatic is a song with a real pulse that builds into something . . . well . . . dramatic, as opposed to languishing in the easy tempo of a traditional ballad form. It's easiest to demonstrate this category with examples that you can go listen to: "Back to Before" from *Ragtime*, "Hold On" from *The Secret Garden*, "One Perfect Moment" from *Bring It On*, "Anthem" from *Chess*, "Empty Chairs at Empty Tables" from *Les Miserables*, "Proud Lady" from *The Baker's Wife* (a bit overdone and challenging for the pianist, so beware), and "Goodbye" from *Catch Me If You Can* are all examples of contemporary driving dramatic songs. Frank Wildhorn is a master of this style (although be careful of using his material in auditions—it's not for everyone). Also take a look at "How Could I Ever Know" from *The Secret Garden* for a good example of a song that combines ballad (the verses) with driving dramatic (the bridge—which, incidentally, makes a great audition cut!). Again, you should find one that comes from a role you could really play now at your age and training and put it into your book. Nothing beats a really exciting, well-acted, driving dramatic song in an audition room.

Contemporary ballads are a little easier to spot and identify. Just remember to be sure to start from a place of: "Who am I? What is my essence?

Which character in a musical can I believably play that would reveal something about me to the creative team?" Let that be your first criteria; not "what shows off my voice best." For contemporary musical theatre composers, take a look at the work of Maltby and Shire; Stephen Sondheim; Adam Guettel; Stephen Schwartz; Tom Kitt; Ahrens and Flaherty; Pasek and Paul; Lawrence O'Keefe; William Finn; Kander and Ebb; Kopit and Yeston; Andrew Lippa; and Michael John LaChiusa for starters. Obviously, there are dozens more, and each year more new composers come onto the scene. It's your job to stay on top of the industry and to know your business. I recommend you create a bookmark on your computer for Playbill.com so that you get into the habit of reading the front-page news of the industry each day. This way, you'll always know what's opening and who's starring in every Broadway show and national tour. It's a great resource to lead you to repertoire!

One more thought about those contemporary composers: You'll notice that I included Stephen Sondheim and Adam Guettel on that list. You may have heard in your training that you should never sing their songs in auditions because they are too difficult for pianists (and quite challenging for novice singers as well!). While this is sage advice to heed, I will offer you the caveat that Sondheim, Guettel, as well as Jason Robert Brown have written some of the most masterfully crafted dramatic songs in the canon. If you can handle the songs technically, and if it really shows you off in a way you want to be perceived in the audition room, I think it's okay to have it in your book. You should run it by an accompanist before you bring it into an audition, just to be sure it's something that can be sight read, but you should be aware that in the professional world of musical theatre auditions, the piano players who are hired to play auditions are generally at the top of the game and there isn't much they can't play. (College auditions are a different ball game, and you would probably do well to avoid *most* of these composers' work.) It's incumbent upon you to prepare and mark the music very clearly to help them play it without hiccups. More on that later in the chapter.

The next set of songs you need to build into your repertoire is what we broadly call "pop/rock." This is a very general term that refers to music that has been written for popular consumption; radio tunes, as opposed to theatrical music. Let me first be clear that pop/rock music is *not* music from pop/rock musicals (i.e., *Hair, Next to Normal, Spring Awakening, Rent*, etc.). Those songs will (almost) never be a part of a singer's audition repertoire because, as I indicated before, auditions for those shows will inevitably call for you to sing actual pop/rock songs, not theatrical songs. The other warning to you in this category is to avoid songs that were once popular tunes but are now part of a musical theatre context. I'm speaking of the "jukebox musical" phenomenon that has exploded over the past decade; shows such as *Mamma Mia, Movin' Out, All Shook Up, American Idiot, Rock of Ages, Beautiful: The Carole King Musical,* and *Jersey Boys.* While this music obviously lends itself well to a theatrical construct, we now identify it with its show context and its character, and it no longer stands alone as a pop song, open to interpretation by you, the artist. I know I keep harping on your audition material showing *you and your essence* off, but nowhere is that more important and more valuable than in the pop/rock genre of music. Pop/rock tells us more about *you* as a human being than any other genre because there is no established character; *you* are the character!

The first thing I suggest you do in your process for discovering great pop/rock repertoire is to accept and embrace that popular music is now a part of our musical theatre landscape once more (it was back in the jazz/Tin Pan Alley era, but it really fell out of the theatre for many years) and it's not going away. Some voice teachers will warn you that singing pop/rock styles of music is dangerous and should be avoided. If you're reading this book, I assume that you know better than to buy into that old myth. You have to be smart about your training and your understanding of style and how technology, such as microphones and recording equipment, enhances and supports the rock singer; but as long as you approach it from an educated standpoint, you can have a long and fruitful career singing rock eight shows a week! If you deny the importance of learning to sing pop/rock, you are shutting yourself out of approximately 72 percent of professional auditions. I highly recommend Matthew Edwards's book, *So You Want to Sing Rock 'n' Roll: A Guide for Professionals,* as a starting place to understanding the vocal technique behind the challenges of this kind of singing.

It is important that you study with a voice teacher who understands contemporary commercial music (CCM) styles and voice function. It is not enough to work with someone who is only versed in classical singing and assume that all of the technique will transfer over. Be a smart consumer and take a firm hold of your career and get yourself into a studio that teaches you healthy belting (if you're a belter; healthy mixing, if you are not a belter) and microphone technique. Subscribe to Spotify or Apple Music and create playlists for yourself and *listen* closely to style—how are singers from different eras and genres using their voices? Listen for style tags such as vibrato, breathiness, vocal fry, slides, "cries," husk, and various other techniques and start trying to imitate the sounds of your favorite artists. I suggest you do this kind of experimentation on a microphone, so that you don't mistake loud volume for style. Things always sound louder on recordings because they are produced and enhanced in the studio. You could easily hurt yourself if you try to belt out an Aerosmith or a Heart song without a mic. You'll be amazed at the sounds you can make *safely* with a microphone a few inches from your mouth.

Once you've embraced your inner pop/rock singer, it's time to start finding material that really works for you, in your unique voice. Whereas with finding musical theatre material, I strongly urged you to begin with character essence and make voice the secondary criteria, I would suggest the opposite for pop/rock music. You need to be on a constant diet of ear candy, listening to all sorts of singers, and taking note of the ones who sing similarly to your sound. You want to sing material that really fits your voice when you do popular music. Then once you find those singers, seek out their songs that have a message or an emotion that you can really grab a hold of and personalize. This leads me to my second major suggestion in building the pop/rock section of your repertoire: Set this book down right now and get yourself on the Rock the Audition website by Sheri Sanders (www.rock-the-audition.com). It will be the single most important resource you can employ in your endeavor to audition successfully in today's musical theatre landscape. Sheri is the foremost authority on finding appropriate popular music for musical theatre auditions to suit the individual performer. Furthermore, her approach to history, context, and style is the best in the business, and she can teach you to interpret the music in a way that honors your authenticity and makes you sparkle in the audition room.

Got it? Good.

Sheri is really the expert on this subject, so I won't even begin to delve into the specificity with which she teaches building popular repertoire. Her book is an entire volume on the subject, including all the styles and genres and their historical context, whereas I'm only offering you a few pages of general advice. So take the following paragraphs as a kick-starter to your process, but definitely go deeper and make this a project. Trust me, it's important.

When we approach the realm of pop/rock, we have to first recognize how broad and encompassing that category is: Popular music, as it pertains to the world of musical theatre, includes '50s rock/"oldies" (*All Shook Up, Jersey Boys, Beautiful: The Carole King Musical, The Taffetas, Forever Plaid, Beehive,* and *The Marvelous Wonderettes, Diner, Grease*); rhythm and blues/Motown (*Memphis, Hairspray, Motown, The Wiz*); disco (*Mamma Mia, Saturday Night Fever, Xanadu, Priscilla: Queen of the Desert*); classic rock (*Rock of Ages, The Who's Tommy, High Fidelity, We Will Rock You*); '80s pop/rock (*The Wedding Singer, Kinky Boots, The Full Monty*); hard rock

(*American Idiot, Toxic Avenger, Bloody, Bloody Andrew Jackson*); country/
rockabilly (*Big River, Pump Boys and Dinettes, Floyd Collins, Always Patsy
Cline*); hip-hop and rap (*Hamilton, In the Heights, Bring It On, Lysistrata
Jones*); and—as Sheri would call it—Faerie music (*Waitress, The Light
Princess, Spring Awakening*). I point this out to you so that you understand
that pop/rock has many different "colors" or "flavors." Some you will be
naturally good at, and others might be a little out of your comfort zone.
The great news is that there is something to suit every voice. You just need
to figure out which colors are best suited for you. And once again, you do
this by listening to popular music and noting the variations in style choices.

I don't believe that it's important for you to represent every flavor of pop
in your repertoire. It is simply unrealistic to believe that anyone can sing
every one of these varieties of music expertly. However, you need to consider which types of shows you plan to audition for and make sure you have
appropriate music to suit those particular auditions. For instance, you may
love Ingrid Michaelson (excellent example of "Faerie music"), but singing
one of her songs would not serve you well for an *American Idiot* audition.
Nor would a great Diana Ross song from the '70s really help you get cast
in *All Shook Up*. Beware that they may release a casting call for any one
of these shows that generically asks for a "pop/rock" song, and it is your
responsibility to read between the lines, do your research on the show, and
make sure to choose an appropriate popular genre to suit the specific musical for which you're auditioning.

Examine what period the musical was either written in or styled to imitate, and find audition material that showcases you well in that particular
style. Casting directors are, first and foremost, seeking authenticity now
when they cast rock shows. They don't want watered down musical theatre
versions of pop/rock singers; they want the real deal.

When *Rent* hit the scene in 1996, everyone heralded it as rock and roll
taking over the Broadway stage. The funny thing now is that if you listen
carefully to the original cast recording of *Rent*, it has all the trappings of
theatre people singing rock music (i.e., tons of vibrato, clear singer's dic-
tion, etc.) with a little edge. Compare this with the recordings of *American
Idiot* or *Rock of Ages* and you'll see how much more authentic musical theatre rock singing has become over the last 20 years. That is the new normal,
and it is expected of you in the room.

When it comes to preparing an audition book for college or other such
generalized auditions, where you're not targeting a specific musical, you
should represent your very best and very favorite style(s) in the pop/rock
category. Very often, when seeing admissions auditions at the conservatory,

we will ask students if they have a pop song. If they don't, we'll ask them what their favorite song is to sing in the car with the radio blasting, and then have them sing a bit of that for us. Nothing gets them to reveal their authentic selves in the room faster than asking them to sing the music they love. So be ready to show that when you walk into these auditions.

One final word on finding pop/rock music: Unfortunately, the majority of sheet music you will find for your favorite radio songs come with terrible arrangements. They very rarely sound like what you're used to hearing on the recordings, and in many cases they sound absolutely awful on the piano. New York casting director Joy Dewing advises actors to listen to "coffee house" or acoustic stations, which have stripped-down covers of pop/rock songs, so you can hear how these songs sound without all of the instrumentation of the original recording. Furthermore, I urge you to seek out someone who can write you great piano arrangements for your audition cuts—sheet music that can be played by any accompanist and will support your authentic pop performance in the audition room, so we don't have to use our imaginations to hear what it's "really supposed to sound like." (Again, I would point you to Sheri Sanders as a great resource.) This is obviously an added expense, but in the long run, for your career, it's totally worth it. Once you have great arrangements of a small handful of your "go-to" pop songs, all you need to do is to help the pianist find the groove with you, and you're off and running on a successful audition.

Some Words of Wisdom
from Matthew Edwards, Voice Teacher

If you look at the Broadway productions from the last ten years you will notice that nearly every style you can imagine has been performed on the Great White Way. Classical shows such as *South Pacific* and contemporary shows such as *The Addams Family* play alongside hard rock inspired shows like *Rock of Ages,* country inspired shows like *Hands on a Hard Body,* pop inspired shows like *Lysistrata Jones,* alternative rock shows like *American Idiot,* rap inspired shows such as *Hamilton,* and the list goes on and on. There are also many new shows such as *Spring Awakening, Next to Normal,* and *In the Heights,* which clearly have strong pop/rock influences. Until this most recent explosion of pop/rock influenced shows, it could be reasonably argued that traditional forms of vocal training were sufficient to help students navigate the musical theatre repertoire. However, as the repertoire has changed, so have the demands on the singer. We've now reached the point that traditional training alone is no longer sufficient for the needs of the contemporary musical theatre performer.

A Little History

Before *Hair*, musical theatre productions were unamplified or used area microphones to supplement the acoustic power of the singers on stage. Without microphones both "legit" singers (those who sang with a classical vocal quality) and the belters or comedic characters (those who sang like they spoke) had to project their voices acoustically to be heard. However, after *Hair* wireless microphones became more and more common, and today you will not find a single Broadway production that does not use amplification.

Cast recordings also had a huge influence on musical theatre vocal quality and expectations. Andrew Lloyd Webber created *Jesus Christ Superstar* as a concept album before it became a stage production. Because audience members had heard the album before coming to the show, they expected that once they arrived at the performance, the live performance would sound like the recording. This became even truer during the British Invasion, when shows like *Les Miserables* and *Phantom of the Opera* created franchises that enabled theatregoers to see the exact same production in multiple cities. Again, the audience members had often listened to the cast recording and expected that the production in any given city would sound the same as a production in any other city. Electronic amplification and enhancement changed the way we experience the voice in musical theatre productions and eventually the way musical theatre performers sang.

The Parts

The voice consists of four systems: the power source, vibrating mechanism, resonator, and articulators. The power source is the respiratory system. Through controlled exhalation, the singer is able to supply the vocal folds with the necessary air pressure and flow to initiate and sustain vocal fold vibration (called phonation). The vocal folds are located behind the "Adam's Apple" and are made of a combination of muscle and gelatinous material that, when sent into vibration, creates a frequency that we perceive as pitch. The vibrations from the vocal folds travel up through the throat and out of the mouth through what is commonly called the vocal tract. As the sound waves emitted from the vocal folds travel through the vocal tract, they are enhanced and amplified, which produce the singer's unique tone quality. Finally, movements of the lips, jaw, and tongue produce vowels and consonants. The interactions of these numerous components are controlled by a complex system of many different muscles that must be strengthened and coordinated in order for the singer to achieve optimal performance.

Traditional vs. Contemporary Training Methods

Traditional voice pedagogy, which draws its roots from the 17th and 18th centuries, was developed for acoustic concert halls and acoustic accompaniment. While many teachers profess to teach "classical" or "bel canto" technique, the techniques are not codified. Some instructors teach a low laryngeal posture, some teach a neutral position, while others do not even address the larynx. The same is true for every other part of the mechanism. What does all of this mean for you, the singer? It means that it is very difficult to know what variety of classical or bel canto technique an instructor is teaching and even more difficult to know if that technique will be beneficial or counterproductive to musical theatre singing.

A Few Specifics

While it was believed in the past that breathing and posture were the same in classical and musical theatre, scientific research has indicated that may not be true. Traditional "plumb line posture" that aligns the singer's ears over their shoulders, their shoulders over their hips, and their hips over their ankles is actually based on 17th-century French military training manuals. Tucking the chin down and in when standing in this position will artificially lower the larynx. Since we know that musical theatre singers benefit from a slightly raised laryngeal position when belting, this posture can actually be counterproductive to the needs of the musical theatre singer.

Classical singers often favor low abdominal breathing. However, we now know that this style of breathing lowers the larynx through something called tracheal pull. Since classical singers often favor a slightly lower laryngeal position, this style of breathing can be quite advantageous. However, as mentioned above, musical theatre performers need to allow the larynx to rise comfortably while singing. A low breath that pulls the larynx down makes this difficult to accomplish. Furthermore, many musical theatre performers have "six" or "eight packs" and find lower abdominal breathing nearly impossible. This is not to say that there is never a valid reason to teach these techniques. If a singer has a thin, nasal voice, learning to lower the larynx will usually help normalize the vocal quality. If a belter is having a difficult time mixing, it is quite possible that the larynx is getting locked high. Again, introducing exercises that encourage a lower laryngeal position can be very helpful. However, these exercises must be chosen for a specific reason and not just because they worked for the teacher when they were learning to sing.

It is commonly accepted that singers have two distinct vocal registers, head and chest, and another quality that combines elements from those two extremes that is called mix. Register is a term used to describe a group of notes that have similar qualities. In chest register, the vocal folds come together on their thick edge and create a vibrant quality that has a lot of "buzz" or ring. In head register, the vocal folds come together on the thin upper edge and create a quality that is light and lacks buzz or ring. There are unlimited varieties of mix, but the most common in musical theatre are chest-dominant mix and head-dominant mix. Chest-dominant mix is used for mix belting (for example, "Defying Gravity") and head-dominant mix is used for legit singing (for example, Laura Osnes's version of "In My Own Little Corner"). In order to have control over all of the varieties of mix that are required for modern musical theatre, a singer must train both their head register and their chest register. Placement alone is not sufficient to strengthen these muscles. Exercises must specifically develop the muscles responsible for both chest and head in order to build the neurological connections and muscular tone necessary for this type of singing.

Resonance is also different in musical theatre and classical singing. While classical singers primarily use dark vowels when singing, musical theatre vowels are brighter. Voice scientists have developed software that measures the frequencies produced by a singer and have written multiple studies that have all found significant differences between classical and Contemporary Commercial Music (CCM) singers. In order to produce these differences in resonance, singers must learn to alter the height of their soft palate, the position of their tongue, and the shape of their lips. All of these systems are controlled by a complex interaction of many different muscles. Unless you spend time strengthening and coordinating these muscle groups, you will likely find it difficult to produce the necessary vocal qualities for success in musical theatre.

The examples above are all related to musical theatre singing, but let us not forget that musical theatre artists are also expected to sing pop/

rock styles as well. Pop/rock styles put a stronger emphasis on rhythm than musical theatre and classical styles. Pop/rock also requires singers to produce unique vocal qualities such as vocal fry, growl, breathy singing, and how to purposely make abrupt flips between registers. These sound qualities require unique techniques in order to be produced without causing vocal damage.

Because of the new demands on contemporary musical theatre performers, most voice scientists and leading pedagogues agree that CCM styles require a unique technical approach that is different from that used to train classical singers. Essentially, classical or bel canto training alone is no longer sufficient to train singers for electronically enhanced singing accompanied by electronic instruments in the 21st century. Singers are vocal athletes; they rely on highly refined coordination and strengthening of specific muscles to sing at a professional level. Vocal athletes are no different than dancers, runners, basketball players, or football players. They require training that targets the specific muscles and coordination necessary for their profession. A ballet dancer would never assume that her training alone would be sufficient to perform jazz choreography. A sprint runner would never think that her training would prepare her to immediately run a marathon. And we have learned from past experiments in the professional sports world that excelling at a sport such as basketball does not mean that one can successfully play baseball. Singing is no different. Just because you are a successful classical singer does not mean that you can just jump over to musical theatre and be successful, and vice versa.

Functional Training

Functional training is the new buzzword in the voice pedagogy world. The concept of functional training has been around for many years but has been slow to permeate the larger voice teacher community. Functional training requires the teacher to fully understand how the voice works and to know exactly what various exercises accomplish. When working with a student, the teacher's approach is very similar to that of a personal trainer. The teacher assesses the student's voice and determines areas of tension and weakness. They then design an exercise regimen that targets those areas that need improvement. Through systematic use of those exercises, the student will begin to notice physical changes that make it easier to produce desired vocal qualities.

What to Look for in a Teacher

When looking for a teacher, first and foremost you want to make sure they have experience with musical theatre styles and vocal techniques. If you are a female, you must learn how to belt and mix-belt. Male singers need to be able to sing with their own version of a belt, which requires them to use a different resonance strategy than that used to "cover" the high notes in classical singing. If you are just starting out, you can spend a couple of years strengthening your technique while learning Golden Age repertoire. If you are a more advanced singer, you need to be learning how to bounce back and forth between contemporary musical theatre, Golden Age material, and pop/rock material. If you want to work on classical repertoire, you can. However, most leading pedagogues agree that there is no inherent benefit for the musical theatre performer in learning to sing this repertoire. Concepts such as acoustic resonance and legato can be taught just as easily through a song such as "If I Loved You" as it can be through "Caro Mio Ben." Musical theatre repertoire and vocal style has changed dramatically in the last thirty years. While classical techniques were sufficient in the past, they are no longer sufficient to handle all of the demands placed upon today's singers. Just remember that vocal health should always be a top priority and there are plenty of teachers out there who can help you maintain your vocal health while learning to produce vocal qualities that are marketable for musical theatre.

Matthew Edwards
Artistic Director, CCM Vocal Pedagogy Institute
Associate Professor of Voice and Voice Pedagogy, Shenandoah Conservatory

Matthew Edwards is associate professor of voice and voice pedagogy at Shenandoah Conservatory and artistic director of the CCM Vocal Pedagogy Institute. He is the author of *So You Want to Sing Rock 'n' Roll* and numerous book chapters and articles on CCM singing. For more information, visit EdwardsVoice.com, CCMInstitute.com, and AuditioningForCollege.com.

So once more, the complete musical theatre audition repertoire book will absolutely include at least one or two of each of the following: standard ballads, standard up-tempos, contemporary ballads, and contemporary up-tempo or driving dramatic songs. It will also include several selections from varying styles or flavors of popular music, all of which you must *love* to sing and all of which demonstrate only your strengths and never your weaknesses. Let me be even clearer about not demonstrating your weaknesses: you are who you are. You have your unique talents and skill set. Perhaps you are a crazy high riff–Queen beltress. Or maybe you're not. It's okay. Be you. Do you. Don't overreach and try to be what you think "they" need. They need you. But mostly, they need you to be authentically *you*. (Steps off soapbox.)

Beyond those bare minimums, you may also choose to include a couple of certain "specialty" songs in your book, depending on how you see yourself working in the industry. One common casting request is the daunting comedy song. My simple advice for when you need a comedy song is this: Think outside of the box. Songs that are funny in their show's context (i.e., Mel Brooks's material, *Spamalot*, *Legally Blonde*, etc.) are rarely funny in the audition room. And the goal of a successful comedy song is to demonstrate your sense of humor and comic timing. Here's a situation wherein if you can make the creative team laugh, you're probably doing something right.

Comedy relies on two factors to be funny—context and surprise. When you choose typical musical comedy repertoire to take into the audition room, you are removing both of these factors, because you lack the context of the theatrical setting in which the joke lands and you also are performing these songs for a roomful of people who already know the punch lines, so to speak. Instead of risking a deadpan room that sucks the life out of your comedy song audition, I suggest you find (appropriate) ways to bring surprise into the room. To that end, I suggest you first examine the musical/vocal style required of the show for which you are auditioning. Then find a song that fits into that arena, but turn the context of the song on its heels.

At Penn State, under the direction of my mentor Cary Libkin, I learned this activity (which I have gratefully stolen and adapted over the years for my own students) lovingly called the "wrong song" exercise. You simply take a song, examine its lyrics in great detail, and create an alternate context that the lyrics can also fully support, but one that is completely unexpected and unintended by the lyricist in its original incarnation. For example, I had a student perform "Till There Was You" from *The Music Man*, but she did it as a mental asylum inmate who was literally hearing birds and bells and so on. I had another student who turned the 1930 Depression-era song "Brother, Can You Spare a Dime" into a strip tease (perfect audition for the Emcee in *Cabaret*!). The exercise may require a little lyric-tweaking or some additional instructions to the accompanist—and always be sure to notate these sorts of changes on the page for the pianist—but the payoff is often resoundingly successful when you shake the auditors out of their expectations and make them sit up and pay attention to your clever choices. The best part is that you can really do this with any genre of music, from jazz standards to pop/rock. The trick is to be fully committed to the context you create and not stand outside of it and comment on your own cleverness. Whether you are in need of a comedy song for a particular audition or not, this is actually a great exercise to get you thinking outside of the box, so have some fun with it and see what you come up with.

A second specialty repertoire genre for those who are classically trained or have the ability to shift into an authentic legit mode is a song that showcases you in an operatic setting. Many stock and regional theatres will include Gilbert and Sullivan in their seasons (most commonly, *The Mikado*, *The Pirates of Penzance*, and *H.M.S. Pinafore*). If they are interested in casting you for a summer company, they may require that you handle classical singing as well as contemporary musical theatre. Also, there are several reputable companies in New York that produce these works annually, including the Gilbert and Sullivan Players and the Village Light Opera Group. Again, if you can do it, it might be another avenue toward a career in performing.

Songs from the aforementioned Gilbert and Sullivan works will suffice in your book. For girls, consider an aria such as "The Sun Whose Rays" from *The Mikado* or "Poor Wand'ring One" from *The Pirates of Penzance*. For men, you may want a patter song (tour de force of words, very common in operetta), such as "I Am the Very Model of a Modern Major General" from *Penzance*. These examples are very common and somewhat cliché in the world of operetta, but for a musical theatre performer to have something simple to pull out, they should be fine. Consider searching deeper, however, and looking into the works of Rudolf Friml, Sigmund Romberg, and Victor Herbert if this style suits your voice and your ambitions.

As you continue to build and hone your book, I want to reiterate what I said before about casting directors asking actors to sing standards and Golden Age music. Many performers find it necessary to dig deep into the catalog of lost, unproduced, and forgotten musicals to find songs that no one has heard. They are so concerned with singing what nobody else is singing, they lose track of good taste. While it is occasionally appropriate and beneficial to have songs that are really your own (especially comedy songs!), it is far more helpful to have songs with which most directors are at least vaguely familiar. This way, they will have some standard against which to judge your rendition of the song and they won't spend your entire audition thinking, "What is this song???" There is nothing wrong with singing a familiar melody, as long as you sing it well.

Of course, that being said, there are some tunes that are so overdone you may want to avoid them completely. Everyone has his own list of "do not sing" songs, but here are some of the big groan-inducers that I think are standard across most of the industry:

"Nothing" from *A Chorus Line*; "Think of Me" from *The Phantom of the Opera*; "I Dreamed a Dream" from *Les Miserables*; "Getting to Know You" from *The King and I*; "Always True to You" from *Kiss Me, Kate*; "Gethsemane" from *Jesus Christ Superstar*; "I Got Rhythm" from *Girl Crazy*; "Anything Goes" from *Anything Goes*; "Adelaide's Lament" from *Guys and Dolls*; "My Favorite Things" from *The Sound of Music*; "Shy" from *Once upon a Mattress*; "Vanilla Ice Cream" from *She Loves Me*; "Popular" and "Defying Gravity" from *Wicked*; "Disneyland" from *Smile*; "Astonishing" from *Little Women*; "Pulled" from *The Addams Family*; and "All That Jazz" from *Chicago*. There is nothing wrong with these songs in and of themselves. And honestly, if you really feel like one or more of these songs really shows you off better than anything else in the musical theatre canon, then by all means, have it in your book. At the end of the day, a casting director's job is to assess you and your talent, not your taste in music. But just know that these overplayed songs do come with a price tag when you bring them into an audition. You have to determine if it's worth the risk.

Finally, some other songs to avoid include anything with dialect (*My Fair Lady*, Adelaide in *Guys and Dolls*, Audrey in *Little Shop of Horrors*), and any songs that either brag obnoxiously ("Gorgeous" from *The Apple Tree*—another of the unfortunate overdone, shoot-me songs; "Me" from *Beauty and the Beast*; "The Greatest Star" from *Funny Girl*) or self-deprecate and make a statement that you are a loser ("Mr. Cellophane" from *Chicago*, "Nobody Does It Like Me" from *Seesaw*, and "You Can Always Count on Me" from *City of Angels*). If you are attending an audition for any of those shows, then you may use those songs. Otherwise, leave them in your "B" book or on the cutting room floor.

STEP 3: LEARN THE SONGS

I am now going to offer you advice on how to approach every song you learn. You will likely read this section and scoff at the amount of work it requires of you, especially in light of the quantity of songs I just suggested for your repertoire. You may want to take shortcuts or perhaps avoid doing the work on songs you already "know." But I guarantee you that if you have not done this analysis, you do not truly know the songs you have been singing. When my students complain to me about how much time this requires, I tell them what my acting teacher Jim Wise always told us in graduate school: If this were easy, everyone would do it. Now begins the real work of the actor.

The first step to learning a song properly is to begin with the lyrics. If you have never heard the song, this step will be easier, as you will not have a preconceived rhythm or tune in your head. If you do know the tune, try your best to separate yourself from it and look at the words as an entity of their own. Begin by writing or typing out the lyrics in paragraph form, taking them out of verse. This will allow you to read the song as a text without any poetic quirks. Next, observe the punctuation in great detail, including periods, question marks, exclamation points, commas, colons, semicolons, hyphens, and so forth.

At this point, I am assuming that you know the story line of the musical from which your song comes and you have thought about the character and the song's dramatic context. Look for red flags such as repeated lyrics, symbolism, metaphor, alliteration, and consonance to point out which words the lyricist felt were important in the conveyance of the song's meaning. Why are those techniques used, and how can you use them to make your performance more powerful? Circle the nouns and think about what they mean to your character so that when you speak and sing them, they come to life clearly. Then begin to consider why the character *needs* to sing this song (remember, in musical theatre characters sing when the emotion is too great to speak). What does he want from his scene partner? What kinds of tactics can he use to achieve his objective? Is there seduction, guilt, reasoning, pleading, bargaining? When you have thought through all of these questions thoroughly, you should begin to memorize your lyrics as a monologue and then practice delivering it as such. Use an imaginary other, a mirror, or better yet, a real live scene partner, and speak the text aloud, paying close attention to words and phrases that need to be emphasized or driven home. And do not cheat: If there are repeated words or verses, you should find a justification for the repetition. Why do we repeat ourselves when we speak? Why do we *repeat* ourselves when we speak? Why. Do. We. Repeat. Ourselves. When. We. Speak? Get it?

Once you have made a full analysis of the lyrics, you are ready to begin looking at the music. Just as you found red flags in the words, I encourage you to do the same with the composition. Even if you don't read music, you can look for clues like high notes and low notes that stand out on the staff, dynamic markings and accents that tell you how loud or soft to sing or how to attack certain notes, and duration of notes (half notes, whole notes, held notes, fermatas, etc.). In good musical theatre composing, these are all indications of the mood or emotional life of the character, and you should use them. As a general rule of thumb, it is safe to assume that rangy (really high or really low) notes and long notes have extra significance and meaning.

The next thing to look at is the accompaniment, or the music playing underneath what you are singing. If you can play piano, you should hammer this out before dealing with the melody line. Otherwise, have someone play it for you. Listen for clues such as tempo and symbolic underscoring. For example, in Sondheim's musical *Company*, there is a terrific song called "Another Hundred People." It deals with the overwhelming population of New York City, and its accompaniment sounds very much like a subway train. The accompaniment can tell you a lot about what kind of mood the composer is looking for. It is a big mistake to ignore clues in the piano line.

Finally, you are ready to plunk out the melody. Remember my warning about original cast recordings: if you rely on them to teach you the melody, you will surely be led astray. Learn the notes and the rhythms on the page perfectly before adding any styling or ornamentation.

Once you put all of this together, you should be ready to fully perform any song you choose to tackle. The analysis will help fuse the singing with the acting, and it will make the difference between a nice voice and a skilled musical theatre actor. Note the use of the term *actor*. It is not enough just to stand and sing. You must invest fully in the character's life with any song you perform, moment to moment. Anything less than this will not be competitive in this cutthroat business. For every song you sing, you should be able to answer the following questions: What show is it from? Who wrote the show? Which character is singing it? To whom is she singing? What does she want from that person? And what just happened the moment before to launch her into song? Trust me, these questions will come up in audition situations, and you do not want to be unprepared for them. So take the time before you even put a song in your "A" book to take it apart and learn it correctly.

Finally, you must go one step further than simply answering the above technical questions and doing the analysis "homework." There is a vital element of *personalization* that you must invest in every song you sing—whether it's jazz, musical theatre, or pop/rock. The last crucial puzzle piece in preparing and delivering an authentic, moving, exciting performance is to do some serious soul-searching and to create a deep, personal connection to your song. By now you know why the character is singing the song, but why are *you* singing the song? So you have chosen to play a character who wants to convince her flirtatious rival to ask her to the Box Social. That's Laurey's context, but what does that mean to *you*? How can you personalize the journey in a way that allows you to feel all of the same yearnings and live under the same high stakes as Laurey Williams is experiencing so that your performance is in earnest and you don't need to make believe you're feeling the character's emotions? Perhaps you've chosen to sing Alanis Morissette's "Head over Feet," which was written about a very personal relationship in that artist's life. How can you make Alanis's song *your song* when you take it into an audition? How can you make her words as though they were your own personal thoughts? Personalize it, using your experience and your imagination. This is the most challenging part of preparing a performance, but it's arguably the most important and effective element you can deliver in the audition room.

STEP 4: CUT AND MARK YOUR MUSIC

Now that you know how to find music and learn it, the final element is to prepare it for the audition room. It is not enough simply to copy it all and place it in sheets. This is where your black marker, Post-It Notes, and highlighter will come in handy.

First of all, you must have the entire song for every selection you choose to sing. The only exception to this rule is if you choose to sing a cutting from a duet in which your character sings an entire section that stands alone; in this case, you may cut out the other character (e.g., "No Other Love" from *Me and Juliet* or "People Will Say We're in Love" from *Oklahoma!*). Otherwise, I'm afraid it's not enough to learn only a small segment of any song. You never know when they'll want to hear more or ask you to jump to the bridge or the modulation (key change), and you'll be embarrassed if you are caught without all the music.

That said, if you are auditioning in the United States (it's different in Europe and Australia, where they generally allow for entire songs), for every song you sing, you should prepare a specific, stand-alone section, generally consisting of 16 measures (half a chorus) or 32 measures (whole chorus) of music. Rarely will open call auditions call for entire songs, so you want to be prepared to show them only what they are asking to see. Cutting songs is an art in itself, and there is no simple, generalized way to explain it. However, I will offer some guidelines.

First of all, do not simply assume that "16 bars" literally means 16 bars—that you should count out exactly 16 measures of music and sing only that much. Sixteen bars is an approximation that says they don't really want to hear more than a minute of singing. If you are singing a ballad or a slow-moving song, chances are you will find a cutting that is close to the actual measure count; but if you are singing an up-tempo, cut-time, speedy song, you can usually get away with doubling the number of measures and it will feel like the same amount of song. The bottom line is this: Don't come in and sing an entire verse and a chorus. Just give them a snippet of the song so they can hear your voice and see you act.

You've probably heard some version of the cliché that the first impression is the most important. Keep this in mind when choosing a cutting of music. You don't want to start out too subtle and take three minutes to get to the "good stuff." You may not get a chance to get that far. So try to show them everything you need them to see in the first 30 seconds. This means that starting at the beginning of the song isn't usually the best idea. If anything, it is usually more productive to start at the song's end and count backward until you come to the beginning of a logical phrase at approximately 16 bars (or however many the audition calls for).

This brings me to the idea of logic. Please consider all the work you have done on lyric analysis. Make sure you are able to show them some acting in the songs you bring in to auditions. This means that the cuttings you choose must make sense and be *complete* thoughts. Nothing burns me more than when singers stop in the middle of a phrase because they reached the measure "limit." Don't leave us hanging on a thought! It's also irritating when song cuts begin with words such as "and . . ." or "but . . .," both of which imply that you're entering in the middle of a thought or a conversation. Make it feel like you are giving us a clear beginning as well as an end in your short cuts.

As you consider where you are going to cut a song, you will want to mark clearly with the black marker a bracket around the beginning and the end and write "Start" and "End" in big, bold letters. Then you should highlight both of these markings to make them extra clear. You can also use Post-It Notes to make your brackets—this way if you decide to change your cut, you don't have a big mess of markings in various places of the music; you simply lift the sticky note with the start or end bracket and move it elsewhere. Just be sure that the sticky notes go inside of the nonglare protective sheet, so they don't fall off.

Other things to highlight in the music include the key signature (the sharps and flats at the beginning of a piece of music) and any changes of key that occur throughout the song, any dynamic markings that will affect the piano accompaniment, any repeats in the music that you are taking or ignoring, and any stylings you choose to observe, such as fermatas, extra rests, or caesuras (train tracks). If you are using any alternate lyrics to what is written in the music, be sure to write these in as well. These highlights will make the pianist take note in advance of elements that might otherwise cause a slowdown or a stoppage in the fluid accompaniment. They will make your performance as smooth as possible, and you will be able to audition with confidence.

Once you have made all the necessary markings in your music, you are ready to put it into protective sheets and add it to your binder. Be sure to line the pages up so that they require the fewest number of page turns possible (or that the page turns happen, when they must, at the optimal places in the song, so as not to disrupt the flow). If you have an excerpt with an even number of pages, the first page of the excerpt should generally be a left page, so that two pages are visible at once. If the excerpt has an odd number of pages, the first page may be either on the left or right, depending on where the logical turns need to happen. And needless to say, a song with only two pages should be placed so that the pages face each other, rather than page one on the right side of the book and page two behind it. Use common sense when designing your book layout.

If you have songs that are fairly long, you may choose to display only the cutting of the song that you will most frequently use, placing the rest of the music behind the cutting in one plastic sheet. If asked for more of the song, you can then take it out from behind the cut pages and display it fairly quickly. Just be sure that if your cutting starts in the middle of a song, you write the title of the song, the show it comes from, and the key signature on the top of the first page of your cutting. Again, this is for the benefit of the accompanist.

When putting the music into your binder, it is completely a matter of preference how you organize the songs. Some may choose to lay out music by genres, as I demonstrated for you earlier. Others may separate ballads from up-tempos or organize chronologically or even alphabetically. Whatever works for you is fine; there is no prescribed method. But you should use tab dividers for ease of finding music quickly. Smart performers also place a table of contents at the front of the book so they do not need to thumb through to see what titles they have, one song at a time, when a casting director asks for other options. My only advice is that you place whatever song(s) you are going to sing at an audition in the front of the book for that particular audition. This will make the pianist's life easier and they will love you for it.

Once again, remember that the repertoire book is an ever-changing beast. It can change over the years as you outgrow songs you've been using or grow into songs you've wanted to use. It can change depending on the nature of the audition that you are planning to attend. It can even change based on your knowledge of the director and his or her preferences. If you take care in building your rep book, it will serve you well for years, and you will always look professional, confident, and polished. Directors will want to work with you.

STEP 5: NOT SO FAST . . . YOU NEED MONOLOGUES!

One of the biggest challenges for my students seems to be finding good monologues. I'm not sure if it's because they really don't know where to look or if it's because they don't think that musical theatre performers need them. Maybe it's laziness—that they don't read enough plays. Either way, I have news for you: You need them if you are to call yourself an actor. Almost nothing will make you look less professional in an audition setting than being asked for a monologue and saying you don't have one prepared. While monologues are not so common anymore in professional auditions in the United States, they're certainly not obsolete. So here are some tips for finding at least a modest selection of pieces:

Like musical repertoire, you want monologues that stem from different genres of theatre (*not* monologue books or the Internet!). You need a mix of light, comic pieces (not stand-up routines) and more dramatic pieces (not suicidal or utterly miserable). Furthermore, you need representation of classical and contemporary theatre.

Begin with Shakespeare. He is the master of dramatic literature, and he is the most commonly produced playwright even today. Consider avoiding plays like *Macbeth*, *Hamlet*, and *Romeo and Juliet*, as these are really too overdone. Instead, look to plays such as *Measure for Measure*, *Twelfth Night*, *King Lear*, *Taming of the Shrew*, *Much Ado about Nothing*, and *Cymbeline*, for starters. Shakespeare has a wealth of youthful characters who are in their 20s or early 30s, so seek them out if that's your current age range, as opposed to playing the older "heavies." And when looking for good material, do not limit yourself to scanning the book for long paragraphs. Often the best monologues come from taking a scene of dialogue and cutting the minor character out. (This goes for Shakespeare and contemporary playwrights as well.) By taking this approach, you are guaranteeing that your monologue involves another person from whom you want something and upon whom you are *acting*.

If you do a great deal of nonmusical, classical acting, you may also want to have a monologue from early Greek or Roman theatre (such as *Antigone* or *The Oresteia*), but normally Shakespeare and his contemporaries, Ben Jonson or Christopher Marlowe, are enough to suffice for classical or verse pieces. Just do your best to have both a comedic and a dramatic option.

The next thing you'll need is some great realism from the masters of realistic drama. These authors include Henrik Ibsen (*A Doll House; Ghosts; Hedda Gabler*), Anton Chekhov (*The Three Sisters; The Cherry Orchard; The Seagull*), Arthur Miller (*Death of a Salesman; All My Sons; The Crucible*), Eugene O'Neill (*Long Day's Journey into Night; A Moon for the Misbegotten; Ah! Wilderness*), Clifford Odets (*Waiting for Lefty; Golden Boy; Awake and Sing!*), Tennessee Williams (*The Glass Menagerie; Cat on a Hot Tin Roof; Suddenly Last Summer; Summer and Smoke*), and specifically for African Americans, August Wilson (*Fences; Joe Turner's Come and Gone; The Piano Lesson; Ma Rainey's Black Bottom*).

Regardless of whether you find monologues that you like in any number of the titles I have listed above, you should read all of them and be familiar with their plots and characters if you wish to be able to hold a serious discussion about theatre with anyone. In addition to seeking out monologues, you should always be reading plays for your ongoing education. However, I promise you if it is monologues you seek, you will find ample choices in those plays.

Finally, find a few pieces in varying styles from more contemporary dramatists such as Kenneth Lonergan (*Lobby Hero; This Is Our Youth*), Theresa Rebeck (*Spike Heels; Mauritius; Seminar*), Rebecca Gilman (*The Crowd You're in With; Blue Surge*), Lanford Wilson (*Burn This; Talley's Folly*), Annie Baker (*The Aliens; The Flick*), John Patrick Shanley (*Women of Manhattan; Danny and the Deep Blue Sea*), and David Lindsay-Abaire (*Wonder of the World; Rabbit Hole; Good People*) to name just a few popular American playwrights. Obviously, this is a list that could go on forever. But do your homework and find plays and playwrights who really speak to you. If you get to New York City, spend an afternoon browsing the shelves of Drama Book Shop (250 West 40th Street) and discover new scripts.

You want to find characters who really speak to you, roles you can sink your teeth into right now at this point in your life. And these monologues you seek should never exceed one minute in length. Even when an audition calls for a two-minute monologue, trust me: a minute is as long as they will need to determine if they like you or not. You don't want to wear out your welcome or talk yourself *out* of a callback.

As with music, there are monologues and playwrights you may wish to avoid because they are overdone or badly written. This is only my personal "hit list," but you may find that many directors agree with most or all of my selections: Eugene's "That's what they have gutters for" monologue from *Brighton Beach Memoirs* by Neil Simon, the "Mr. Cornell" monologue from *The Star Spangled Girl* by Neil Simon, the "Jack and Jill" monologue from *Butterflies Are Free* by Leonard Gershe, the "Mother's ashes" monologue from *I Think You Think I Love You* by Kelly Younger, almost anything over-the-top by Christopher Durang or David Ives, *The Diary of Anne Frank*, and Tom's final speech and Laura's "Blue Roses" speech from *The Glass Menagerie* by Tennessee Williams are some of the really painfully overdone pieces we see in auditions.

Finally, for every monologue you add to your arsenal, I urge you to type out the speech and keep it in the back of your repertoire book. You never know when you'll be sitting in the waiting room at an audition that only called for a song, and three people ahead of you will walk out lamenting that the director is asking to hear comedic monologues in addition. What a relief that you can pull out any of the pieces you have learned and quickly refresh them before going in to the audition room.

Now you have all the keys to developing and maintaining a well-polished repertoire book. These tips will serve you throughout your entire career, whether you are in high school, college, or the big city. Spend the time thoroughly preparing every piece that you add to your "A" book, and I guarantee you will audition with more polish and confidence than ever before.

Suit the Word to the Action

Assuming you've developed a thorough repertoire book filled with songs you love to sing (which you sing well), choosing a particular song for a specific audition should be fairly simple. Just remember this bit of advice: *Let the song suit the audition as well as the performer.*

For example, if you are auditioning for a production of *Good News*, a 1920s high school flapper dance musical, you would be best served finding an audition piece that both embodies the spirit and essence of that show and also displays your appropriateness for casting in it. Material from shows such as *The Boyfriend* or *Thoroughly Modern Millie* would be a smart choice, since they are set in the same era with the same style and they contain characters of similar age and type. Material from *Grease*, although it's a high school–age musical, would be wrong because of its 1950s music; and material from *Show Boat*, although it's from the 1920s, is not right because of the completely different ages and types of characters in that show (not to mention the musical's vast stylistic differences).

You show a great deal of professionalism and savvy if you come into an audition understanding the casting needs of the specific show and choosing material that shows the director how good *you* would be in that production.

SUMMARY

- Your repertoire book is a vital part of your presentation and should say as much about who you are as it does about what you can do.
- Have an "A" book that you bring to auditions. Know every song in this book inside and out and make sure they all represent you well. Your "B" book is where you store works in progress and material that is not audition ready.
- The professional performer's repertoire should contain representation from standard ballads, standard up-tempos, contemporary ballads, contemporary up-tempo or "driving dramatic" songs, and various colors of pop/rock music, depending on what suits your voice best.
- Consider including "specialty pieces" in your rep, such as a great (outside-the-box) comedy song or an operetta piece, if you do them well.
- For today's musical theatre landscape it is important that you study or coach with someone versed in contemporary commercial music (CCM) styles.
- Always do a great deal of analysis on every song you sing, including context, character details, point of view, and above all, personalization.
- Keep your music well organized in nonglare plastic sheets and mark it clearly for ease of accompaniment. Have tab dividers and a table of contents.
- Find monologues of various genres from published plays and be ready to deliver them whenever auditions may call for them.

3

WALKING THROUGH
THE AUDITION

ANYTHING THAT CAN GO WRONG . . .

The nervous actor paces back and forth outside the studio. He is trying—and consistently failing—to review his song lyrics as the tenor in the room begins what the actor is certain is his *third* song. The young man struggles to hear himself think over the beating of his own heartbeat, which is now filling his ears.

The audition called for only 32 bars. What the hell are they doing with him in there? Are they asking everyone to sing more? What else should I sing if they do want another song? I really wasn't intending on having to pick another song. What if they don't ask me to sing more? Does that mean they're not interested in me? I have to nail this audition. I'll just go in there and show them I—

The door opens and the actor is brought back to reality at the sound of his name being called by the monitor. He takes a deep breath and tries to shake his nerves out through his fingertips. He steps into the room and immediately spots the accompanist reading the *Times* drearily at the piano. He makes a beeline to the upright and gently thrusts his music book under the nose of the musician, opening the binder to the last page of "She Loves Me." (He was going to sing "I Met a Girl," but he heard no fewer than three people sing that selection in the hour he'd been waiting!)

"Just start there and go to the end," he tells the pianist, pointing to the red marking on the page. The actor then crosses to the center of the room and for the first time notices the three people sitting behind the table, looking utterly indifferent.

"Should I just start?" he asks, trying to smile confidently.

"Whenever you're ready," replies the man seated at the center of the table. The actor wonders for a moment if this is the director. Should he say something to him? Look at him? Break the ice?

"And tomorrow . . . tomorrow . . . aaaahhhhhhh . . ."

That accompanist just started playing! I wasn't ready. Does he know how ludicrous this must sound, so rushed?

The breathless actor struggles to keep up with the break-neck tempo that this cruel musician has set.

"She . . . loves . . . meeeeeeeeee."

With heart pounding wildly, the young man forces a smile. Had he sung the right words? Was he in tune? It's all a blur to him at this point. No matter, though; it's over. A minor wave of relief washes over the actor. His reverie is broken by the man whom he suspected was the director: "Thank you," the voice intones with a hint of mock enthusiasm.

"Thank *you*," the actor forces as he turns on his heels to leave, eager to put a great deal of distance between himself and this entire experience. But just as he reaches the door another voice calls out his name. He stops, and in an instant he feels overwhelming redemption.

They did like me. They want me to sing more. They want me to come back here tomorrow and read for the leading role.

"You forgot your music." It's the voice of that damned accompanist who had just ruined the actor's audition. But what can the young man do at this point? Blushing, he smiles awkwardly and retrieves his binder. He is grateful to hear the door close behind him following what has been a painfully long, excruciatingly silent trek back to the piano and out of the room.

He is glad it's over. He packs his book and his water bottle back into his bag and begins the walk back to the midtown office where he is temping for the day. If he walks fast enough, he might still have time before the end of lunch to check the paper for any good auditions the next day.

Depressing, isn't it? And yet, this is a daily occurrence for hundreds of actors in dozens of cities. But it doesn't have to be that way. The actor in the story simply hadn't found the joy in auditioning. He lost sight of his purpose and he dug himself an emotional, psychological abyss before he even stepped into the room. His confidence shot before he began, he didn't stand a chance in there.

A few pieces of advice may have set that poor young man (and multitudes of fellow actors) on a better track to success in the audition room:

Tip 1: Prepare, Prepare, Prepare

I know I'm being redundant, repetitive, and redundant on this point, but it cannot be overemphasized. You *must* know every song in your book by rote. That means you don't have to spend the time leading up to your audition reviewing notes and lyrics. There will never be enough time to cram, and you will forget the song when your nerves kick in. If you know your songs backward and forward, in your sleep, you can put your focus elsewhere . . . like on the *acting*, perhaps!

Further to that point, you'll remember that our tragic hero had originally prepared to sing "I Met a Girl" (a great Golden-Age up-tempo song from *Bells Are Ringing*), but he switched at the last moment to avoid choosing a piece that several others had already performed. Switching at the last minute would not have been problematic had he been confident with every song in his repertoire. But more poignantly, he shouldn't have been intimidated. If six women sing "I Enjoy Being a Girl," do any of them do it exactly the same? Your job as an actor is to interpret and act every song you perform as though it were happening to you right in that very moment, for the first time. (Remember our talk about personalization from chapter 2?) If you can do that, I promise you your rendition will be unique and special. If you can't do that, it doesn't really matter what you sing or how many others sang it before you that day; you'll fall flat. *Just remember, they're auditioning you, not your song.*

Tip 2: Keep Your Focus in the Right Place

Nobody gets cast from a first audition. It just doesn't happen. Your purpose in an audition is to show the creative team you at your very best and most authentic. Your subliminal message to them is "This is who I am. This is what I do. This is what I love." (Thank you audition guru VP Boyle for that mantra!) Getting a callback is the *most* you can hope to achieve from that first meeting, and furthermore, just showing yourself off well is the measure of a successful audition, callback or not. If you try to do too much, you'll overshoot the mark and wind up shooting yourself in the foot. Broadway actor Alex Brightman (*Wicked, Matilda, School of Rock*) wisely advises: "When you walk into an audition room, you don't have the job. That's a fact. So if you walk out of the audition room without the job, you haven't lost anything. Most people think they just don't have the job *yet* but it's simpler than that." Think about that for a minute.

Our fictional actor was so concerned with getting the job ("nailing it") and comparing himself with the other actors going in ahead of him that he lost sight of his own mission and his authenticity. Similarly, when actors go in needing a job too much and trying to be exactly what they think the director wants, it almost guarantees failure. It's as though the directors can smell the neediness, and that is a tremendous turnoff.

Besides, you'll never know what they're really after—it's not for you to know, so stop trying to figure it out. Let go of the things that are not in your control, and focus on the aspects that are. Just relax. Remember that this is your daily opportunity to do what you love—perform. You don't need to show them any more than you at your very best.

Tip 3: Be a Person in There

An unfortunate majority of actors follow the path of the hypothetical man in my story, from the door to the piano to the imaginary "X" on the floor to the piano to the door, without taking a moment to connect with the artistic team on a personal level. Would you put your baby in the care of a rigid automaton that shows no outward display of compassion, empathy, or emotion? Neither would a director.

Stop trying so hard to show them what you *think* they want to see—you will never be able to know what they want or how to manufacture it. The truth of the matter is that most of the time, they don't even know what they're really looking for until you walk in and show them. I'll tell you a quick story to demonstrate this point—and this is a very common occurrence. Last year, I had the opportunity to direct the college/regional premiere of *Green Day's American Idiot* at Shenandoah Conservatory. It was the first production after the closing of the Broadway national tour, and we were getting a lot of attention for it. As most directors do, I created lists of actors whom I wanted to consider for each role in the show, based on what I thought the parts called for and what I knew of my students. One young lady in her senior year didn't even come across our radar for the role of "Whatsername," because she wasn't at all what I envisioned the character to be. But I'm sure you can guess what I'm going to tell you: She walked in with such authentic determination, and she offered us *hands down* the very best audition we had seen. Immediately, my vision of the character changed. We called her back, and after she sang material from the show, we immediately knew that it had to be her—we really didn't need to see anyone else's auditions. It was so thrilling and unexpected. (And in the end, believe me when I tell you that she *delivered* in performance as well!) The moral of the story is when you get out of your head, stop trying to do it "right," and just be yourself, you become far more appealing to the artistic team. Perhaps the secondary moral (for all those girls who didn't get the part) is yet another reminder that some things are 100 percent out of your control. We had four or five other really stellar candidates for the role. But it didn't matter how well they sang because once Lara auditioned for us, our minds were made up.

So all you can do is let them know who you are and what you have to offer. Then it's up to them to determine if you match what their show needs this time around. If you aren't cast, it's no judgment on your talent; but you've done yourself a service by showing them your humanity. I can't tell you how often directors pass on an actor because she isn't right for a particular show they're casting, but they keep her in mind and call her in later for a more suitable role. What makes an actor memorable and impressionable enough to earn casting clout for future projects? *Vulnerability, authenticity, and personality.*

Tip 4: Own Your Audition

Nobody in the room wants you to fail. They are trying to cast their show, so your collapse and humiliation benefits nobody, least of all the artistic staff. If you keep that fact in mind and remain present from start to finish, you'll greatly improve your chance for success. In the pages that follow, I'll walk you through the steps for controlling as much of your own fate as you can in an audition room, but for now just remember that it's your time.

The performance is only one part of the audition process. Communication makes up a large percentage of the overall experience. As we move forward in the following pages, we'll spend some time dealing with this issue as it pertains to all of the people in the audition room. For now, suffice it to say that if you feel like the pianist is rushing your song and making a mess of your audition, it probably began with poor communication on your part. If you feel as though the creative team is ignoring you and focusing on their fingernails or their lunches, it probably began with poor communication on your part.

A VERY GOOD PLACE TO START

There's an old adage in the theatre that says: "Your audition begins *the moment* you walk in the door." This point cannot be overstated. Many actors feel that they need to deal with the accompanist first, and then get their bearings in the room before finally being ready to look at the artistic team, with a big old fake smile plastered on. This is a major fallacy. The director has a very limited amount of time to gather as much information as possible about you. Although this information includes singing and acting ability, it also comprises a great deal of personal information. The director wants to know if you have a sense of humor, if you are outgoing, if you are confident, if you are intelligent, if you can be present and compelling, if he or she wants to work with you every day for the next five to eight weeks. If you walk into the room silently, with your head down, and march directly to the accompanist, the director learns little about you beyond a certain ability to radiate anxiety.

Why not use every second to your advantage? Get them on your team before they even hear you sing. Have them liking you so much that they think: "God, I hope she can sing!" This process begins by *owning* and *warming the room* when you enter. It is your audition, and you must appear as though you are comfortable with the entire process. Nothing surprises you or throws you. (Note: This doesn't mean that you shouldn't be nervous. *Everyone* is nervous at auditions! Auditions are the most artificial and awkward conceits. So get over the idea that you'll be able to breathe out your nerves and be totally calm when you enter. Rather, embrace the nervousness as part of your human condition, and allow yourself to be honest, authentic, and present instead.) When you walk through the door, walk in as though you were meant to be there. Carry an air of confidence and sincerity that emanates through the room. I once heard an audition coach refer to this as creating a "shoulder-lowering experience," and I love that idea of helping the creative team relax and let go of their tension when you enter. Always begin by acknowledging everyone in the room with a polite greeting. This is, at the very least, a basic courtesy you would extend to a room of people in any given situation, especially one from which you are seeking work. After all, directors, pianists, and choreographers are people, too, and we don't want to feel we've been treated rudely.

Once you step into the room, you must remain in active, present listening mode. You may run into a sullen group of people who are holding a conference and ignoring you when you enter: Just move on. You may find that they perk up upon hearing your polite greeting and respond with further conversation: All the better for you. You may simply get a curt grunt with no encouragement to take the chatting any further: Don't let it throw your process or kill your mood. Whatever the case, you should remain open and respond to whatever they throw at you. If they want to talk to you, don't run to the piano and anxiously try to move things along. Stop and talk to them—you may be the only one all day who has! The more they can get to know you outside of your performance, the better. The bottom line is this: *Always remain present in the audition room.* This means really listen to what they say and respond to them like a human being. It's part of the test of a good actor, this ability to be present. Additionally, the theme of the audition should be "face time." The more they get of you and your face as a first impression, the better. So if they want to talk, let them talk to you. And remember to be authentic—this is not the time to put on a character or a show.

That said, be careful not to overdo it. Some actors try to be too fake and chummy with me in an audition, and it's a big turnoff. (It's one thing if we have a previous relationship, but if you don't know me, don't pretend I'm your best friend.) Don't start telling jokes and trying to be cute; don't *ever*, under any circumstances, go for an unsolicited handshake—in fact, it's best if you do not ever approach the table unless you are asked to do so, and in general, don't try to drag out more dialog than they're willing to exchange with you. Again, just let them take the lead on whether or not there will be conversation, and be open and responsive to what they give you. They may ask how you're doing. They may ask you personal questions. If so, they just want to get to know *you*, so don't put on an act.

When David Rotenberg teaches his acting for the camera course at Pro Actors Lab in Toronto, he tells his students that their job on camera is to "always be present." He likens the actor to an athlete, stating: "A ball player couldn't hit a baseball traveling at 95 miles per hour if he weren't present." This is exactly the kind of focus you must have in an audition for the theatre. If you're up in your head looking for song lyrics, or you're thinking about what you're going to do once it's over, or you're wondering what the choreographer is thinking as she gapes wide-mouthed at you while you sing your high notes, then you are not present. You cannot act well and stay in the moment if you're not present, and you certainly won't do well at light, personal banter before or after your audition pieces. If, however, you can make those folks behind the table feel as though they are the most important people in the world to you right now and their project is worthy of all of your attention right now, then you are sufficiently present. Concurrently, if you can deal with them on a personal level and really be yourself throughout the entire experience, then you are sufficiently present as well. It's no easy task, but if this were easy, everyone would do it! It will take a great deal of practice and some degree of failure before you nail down these concepts and put them into muscle memory.

One more thought on *when* your audition actually begins: Sometimes your audition may begin *before* you walk in the door. If you are in the holding room and one or more of the artistic staff comes into the room on a break, in a small sense, you are auditioning for them. If you pass the director in the hallway and smile at him, in a small sense, you are auditioning for him. If you are at a college entrance audition and the head of the program addresses the entire group of potential students before the dance combination is taught, in a sense, you are auditioning for her. The point is, don't let your guard down. Be on your best behavior and always be aware of who is around you. You don't want to begin your audition carrying the stigma of "the guy who was chatting while the director was giving instructions to everyone." Be attentive, and by all means *be nice to everyone!* I'm certainly not suggesting you become sycophantic or disingenuous, and I do not want to discourage you from being bold and daring in an audition; rather, I want you to avoid being rude or offensive outside of the audition room. You really never know with whom you may be speaking.

PLAY ME THE MUSIC

I am not exaggerating when I tell you that the piano player should be your best friend in the audition room. I say "should" because whether he is or not is entirely up to you. But if you play your cards right, you may gain a major ally in your audition. Whether a piano player is attached to a project, or (as is more often the case in professional auditions) he is hired just for the day to accompany auditions, he is an extremely important figure. Think about it: If you are auditioning for a musical, this person is literally your partner through the singing portion. Yet countless people, just like the unfortunate guy in our story, treat the accompanist as some sort of servant whose job it is to play what you set in front of them, no questions asked.

I'll let you in on a little secret, though: piano players are human beings, too. (That's totally true!) Although you may not require their approval to be cast in a production, treating them disrespectfully can be a major deterrent to your job hopes. Besides the fact that many of them will tell the director what a jerk you are if you mistreat them, there's also the risk that they won't put very much effort into helping you succeed in your performance. Talking down to them, snapping your fingers at them, and generally treating them like they aren't there is the best way to ensure you'll get no extra help from them.

On the other hand, think of how much a good accompanist can help your cause if he decides to really follow you as you audition. If he is sympathetic to your nerves and in tune with your rhythms, it becomes like a scene with the two of you playing off of each other. The best thing an accompanist can tell you after you finish your audition is that he had fun playing for you. Chances are, if he says this, then you had fun as well and so did the director. So why not go for this optimal experience every time? It isn't hard to ensure a happy pianist—it just takes a touch of personalization and humanity, not to mention a wonderfully organized repertoire binder with music marked properly (review chapter 2!) in nonglare sheets.

Once you have entered the room and acknowledged everyone behind the table with a cordial greeting, you'll be given time to confer with the accompanist before you sing. When you get to the piano, make sure you greet the piano player genuinely and kindly—he's been working harder than anyone else in the room all day, and he'll appreciate your sincerity. (Insider tip: Go the extra mile. Find out from the monitor outside the room who is playing for auditions. Then when you approach the accompanist, make eye contact and greet him or her by name! The sincere personal touch will really mean a lot.) This is where owning your audition comes into play. Make certain that you communicate exactly what you need from the pianist in the audition. Begin by gently displaying your music in front of him and telling him what song(s) you'll be singing. A professional accompanist will likely be familiar with many of your selections, but either way, it's always good to start by saying "I'm going to sing 'Such and Such' from the musical *So and So*" (or "by So and So," if it's a pop song). This way you can make certain the pianist knows what he's being asked to play, especially if you're starting from a point other than the first page. Do not ask the piano player if he or she knows the song. Whether they know it or not is entirely irrelevant and it just wastes time.

The next pieces of information you'll need to convey are your starting and ending points as well as any jumps or repeats you'll need him to take. Unless you're going straight through from beginning to end with no repeats or cuts whatsoever, all of this information should be clearly marked with your marker/sticky notes and highlighter for ease of sight-reading, and you should take the time to point it out *briefly* to the pianist. Further, don't assume that because you've marked a cut in your music the musician will be able to follow you on the spot without some warning. Cover your bases and talk it through, making sure that you are clear about how you want to sing the song. If there is a modulation (key change) or any other oddities in the song, you also want to bring that to the pianist's attention and have it highlighted in the sheet music as well, so that they are warned in advance and can continue to follow you.

Tell him how you want to begin. Frequently, an actor will wish to begin in the middle of a song or skip any musical introduction at the top. It is common in these cases to ask the pianist to start you off with a chord or a starting pitch, so that you know what note to come in on. If you do not ask for one, you should assume that the accompanist will play exactly whatever intro music is written, and you may find yourself standing there waiting for the song to come around to your entrance. Be sure you know what you want going in, and practice it that way. (Note: Be very careful of getting your first pitch and starting in the clear. It's often hard for the pianist to jump in and pick you up, and your nerves may cause you to be out of key. I usually recommend getting at least a one- or two-bar intro. This will help you get into the moment more as an actor, too.)

Next, you need to convey the tempo. Don't assume the accompanist knows how you do your song, even if—as is sometimes the case—he tells you "I know it" when you put it in front of him. Everyone takes songs at their own tempos, so you must make certain that you and the pianist are in-sync about this information. Do not ever snap at him and count (*one two three, one two three*) to establish your tempo. Rather, sing a little snippet of the song to him while tapping the piano top, your chest, or your leg, so that he can hear exactly how you intend to line the words up with the rhythm/tempo. Just a couple of lines will usually do, unless of course, there is a change of tempo somewhere in the song; in which case, you'll want to point this out as well.

One other option—particularly with pop/rock music—is for you to sing the actual accompaniment to the pianist. Sheri Sanders talks about helping the pianist "find the groove" of the song, and sometimes the easiest way to communicate that effectively is to use syllables to verbalize what you want the accompaniment to feel like, while you tap your leg and move your body. This can be as simple as: "So the feel of the song is 'Ba da baa baa baa, Da da daaa, Chicka daaa.'" You'll find this way of delivering tempo information to the pianist is actually a lot of fun and it can set a great tone for your mini-collaboration.

As you give him the tempo, be sure to pay attention to his response. If he nods and says, "I've got it," then move on. There may also be times when you'll want the pianist to follow you—for instance, if a song begins freely before the rhythm is established. Again, make sure you are clear with him that this is your expectation, and be specific about when you want the song to be played at tempo. Beware of nerves during this conversation. Many actors, jittery and anxious, end up setting a brutally fast tempo (probably matching their heartbeat) and then struggle to keep up. *It's often a good idea to suggest a slightly slower tempo than you actually think you want.* With practice, you'll find out how best to handle this exchange.

So thus far, you have a good deal of information to present at the piano. The good news is, most of it is printed or marked on the page; you only need to point the pianist's attention to it and you're covered. In a worst-case scenario, you forget to mention a key or time change, and the accompanist stutters and then makes the adjustment. Give most piano players the benefit of the doubt that they are there because they can competently read music. However, there is one piece of information that cannot be found anywhere in the sheet music, which you *must* remember to address before you begin. Remember what happened to the actor when the song just started playing with no warning? This common snafu can be avoided by establishing a starting signal with the accompanist.

Some people prefer to nod in the direction of the piano, indicating readiness. This method makes it challenging for the actor to really begin focused on the imaginary scene partner and the "moment before," and it usually takes a good five seconds before she finds the character in the song (especially when the piano is behind her in the audition room, causing her to start with her focus upstage). Others will actually count in the song—I don't need to tell you why this is a bad idea in any genre other than pop/ rock. A better alternative would be to ask the pianist to wait just a second after you get to the middle of the room and then begin. Or perhaps you'll tell them to watch for you to take a breath and lift your head. This way, you are in character from the get-go, and the pianist will clearly know that you are ready to perform. You'd be surprised at how effectively an inhalation can signal the upbeat preceding the downbeat of your music if you and the accompanist are really connected. Whatever way you choose to begin, just make sure to let the pianist know so he doesn't have to guess—for example, "I'll inhale for an upbeat after I center myself."

If you can communicate your needs politely and thoroughly to the accompanist, you give yourself a major advantage before you even sing a note. If your music is cleanly photocopied, marked appropriately, placed in nonglare sheets in a binder, and set up for the fewest page turns, you will appear extremely polished and professional. If you calmly walk the piano player through exactly what he'll need to know to play your music well, you will make a great impression and he will try hard for you. He may even put in a good word with the director. (One more insider tip: Consider also writing "Thank You!" on the sticky note that marks the end of your song cut. It's just a little extra kindness that can make a big difference.)

Finally, if you are singing multiple songs or doing a package that includes a monologue as well (as is the case in most college auditions or big, combined unified auditions such as Southeastern Theatre Conference [SETC]), do all of your instructing to the pianist before you begin the audition. Just tell him in what order you plan to perform your pieces and how you will signal him to begin each of your songs. Be sure to have any cue lines clearly written in your music if a monologue is to precede a song. Once you introduce yourself and begin to perform, you won't want to lose your momentum and return to the piano. Believe me when I tell you that all of this thorough attention to detail on your part can enhance your chances of success tenfold.

So let me summarize what may have seemed like a very long process: You greet the pianist, preferably by name. You tell him what song(s) you are singing. You show him starting and ending points along with any cuts, jumps, or repeats. You explain a tempo by singing a snippet of the song while tapping the piano or your body. You ask for a starting note, a chord, or the written introduction. And you tell him when you want him to start playing. You may also wish to ask if the piano player has any questions when you are finished explaining everything. Finally, and most important, thank the pianist before you walk away to sing. A little courtesy goes a long way in this business.

This entire exchange needs to be both thorough and quick. You do not want to keep the creative team waiting long. I suggest you always spend time practicing this exchange at the piano so that you have it streamlined down to an art. Let's take a look at an example:

> Good afternoon, Mark. How are you? (*Wait for a response. Don't just ask someone how he or she is if you don't care for an answer.*) I'll be singing "Brother, Can You Spare a Dime." I'm starting here at the bridge and going straight through to the end here. There's a modulation into the last verse. And I take it at this tempo [I sing a bit and tap my leg]. And if you could please play me the first measure as a vamp after I take a breath and pick up my head, that would be great. I'll come in on the second or third repeat. Do you have any questions? Thank you so much.

Read that paragraph out loud. How long did it take to get through all of that information? Twenty seconds? Twenty-five? Even if you have something a little more complicated or if you have a second song to explain, it is imperative that the exchange at the piano not be much longer than that. Again, practicing this little speech and marking everything clearly will make for the smoothest interaction.

Some Words of Wisdom from
Joey Chancey, Broadway Music Director

Recently, I supervised an audition process where we were casting four National Tours. I saw over eight thousand performers for those shows, during which I saw the range of the spectrum: people falling on the floor; someone jumping on the table we were behind; there were props, indecent choreography, unnecessary costumes, and even someone coming to lay his finger on the director's nose. All highly entertaining, but a big turnoff. However, all that aside, it proved over and over again that when the auditionees came in with clean copies of their music, clearly marked, and took the accompanist through the routine, their songs went well. Do whatever it takes to set yourself up for success in an audition . . . like reading this book!

Joey Chancey
Professional Music Director
2007 BM in Music Theater Conducting

On Broadway, Joey has conducted and played for *Beautiful: The Carole King Musical, Gigi* (2015 revival), and *Annie* (2012 revival). He has toured North America conducting the national tours of *La Cage aux Folles, A Chorus Line,* and *The Wizard of Oz.* Recent symphonic conducting includes Faith Prince and Anthony Warlow's *Direct from Broadway,* a concert tour through Australia (Sydney Opera House, Melbourne, Adelaide, Brisbane, and Perth).

COMMUNICATIONS BREAKDOWN

No matter how thorough you are about your instruction to the pianist—no matter how good the pianist may sight-read—there is always the chance that things will go wrong. In a perfect world, assuming you follow all of my prepping guidelines, you should sail through the audition. But let's face it, it's not a perfect world, and not every accompanist you meet will be Sondheim. Many of them won't even be able to play Sondheim!

Keep one phrase firmly planted in your humble mind for those days when you encounter the musician who is all knuckles at the ivories:

"Sorry, my fault."

I know what you're thinking: "But it isn't my fault. This guy is playing a cut-time like it's a slow waltz! He can't read!"

"Sorry, my fault."

"I told her to give me a chord after I say, 'Yee haw,' and she just started playing the damn song before I could even draw a breath!"

"Sorry, my fault."

You take responsibility for your entire audition and they'll know you're a pro. Any director will understand a shaky start. (Again, it's that whole authentic, human thing!) If you need to stop and start over in order to straighten things out with the pianist, they'll allow it, if you handle it professionally. See friends, here's the trick: If the pianist is lousy or simply gets a bad start on your piece, chances are, everyone in the room knows it. You only show yourself as rude and unsympathetic by leveling blame or dirty looks or, heaven forbid, *snapping* in the general direction of the piano. If, however, you excuse yourself and restore communication in a nonconfrontational way, I promise you they will respect you for it and forgive the false start. Not to mention that the pianist will likely redouble his effort on your behalf. Just know that it happens to everyone at all levels of this business. A casting director once told me a funny story about a very famous Broadway actress coming in for an audition and beginning her song out of key. She stopped the pianist, started the song again, and was immediately able to tell that she still was singing the wrong pitches. Once more, she stopped. Then she looked at the creative team, pulled the oversized hat she was wearing off her head and said, "I can't hear myself under this stupid hat." Everyone in the room broke into laughter and they all shared a really fun, sincere moment with a true diva of the stage. Then she sang again and nailed it! (I guess the insider tip is: Don't wear a big hat in your auditions!)

In the very rare case that it is simply not your day and you'd be better served with a monkey at the piano, it is necessary for you to bite the bullet and plow through your audition after starting over once or twice. For, in the end, the pianist is not being auditioned; you are. So just sing your song, trying your utmost to work with what the musician is offering, and make sure to *stay in character* and remain gracious. (Sometimes, I've even seen actors say, "Let's try a different song." But again, the smart ones take the blame off of the pianist by admitting that what they brought in wasn't the easiest song to sight-read.) Most likely the director will know that the pianist is at fault for the bad accompaniment, and your audition won't be a wash. The surefire way to run your audition into the ground is to snap, throw dirty looks, roll your eyes, or make comments about the pianist. So don't do it.

I don't mean to frighten you by making the accompanist sound like a terrifying disaster waiting to happen. Moreover, I hope that any pianist reading this chapter understands that my experience has found these underqualified musicians to be in the very small minority. Most pianists are absolutely capable and eager to help you succeed even if you toss a softbound, unmarked anthology of songs in front of them without so much as a word of explanation. I've never seen a piano player throw her hands up in disgust and bang the keys in rage when a foolish actor has brought loose, unattached sheet music to an audition and it starts to find its way all over the floor of the studio. Musicians are certainly not unsympathetic to the singer's plight, and they will do their best to help you as much as they can. It's just important that you are sensitive to their needs and that you go in prepared to face minor setbacks. They're infrequent, but they do happen. You greatly lower the odds of meltdown by being organized and professional.

AND NOW INTRODUCING . . .

You're off to a great start. You've walked in, smiled and greeted the artistic team, and headed to the piano. You've given the pianist your music and talked him through starting and stopping points, key changes, tempo, and so on. Now you find yourself standing in the middle of the room, ready to plunge headlong into your audition performance and blow them away. What do you do now? Do you just start singing? Do you make conversation? Is there a script you're supposed to follow? Do you wait for some sort of cue from them?

Believe it or not, this simple moment of transition seems to cause a great deal of grief for many actors. What exactly *are* you supposed to say before you begin? Should you introduce yourself? Should you tell them what musical your selection is from? Should you tell them which character you'll be portraying, or perhaps offer a little bit of set-up information? I've seen auditions in which the actor took more time explaining her monologue than actually reciting it. (Shoot me!) If you are asked to do multiple selections, should you introduce all of your pieces at the beginning or is it better to present the titles individually before you perform each of them?

When I wrote the first edition of this book, I suggested a practiced habit of "slating," or introducing yourself and your material in a simple, concise way. ("Hello, I'm Jonathan Flom and this is 'She Loves Me.'") Looking back on that advice, I disagree with what I originally prescribed. I've spent a good deal of time in New York audition rooms over the last six years, serving as a reader as frequently as possible in order to stay current with industry trends. And from what I've observed, the old-fashioned slate method that they used to teach us in schools is really obsolete. For starters, most of the time, when you walk into an audition (professional or college), a monitor will usher you through the door and introduce you to the creative team. ("This is Jonathan Flom.") In other circumstances without a monitor, you will be coming in with an appointment and they will have your headshot in front of them and greet you by name as you enter. ("Hi, Jonathan. How are you?") They are interested in making you comfortable and keeping it fairly casual so that you can relax and do your best work. Surely you can understand how silly and mechanical it feels to then stand like a soldier and introduce yourself in a rigid, formal way once a more informal introduction has already been established. Remember, the key is human authenticity. So just remain present (remember that rule?) and pay attention to what precedes your actual audition performance. If you walk in to silence or you are completely ignored by the people behind the table, you may wish to begin with a very polite and simple introduction, such as the one I mentioned above. But you need to use your good sense and judgment to know when that's necessary or appropriate. (To be honest with you, in the business, it is more common for actors to simply walk away from the pianist and begin their song with no conversation. Or some deliver an easygoing icebreaker with pop/rock auditions such as, "Hey there guys. I'm gonna do a little Ryan Adams for you." Either is totally acceptable!)

Do be sure that if you are going to say your name, you do so slowly, clearly, and with confidence. It's amazing how we take something so common for granted, but you'd be surprised at how many people slur, mumble, and butcher their own names, rendering them unintelligible. Sometimes, I've even had to look at the résumé in front of me to understand the name that has just been mispronounced. Many actors drop out in vocal energy at the ends of lines, so we hear "Hi, I'm Jonthn Fl . . ." The other common faux pas with the name is to give it the (very American) inflection of a question. You know the type: "Hi, I'm Jonathan *Flom?*" I know I'm being nitpicky, but it really makes a difference if you can state your name confidently and let it land. But as I said, it will be a rare time in your career when you'll need to stand and slate.

Just know that in an audition, they really don't need a whole lot of information from you. We all know who you are and why you're here. If they ask a question (i.e., "What will you be singing today?"), then answer their question. Don't tell them what show or what character or what composer. In most cases, they either know what show the song is from already or they don't care. If they want to know what it's from or which character sings it, or who wrote it, they'll ask you. Otherwise, just keep it simple.

The one major exception to the no-slate rule of thumb is the giant combined audition scenario—i.e., SETC; StrawHat Auditions; Unified Professional Theatre Auditions (UPTA); New England Theatre Conference (NETC); and other such mass auditions, in which actors come in with a set, timed audition package and present it for a room full of representatives from theatre companies or colleges. These events all have their own guidelines about how actors are required to slate; most frequently they want actors simply to state their name and audition number, and then the clock starts ticking. In these auditions, you are generally in a hotel ballroom with very unforgiving acoustics, so it's more imperative than ever to get your name stated clearly and articulately. Before you go to one of these auditions, practice getting yourself to the center of the playing space, taking a breath to focus your mind and energy, and then loudly and proudly announcing, "Good morning/afternoon. My name is <first name> (slight pause) <last name>, and I am number <audition number>." Notice that I encourage a little stop between your first and last name. This is to avoid the nervous habit of running one's name together as one garbled word. I've sat in these giant combined auditions many times, and you'd be surprised what a difference it makes when someone walks up onto that stage and says their name clearly with great energy . . . especially if that person is the four hundredth actor we've seen that day!

THE TWO-MINUTE DRILL

We're now ready to deal with the meat of the audition: the performance. Interestingly, by the time you arrive at this point, there is very little that you can do to control your fate. You either sing the notes well or you don't; you either make compelling acting choices or you don't; they either think you're right for the role or they don't. With the exception of role appropriateness, which is completely out of your hands, everything rests on the preparation you have done leading up to this moment. If you have trained your body, voice, and imagination; if you've read and understood the audition call; if you've invested in good headshots and created a clean, polished résumé; if you've prepared your repertoire book professionally and chosen selections that show you off at your best; if you've entered the room confidently and dealt with everyone in a proper manner, then what remains to be done should be a cakewalk. Stand and deliver, as the saying goes. And have fun up there.

There are a few guidelines I can offer to help you get the most mileage out of your audition performance, but even most of these suggestions go back to preparation. The bottom line is that you want to do all of your work before the audition, then stay out of your own way once you're in there. The minute you get up in your head (i.e., wondering if they like you, thinking about correct lyrics, judging your performance), you cease to be present and you run into trouble. That said, here are some bits of audition wisdom to consider:

1. Get off "The Dot"

I totally stole this from Broadway audition coach VP Boyle, and I love it! When I was in school, we were always taught (along with our rigid slate) to stand in the center of the room, about 10–12 feet directly in front of the middle of the artistic team's table. We were told to make eye contact as we introduced ourselves and our pieces, and then we were told to focus on a spot just above their heads to establish our imaginary scene partner and play our audition piece(s) to that spot on the wall.

While this is not completely "wrong" (you absolutely must make eye contact with them when you're making conversation, and you absolutely *must not* use them as your scene partner when you perform your material!), it does have quite the tendency to be completely lifeless. VP refers to that spot on the floor that sucks your soul out of your bottom as "the dot" and he encourages actors to *get off the dot*. Remember that this is supposed to be representative of a human experience (dare I use the word *authentic* once more?), and nothing can be less human than you drilling your feet into the floor and boring a hole through the wall with your laser eye-beams.

Consider shifting the room just slightly—perhaps begin your piece slightly off center. Establish your imaginary scene partner over the heads of the creatives, but then remember that when we are talking to someone in "real life," we don't stare them down the entire time. We begin by looking at them and then we look elsewhere as we think of what to say next or as we remember the story we're telling them or as we avoid eye contact for the difficult thing we have to ask them. Then we come back to their eyes when we need to make a point or to check in and see how they're reacting. (This check-in is *majorly* important, and we'll discuss it more soon.) The bottom line is that you do not need to stand completely straight forward, feet pointing toward the table, and play directly center to the back of the room. You want to avoid playing in full profile or upstage, away from the table—they definitely need to see your face—but you need to practice ways to make this experience feel less like an audition and more like a human interaction. Make sense?

You should let the style and genre of your piece dictate to a great degree where you stand and how you position yourself. If you're having a difficult talk with a loved one about a sensitive subject, then it may very well be appropriate to find a stationary spot in the room and plant yourself (again, slightly off center with the body angled just a little bit is far more compelling than straight on); however, if you're doing a pop/rock cut it may be more exciting to start your song at the piano, really getting into the groove with the accompanist, and then move more fully into the space throughout the course of the song. I encourage you to play with some variety when you prepare your auditions. See how it feels to play in different parts of the room. Obviously, you need to consider being fully seen and heard, but beyond that, there are no hard, fast rules about standing on a red "X" and being still (unless you are being put on camera and they specifically ask you to stand on a spot for framing purposes).

2. The First 30 Seconds Is Everything

It's cliché, I know, but the reality is often that we have an instinct about an actor in as few as 15 seconds! Directors won't be so rash as to cast someone based on 20 seconds of a song, but we can generally decide in that time frame if someone *isn't* what we're looking for (or if we want to bring them back in to work with material from the show we are casting). Many students ask me what they should lead with: Up-tempo or ballad? Comedic or dramatic? Monologue or song? The answer depends on what you're auditioning for and which material you're presenting. And the best advice I can offer is get 'em hooked quickly. The notion of "save the best for last" has no place at an audition. Broadway composer Ed Linderman suggests you try to use an uplifting, joyous, or fun song as a first impression, so that they like *you* and want to see more of your talent. I can't say I disagree with this philosophy. But again, it'll depend on the circumstance.

If you are auditioning for a specific role with certain requirements (i.e., belting to an E; comic timing; rock chops), you should make sure you demonstrate at least a teaser of your ability to meet the demands of that role. You don't need to show us *everything* in that first audition—save some for the callback for sure—but you should at least let us know pretty quickly that we could consider you for the part.

When auditioning for colleges or at one of the aforementioned general combined auditions, remember to make those first 30 seconds a real statement of *who you are*. Draw us in with your charm and personality and make us want to get to know you more. Don't just sing *at* us and show off; that is very unappealing. It's an audition, not a belting contest, ladies!

3. Always, Always Act the Song

A pretty voice is one thing, but good musical theatre demands more. Acting is what separates good musical productions from bad ones. You must make solid acting choices for every song you sing and fully invest in the character. Ask yourself these questions for every song in your repertoire:

Who am I?
To whom am I singing?
What is my (specific!) relationship with my scene partner?
What do I want from this person? ("If I could write the end of the scene, my scene partner would _____.")
What happened just before I start to sing that causes me to speak?
What is the obstacle keeping me from getting what I want from my partner?
What tactics can I use to overcome the obstacle? Tactics are the actions an actor uses to achieve her goal (i.e., to tease, to flirt, to seduce, to lecture, to soothe, etc.). They should always be active verbs.

These are the most basic building blocks of scene work, and they must be applied to musical theatre to make it rise above meaningless fluff. I strongly urge you to read *A Practical Handbook for the Actor* (Bruder et al.), *Sanford Meisner on Acting*, and *Acting in Musical Theatre* by Joe Deer and Rocco Dal Vera. These books offer the most comprehensive approaches to truthful acting, which can and should be utilized in musicals as well as non-musicals.

The caveat to the act-the-song rule is that pop requires a slightly different approach. You don't necessarily perform popular songs with the kind of moment-to-moment specificity of circumstance with which you'd approach a theatre song. You'd look kind of weird singing a rock and roll song and *schmacting* out every lyric as though it was meant to be a two-person scene. (Usually it gets weird particularly when an actor tends to *indicate* every lyric with a physical action.) That being said, we still want to know that you've created a personalized story in your head and that you have a person to whom you are singing and something you want from them. Beyond that, pop rock is more about creating a mood and an energy to convey your story. Again, I encourage you to turn to expert Sheri Sanders and let her help you "Rock the Audition" when it comes to these tunes. I would also suggest that you use the magic of YouTube and television channels like Palladia where you can watch tons of concert footage and see how rock stars perform their songs. You can bet that even in a concert setting, pop and rock singers have a subliminal need from the audience (they may want everyone to get up and dance or fist-pump or sing along, or they may want their fans to get immersed in a story and empathize). What is your story when you sing pop songs? What do you want us to feel as we listen to your performance? You're not playing a character when you deliver pop in an audition; rather, you are being your authentic self and creating a story and an interaction that are *personally important* to you.

I mentioned the "check-in" a few pages back, and I want to bring it up once more here. In life, when we want something from someone, we consider the nature of our relationship and our history with that person, then we determine a course of action—the best way we can possibly go about getting that person to do what we want. (I may use guilt on my mother, where I would use shaming to get a similar objective from my younger brother, or flattery for my girlfriend.) We don't necessarily dissect the process on a conscious level, but that's how it works. When we act, we need to employ the same devices. But what I described above is only the first half of the equation. Once we make an attempt to get what we want, we need to remain in active listening and observing mode to see how our tactics are working or not working on the other person, and then adjust accordingly. You've probably heard the old saw that "acting is reacting." Well . . . *react* then! Even when you are doing a solo piece, we need to see that you're allowing the other person to hear what you are saying and be affected by your words. You have to help us get out of the artificial audition room and imagine you in a truthful, fully engaged scenario. Paint a picture for us that involves two people. And in order to do that, we need to see how you make adjustments throughout your audition material, based on what the other person is doing, saying (or not saying!). Sometimes you may have to change tactics mid-stream—you were using guilt on your mother, but she bristled and put up her defenses, so you switch to buttering her up instead. Again, this check-in process keeps you alive and present, and you may even surprise yourself at where your imagination can lead you in an audition. Consider allowing these organic (imaginary) interactions to occur, as opposed to staging them or forcing them.

4. Make Your Transitions Smooth

Earlier I talked about warming the room and avoiding the awkward transition from cordial greeting and conversation into performance. The two words to keep in mind when planning your transitions are "breath" and "focus." If you establish a solid new focus (on your imaginary partner) and inhale before launching into any piece, it should give you enough of a transition without seeming gratuitous. In fact, it will not only serve to inform the creative team that you are now moving into a character with a distinct objective and set of actions, but in a musical audition it will also alert the pianist that you are prepared to begin your song.

Some actors will opt to use a chair for part of their audition. This can be an effective way to break up the monotony of staring at a person standing stationary for a long period of time. Sitting down on the chair or rising from it can serve as a strong transition. However, do not opt to use a chair *just* to vary it up—use it only if it serves the action of the piece. And be sure that when using a chair you do not allow your energy to sink into your bottom; keep your energy forward and pointed outward.

I advise against turning upstage or bowing your head and closing your eyes and taking a long "actor prepares" moment before launching into a piece. Find a way to keep your energy and presence in the room once you've warmed it up with your personality. It will take practice to make this transition less awkward, especially when you are presenting a heavier, dramatic piece of material.

You'll note that I very specifically told you to inhale before beginning each song or monologue. Many actors will begin with a great big inhale and then let it out, sometimes even with a sigh, especially if they are performing a particularly dramatic piece. Stand in front of a mirror and watch what happens to your posture when you start on an exhale, versus when you start on an inhale. You will see your shoulders collapse on the sigh and you will find that you have much less breath support with which to speak or to sing. It's no wonder, since you just let all of the breath out of you! Inhalation is empowerment (*breathing in* is also called inspiration!); exhalation is defeat. Which would you prefer to watch? We want to see characters who play to win, rather than those who accept defeat and wallow in the problem.

At the end of your pieces, be sure that each song and monologue has a "button" to it as well. A button is like a period at the end of a sentence. It states unequivocally that you have reached the end of that particular piece and your character either achieved her objective or said her piece. Sloppy segues occur when a song or monologue lacks a button. In these instances, it's often hard to distinguish when one piece has ended and you are either back to being yourself or into your next piece. Many inexperienced actors try to make up for a weak ending by breaking character and directly informing the auditors they are finished. These novices conclude by saying "scene" or "that's it." I can't tell you how ugly this is! When you need to tell us that you are finished acting, it means you are not acting very well. I wish amateur drama teachers would stop encouraging their students to say "scene." Finish with a button, letting the last line land for a couple of seconds, and we'll know you are done. You may choose to say "thank you" at the conclusion of an audition selection, but only after you've let the final moment linger and the piece has concluded. (Also please note that your song is not over when you are done singing. It is finished when the pianist has taken her hands off of the keys. Too many actors finish singing and then just stand there awkwardly, out of character, while the accompanist plays the remainder of the music. Stay in it to win it!)

5. Don't Become a Prop Act

Unless you are dead-set on auditioning with a selection that absolutely hinges on a small hand prop (for instance, the character says something like, "As I tear up your letter" or "here, take this tissue and wipe your tears"), don't plan on using anything in your audition. As I already stated, a chair is usually available to you, but beyond that, just bring your acting and let it work for you.

6. Don't Be Afraid to Just Plant Yourself

Standing solidly on two feet and not fidgeting is a sign of confidence and strength. You certainly don't need to remain rooted in place throughout your entire audition; however, you want to find moments when you are able to display stillness.

Once you are engaged in your song or monologue, be sure that any movement you make is character driven. In other words, don't pace aimlessly back and forth. If you choose to pace the floor, it must be as a result of a chosen action: for example, *My character is diligently trying to sort out a complicated dilemma.*

Similarly, if you perform a song that specifically requires dance in the lyrics or it's naturally implied in the accompaniment ("What Do I Need with Love" from *Thoroughly Modern Millie*; "All I Need Is the Girl" from *Gypsy*; "I Can't Stand Still" from *Footloose*; "Hit Me with a Hot Note" by

Duke Ellington), you should feel free to move, especially if you want to show the director that you are a dancer. But again, it must be character driven and it must fit the circumstances rather than simply being a nervous twitch. Furthermore, you must be able to perform the song without the movement if asked to do so.

7. Say "Yes" to Direction

It is not uncommon for a director to ask an actor to make a different choice in an audition, in order to see if the actor can take direction. If you find yourself in such a situation, no matter how bizarre you find the director's adjustment to be (e.g., "Can you do the piece again and wring this piece of cloth in your hands as you sing it?"), the appropriate response is, "Yes, I can do that." Of course, the second part of the equation requires that you actually make the adjustment, but having a positive attitude is definitely half the battle.

Inexperience causes many actors to seize up with fear when a director asks them to approach a piece differently than they have rehearsed it. They jump to the conclusion that they've done it wrong or badly. These actors fail to embrace the golden opportunity they have been given: first, a chance to show they are directable, and second, more face time with the director. In this respect, an adjustment is almost as good as a callback.

Don't be so stuck in your original choices that you are unable to make the change(s) that the director asks of you. Often, an actor has done all of her proper preparation leading in to the audition, but when asked to take an adjustment, she is only able to make the smallest of modifications. If you can't release your hold on exactly how you've decided to perform a piece, you'll likely be eliminated from contention for a job, since so much of our work in a rehearsal process will hinge on your being able to take direction. So when you are offered a suggestion or an improvement in an audition situation, be sure to make a bold, clear adjustment and find a way to personalize it so that it doesn't seem artificial. This is a skill that you must master with practice.

8. Do Not Apologize for Your Work

The only apology you are allowed to offer in an audition is the aforementioned "sorry, my fault" when the accompanist situation goes awry. Beyond that, you must present a confident, positive image. This means *eliminating any and all excuses* from the audition studio.

Do not try to explain how sick you've been when you arrive with a husk in your voice. Do not try to explain how the trains were all delayed when you arrive late. (Don't arrive late!) Do not try to explain why you messed up when you forget your lyrics or botch an audition piece. It is so tempting to want to convince the director that she is not seeing you in optimum performance mode at the moment and that you can do better. I assure you this is self-destructive, so don't do it.

If you are sick or recovering from illness, you have two options: Either skip the auditioning and wait until you are well enough to resume performing again or go in there and sell yourself like you would on your best day. Directors are not stupid. If you are sick, chances are they'll recognize it. They may ask you if you are under the weather (in which case, of course, you answer honestly without embellishing), and they may ask you to reaudition when you have recovered. But whatever they do, they will respect you for putting on a brave face and being a professional. Truth be told, it's often all in your mind that you don't sound healthy. Many actors are surprised to find that they have earned a callback in spite of congestion or other symptoms. It's not usually as detrimental as one might assume. I've seen some of the most interesting acting choices made by the actor who was sick and had to concentrate on something other than the quality of her voice. You should work on learning to sing through illness. Sometimes it requires an extra hour of warm-up; sometimes it means steaming. You need to discover what works for you and be sure to fully prepare for any audition you attend.

As for running late, the best thing I can tell you is *don't. You must arrive early to auditions and rehearsals.* Tardiness is not tolerated in this business, and it will lose you jobs if you develop a reputation. In the event that you are unavoidably delayed, try to call the studio and get a message to the monitor—it may be possible to have your slot moved to a later time if you are courteous enough to call and give notice. If you can't call ahead, your options are to show up late and hope for the best or skip the audition all together. If you do decide to go in late, just do the work and leave it at that; no proverbial song and dance. No matter how good (or true) your story is, the minute you begin making an excuse, you dig yourself into a hole. Another saying in the theatre goes: If you're 15 minutes early, you're on time; if you're on time, you're late; if you're late, you're unemployed.

The other apology I see actors make regularly is the old "I blew that one." Either the actor verbally comments on his own performance or he rolls his eyes or laughs, signaling a disappointment in his work. Eliminate these tics from your muscle memory. I don't care if you completely forget your words, sing off-key, or trip over your feet in the dance call; you just keep going like you meant for it to be that way. You don't need to tell them you messed up—they'll know it or they may have missed it completely. Either way, you need to demonstrate that you can recover from a mistake. After all, that is what you'd be expected to do during a live performance. If you can do that, I promise you any error you made in your audition will likely be forgotten. Not to mention the fact that usually when we mess up in an audition, it shakes us out of our robotic process and provides at least one moment of authentic human behavior. Sometimes, in fact, the error is actually what lands us the next audition.

PUT IT TOGETHER AND . . .

I realize that I have given you a whole lot of information to process, digest, and carry with you through every audition. What's more, I'm telling you that you must stay out of your own head whenever you perform. The only possible way to achieve such synthesis is to practice . . . a lot! You will have off days and failures, but if you take the time to reflect after the fact and make your next audition sharper, then nothing is lost. Think of the baseball player who leads the league with a .333 batting average. He *fails* two-thirds of the time he comes to the plate! But he improves by reflecting on the mechanics involved in his failed at-bats and by making adjustments in the future. The same technique can work for the actor.

As I have said, thorough preparation will really carry you through an audition. If you have walked through everything from dealing with the accompanist, to figuring out where and how to begin your audition, to performing your pieces, you won't have to keep focusing on all my little rules and tips in the audition room: It will all become second nature. Once it is, you will be free to have fun in your auditions; believe it or not, this *is* possible!

In preparing the first edition of this book, I shared some of this chapter's material with an undergraduate classmate of mine who had been making a steady living on national tours and regional theatre for over nine years. As we talked through all of these guidelines for handling the audition, he actually told me that he hadn't *thought* about any of it for the last seven years at least. It had all become so engrained in him through experience that he was free to relax and really fly through his auditions without having to focus on the steps of the process. He also told me that as he had gotten to know more and more casting directors in New York, he felt increasingly confident in taking bigger risks and having more fun when he went in for them.

It really is simple, this daily grind that performing artists put themselves through. When you follow Meisner's acting advice and put your attention on your actions and your objectives, you will be truly free to perform without getting in your own way. Self-consciousness is literally an awareness of one's self. It logically follows that placing your consciousness elsewhere would then alleviate the symptoms associated with self-consciousness. And once you can embrace the audition as your daily chance to do what you love to do, then your joy will be contagious and directors will want to work with you.

THANK YOU FOR LETTING ME . . .

The final step in navigating a successful audition is getting out of the room gracefully. I liken it to an Olympic gymnast who, in order to earn deserved high marks for a killer floor demonstration, must be sure to "stick the landing." Likewise, you must "stick the landing" at the conclusion of your audition and eliminate the awkwardness as you go to exit. But how?

First, think of the wrap-up as just another transition. Only this time, instead of going from one selection to another, you're going from performing a character role back to being your gracious self. The easiest way—really, the only way—to make this segue is to button your final piece, take a beat to let it land, and then say, "Thank you." No further discussion is required on your end; no "that's all" or "scene," or any other extraneous commentary. Just a simple "thank you" and a smile will do. Furthermore, if the people behind the table thank you for your work, why not say, "you're welcome," as opposed to the disempowering extra "thank *you*" that actors always offer back? Last time I checked, "you're welcome" was the appropriate response to someone's gratitude. But actors don't often feel worthy, so they want to keep behaving as though the creative team has all the power and they are owed some sort of overwhelming obeisance. Sure, thank them and be grateful for the opportunity to audition, but don't be afraid to accept their mutual appreciation for your work. You deserve it!

Another common mistake that many novice performers make is that they try to flee the scene as quickly as possible once they complete their audition. I have literally had to chase down actors outside the studio just to ask them some questions following their audition. So stay put for a couple of seconds after you thank them. Nine times out of ten, someone behind the table will return your thanks, and a nod or a smile will indicate that they are finished with you. However, you have to remain open to the possibility that they may want to talk to you or even to hear you sing more. (Remember: Be Present.)

Don't get me wrong; I'm not suggesting that you hang around until they finally have to ask you to leave. And you certainly don't want to ask the awkward questions, "Is that all?" "Am I done?" or the really annoying, "Did you want to hear me sing something else?" (Please don't put directors in the position of having to tell you that we don't want to hear you sing any more.) It's a delicate balance, but you have to learn just when to head for the door. It's basically a matter of being able to read people. For example, if you finish your last piece and you find them whispering or passing notes or examining your résumé without a word in your direction, you may assume that there is a possibility they'll have something more for you. In such a case, just hang tight until their attention returns to you. Maybe grab a sip of water and talk to the pianist.

Otherwise, say your "thank you," after you finish your song or monologue, allow them a beat to respond, and once they have done so, head for the piano to retrieve your music. Do not neglect to thank the pianist as you take your book.

The walk out of the room can feel like a long, awkward silence for everyone. So move with purpose, but don't run. You may want to be careful about wearing shoes that "clump" at an audition; you wouldn't believe how pronounced this noise becomes in a quiet, hardwood-floored room! When you reach the door, you can wish them a good afternoon. It's never a bad idea to leave them with a cordial smile as you exit. But don't say more than that. They are very busy, and you don't want to overstay your welcome.

The bottom line is this: Just as the audition begins when you walk in the door, it continues until you walk out the door. So keep your game face on until they've finished seeing the back of you. Furthermore, avoid commenting on your work outside of the studio. I hear many performers, before the door is even closed behind them, sharing the horrors of their auditions with friends in the hallway. I don't want to hear how you "sucked in there" or "what a stone-faced jerk" the director was or "how lousy the accompanist played." Save it for when you are clear of the audition building. Until that point, just smile and tell anyone who asks that it went well. It's the professional thing to do, and it avoids the possibility of saying anything damaging within earshot of the wrong person.

Finally, once you're clear of the audition room, *let it go.* You have now done everything you possibly could do as a first step toward booking a job. It is no longer in your hands. You should reflect briefly on what you thought went well and what might need some tweaking, but only long enough to add an entry to your journal: who was in the room, what you wore, what you performed, how it went, including any feedback they may have offered. Then you must let it go. I know I keep telling you that the goal is a callback, but even that is out of your hands at this point. Treat yourself by sitting down for a coffee or an ice cream and a good book, or something else you love. You prepared, went in there, and showed them you at your best and most authentic. Now it's up to them to decide if you are what they need. If you reward yourself for going in there prepared and doing your best, you will always look forward to auditioning.

SUMMARY

- You can't be too prepared! Know your songs well enough that you don't need to think about them before going in. Relax and focus on acting choices.
- The audition begins the minute you arrive on site, not when you introduce yourself.
- Greet the creative team when you walk in the door.
- Treat the pianist with care and respect—he or she is your partner in an audition.
- Be sure to be thorough with the accompanist—point out tempo and key changes, give a clear starting signal, and note any jumps or repeats.
- Skip the slate routine and just start your audition. At most, say, "I'll be singing <title of song>."
- Hook them in the first 30 seconds of your audition.
- Always *act* the song.
- Stay off "the dot."
- Establish an imaginary scene partner for every piece, and stay open and visible.
- Be certain all movement (pacing, sitting, dancing, etc.) is character driven.
- Say "yes" to any direction offered to you.
- Never make excuses or apologize for your work.
- After buttoning your final piece, simply say, "Thank you," and wait a beat for a response. Then retrieve your music, thank the pianist, and leave the room gracefully.
- After the audition is done, make a journal entry and then let it go. Reward yourself for preparing and attending the audition, but don't harp on it after it's done.

4

CALLBACKS

MISSION ACCOMPLISHED

I once told you that an actor's goal at an audition is always to earn a callback (refer to the first edition of this book). Despite providing a catchy title for my book, the reality is that getting a callback is just as much out of your control as getting hired. I want to instead offer you a new mind-set: The goal of an audition is to prepare like crazy, walk in the room, and deliver the most authentic performance you can give. That's totally in your control. Getting called back and being cast is of course the greater hope, but there are too many variables involved in those decisions that are completely out of your hands; pulling your hair out over it during your audition doesn't help at all. Just get them to want to see more of you (for this or future projects), and you will have been successful.

You may receive notification of a callback in one of several ways. Some directors will decide on the spot if they want you to return—often, they will even hand out callback sides (pieces of the script or score) at your initial audition so that you may look them over for a night before returning—another argument for not rushing out the door at the end, wouldn't you say?

In the profession, the other common occurrence is to receive a call or an e-mail from the casting director, artistic director, or director of the production (or via your talent agent, if you have one) inviting you back for another audition. This call/e-mail could come the very evening you auditioned, within a few days of your first appointment, or as far away as several months from your initial contact! (Take a look at the documentary *Every Little Step*, which offers incredible insight into the casting of the Broadway revival of *A Chorus Line*. Those actors waited nine months to hear anything between rounds of auditions, because there was a time when the producers thought the show would not happen. So anything is possible!)

One other possibility is that some directors will post a physical callback list once auditions are complete, and you will be expected to check to see if you made the list. This is most common in high schools, colleges, and large convention-style auditions such as StrawHats, SETC (Southeastern Theatre Conference), or UPTA (Unified Professional Theatre Auditions).

However you are invited to attend the callbacks, you will likely have very little time to prepare. It would be wise, then, to gather as much information as possible when you are asked to return. If you are offered a callback in person or over the phone, be certain to ask what the callback will entail: Will there be dancing? Would they like you to prepare any other selections? Are there sides from the show available to peruse? Some of these questions may already be answered for you without you having to ask, but you are responsible for keeping a checklist of such pertinent information. To that end, I suggest once more that you invest in a journal to keep a record of audition information.

If your name is posted on a list, all of the necessary details of the callback will usually be outlined on the callboard as well. Be sure to read carefully so you know what to prepare for the following day.

Once you have all the information available regarding the callback, you must put what little time you have into doing as much preparation as possible. If you haven't done so already, try to familiarize yourself with the libretto and music of the show you're going in for. Focus on the specific character or characters for which you are being considered so that you are able to make some bold, intelligent acting choices when you read or sing. Don't lose face by asking the director to explain to you who your character is and what the character wants, if that information was readily available to you. Instead, *show the director that you did your homework*. Don't approach the callback like a blank slate and make weak choices or no choices at all; rather, be bold and answer all of the acting questions I laid out in chapter 3, even if you don't know the exact context of the show. Sometimes you might make the "wrong" choice, but in those instances, the director will usually offer you an adjustment. "Strong and wrong" is better than weak and boring and generic.

In the case of the big combined auditions, you will likely be called back for a summer or year-round season. In the interim between receiving your callback and visiting the theatre company's room, be sure to do some quick research on their season and make some educated guesses as to how they might see you fitting in. With smartphones in every pocket, you have no excuse to go into any appointment ignorant.

If they have given you sides, do your best to become very familiar with them—if possible, recruit a buddy to read through them with you. By no means are you required to memorize the sides on short notice (but if you've had more than a few days, you'd better go in memorized!). Doing so demonstrates an obvious commitment to the project, but I've never known of casting choices hinging on an actor being off-book. Whether you have the time and the inclination to memorize material for a callback or not, you should *always hold the script pages in your hand*—even if you never refer to them; it's just common protocol. Too often, actors end up trying to wow a director with their memorization skills only to find that they forget the lines once they are acting opposite a partner. Think about it: no matter how much you cram, one night isn't usually enough time to know a scene by rote and be able to interact honestly with a partner. In the moment, when the partner makes a choice that you hadn't anticipated in your imagination, you are bound to lose your words. You avoid a slowdown or complete stoppage of the audition if you keep the script pages nearby for quick reference.

On the flip side, if you are given sides with little or no time to prepare them, be sure to ask for a few minutes to look them over. Step out of the room (if possible) and read them out loud, so you get the feel of the words in your mouth—this is a very different experience from hearing it in your head. Since you won't be able to have your eyes off the page the entire time, look for the operative, pivotal moments. What is the "meat" of the scene or the big turning point? Try to commit those important bits to memory at the very least so that you are able to deliver them with your eyes up off the paper when you go back in. It usually helps to have a pencil (do ask if you can mark up the script before you write on it) so that you can circle key words or phrases that you know will need to be delivered with power and with your full energy going out to the scene partner. Cold reading is a skill set that you'll want to practice and hone so that you aren't the actor whose nose is buried behind a piece of paper throughout the audition. No one books a job by being able to read words off of a page well. You must find a way to interact with the scene partner—real or imaginary—and show the director that you are in reaction mode, as opposed to simply delivering lines.

If you are given musical cuttings for a callback, you must do your utmost to learn the tunes. If you read music, sit down at a piano and plunk it out; if not, try to find someone who can do it for you (perhaps your vocal coach). You can also utilize actor services available online to help you learn your material. Voice teacher and musical theatre coach Warren Freeman runs a company called Get on My Sides (www.getonmysides.com), through which he offers clients quick turnaround on coaching tracks. You send him the sheet music and he sends you digital versions of the melody as well as the accompaniment track. He has been a lifesaver to many Broadway performers, so you'll want to bookmark his website. As a last resort, you may refer to the original cast recording, but I've already warned you about this pitfall, so use it sparingly. If you are going in for a new musical, a cast recording may not even be available.

On occasion (in school settings, primarily), musical sides may be taught at the callback. In these cases, the musical director will play through the music and answer questions before individuals are asked to sing for the director, but you must not rely on this crutch. Take it upon yourself to learn the music before the audition and then use any teaching time at the actual call to review for yourself. You'll find there is a lot less pressure when you aren't struggling to hear, learn, and remember notes and rhythms on the fly. Once again, you'll be free to focus on making solid acting choices, which will set you apart from the rest of the pack. If you are forced to learn a song at the callback, ask the musical director if it's okay to record the melody, so that you may step outside and review it while waiting your turn to sing for them.

Sometimes you will be asked to return for a second audition, but you won't be given any materials to prepare. This is often the case in the profession when casting involves a prescreening process. You may audition first for a casting director or her assistant, and then be asked to come back for more of the creative team (the director, music director, choreographer, writers, the producers, and so on). I've seen friends go in for upward of *seven* auditions before a decision was made!

The same is true when attending URTA (University Resident Theatre Association), the national screening for graduate training programs, and conferences such as SETC, NETC, StrawHats, and others. You audition for a panel of many, and you are called in for appointments by any schools or theatre companies that are interested in you. At these appointments, they may ask you to do your audition materials once more and offer you some directorial adjustments. Or they may simply want to chat with you and get to know you.

If you are asked to come back for a second look and you are not given any sides, you may assume that they will want you to present the same audition material that you performed the first time. Furthermore, when this is the case, you should not try to reinvent yourself. Rather, unless they ask you to change anything, make the same choices that you utilized to earn the callback in the first place—they obviously saw something they liked. Essentially, the "second viewing" type of callback I'm describing should be handled just as you would handle a first audition. You must be prepared to present other selections if asked, and you must take directorial adjustments if any are offered. The only difference between this call and your initial audition is that you can go in confident that you already have someone behind the table who thinks you are a good match for the project.

Sometimes you may receive a callback without even auditioning. Remember when I told you that actors will audition for a project, not be right for it, and get a call from a director later on for a different show? Or perhaps a casting director saw your work in another production and wants to call you in for something he is casting. I always say that one of the best ways to audition is to be seen in a show. If you find yourself in one of these situations where you are asked to come in and audition, treat it like a callback. Get all of the necessary information about what will be asked of you, and prepare with the confidence that somebody in there really wants to see you for this show.

THE CLOTHES OFT PROCLAIM . . .

Unless you are specifically called back to dance or to move, which would require you to come in dance attire, the general rule of thumb is to wear what you wore the first time. Believe it or not, some directors will see so many actors at an audition that you will be remembered based on your outfit. (*We're calling back the guy in the light blue collared shirt for "Bobby."*) You do the director and yourself a service by presenting the same look when you return.

An obvious exception to the rule is the instance when a director or casting director asks you to dress a specific way or to style your hair or makeup differently for the callback. Barring such a request from the creative team, it is important to keep in mind that they called you in because they liked what they saw the first time. It may have been your acting, your singing, or your look (hopefully, all of the above!), but you may never know what interested them about you. Any unsolicited change in your overall presentation may skew their opinion of you, and they may decide you aren't what they were seeking.

As is the case with any audition you attend, it's never a bad idea to have dance clothes and a change of shoes with you, just in case. You should try to anticipate any possibility at a callback.

IT'S JUST A JUMP TO THE LEFT

If you plan to spend your life (or any portion thereof) auditioning for musical theatre, you are bound to encounter many dance calls, either as part of your callback process, or as an initial entrée into the casting pool for some shows. These can range in scope from the simple "singers who move" to the much more challenging "dancers who sing" to the quick elimination exercise of "step forward and give us a double pirouette on both sides" that occurs before you learn the opening number of *A Chorus Line*. Whether you have two left feet and get by on your voice and your good looks or you've been dancing since you came out of the womb, you need to learn to love the dance call and you need to understand how to navigate this part of the process like a pro.

First of all, let's take a closer look at the possible scenarios you may encounter as first auditions. I mentioned the "singers who move" and "dancers who sing" calls. It is very common in the profession for open audition calls to be broken down in this way. This set-up allows highly skilled dancers to show off their best stuff rather than being eliminated from contention because their voices aren't quite as strong as the "singer-singers." Likewise, it gives the actor/singer the opportunity to demonstrate her talent, preparation, and suitability for roles in the show that might not require as much proficiency in dance. When performers are asked to return after these initial open calls to a second appointment, the dancers would be asked to sing and the singers would generally be given a simpler movement combination than their counterparts.

You need to be able to intelligently and honestly assess your particular strengths and skills to determine which of these auditions you should attend in order to give yourself the best odds for getting called back to demonstrate the entire range of your training. For some of you, it will be cut-and-dry: You've been a dancer all your life, and you are relieved that you can go to a dance call and be almost guaranteed a callback, with the vocal expectations being slightly lower on you; or you struggled through your dance training in school and you hope that if you make it to a callback the choreographer will be merciful. But if you've trained in all areas of musical theatre and you consider yourself equally proficient in dance and voice, your choice may not always be as simple. Students ask me all the time, "There's an audition coming up for [insert show title]. Should I go to the dancer call or the singer call?" To some extent, you have to hedge your bets and just make a choice, but a smart actor will do her homework and have a basis on which to make this decision.

Take a look at the specific show, its period and style, the role or roles for which you would want to be considered, and the choreographer's body of work (YouTube is your friend!). Use this information to make the most informed decision as to where you stand the greatest chance of being asked back for more. For instance, if you know Randy Skinner is putting out another national tour of *42nd Street* and you want to be considered for Peggy Sawyer or Andy Lee, you best attend the dance call and tap your feet off! However, if you were looking at Julian Marsh, Dorothy Brock, Burt, or Maggie, then the obvious thing to do would be to go to the singer call. Sometimes it may not be quite so obvious. Let's imagine that Andy Blankenbuehler is choreographing another original musical by Lin-Manuel Miranda. It's a new piece, so you can't listen to the music or look at You-Tube clips to know how challenging the dancing will be. Go to the Internet and seek out clips of Andy's other work to get a sense of his style and how challenging and athletic his choreography is (you may be a highly trained dancer but find that your training is not best suited to his particular style). Look also at Playbill.com and see if you can find any articles previewing the new musical so that you have an idea of what kinds of roles they may be casting. Then choose your audition call based on where you think you're more likely to be a fit for the project.

The other factor to consider in all of this is relationship history. What I mean is, when you live in a city and you do your job of attending auditions *all the time*, after a while you will have gone in for most of the big choreographers and you will know which ones gel with your abilities and which ones make you feel inept. *Who's choreographing? Stroman? I never make it past her dance calls—I'll go to the singer/mover audition!*

Part of your work as a professional, fully prepared actor is to know who's who in the business. I've already mentioned Playbill.com several times (have you bookmarked it yet?) and suggested that you read the headlines daily to know what is opening and who is directing, choreographing, and casting. If you're doing that, then you're building up a mental list of all the major choreographers in the business. Go see their shows when you have a chance or look for clips on the web so that you start to learn their specific approaches to musical theatre dance and get a sense of whose work appeals to you. Knowing the styles of today's top choreographers (i.e., Warren Carlyle, Steven Hoggett, Joshua Bergasse, Christopher Gattelli, Casey Nicholaw, Rob Ashford, Susan Stroman, Andy Blankenbuehler, etc.) and their predecessors who are still being imitated or restaged to this day (i.e., Fosse, de Mille, Bennett, Robbins) will help you be prepared for what to expect when you go to their auditions. Furthermore, it will also help you decide which dance classes you should drop in and attend when you are in the city. You can often find sessions offered by the choreographers or their associates at Broadway Dance Center or Steps, for example, where you can go and get practice at the audition combinations before actually attending a call.

The bottom line is this: Train, study, train, study, and keep your body in peak physical condition. Ballet training is the core of so much Broadway choreography. Both classical and contemporary jazz will help you drill style and pick up combos quicker. Proficient tap is almost a nonnegotiable requirement for the musical theatre industry now. Hip-hop is becoming more and more prevalent on the theatrical stage. Partnering and social or ballroom dance, such as tango, waltz, and Latin styles are utilized all the time. So the more you know, the wider you can cast your net for work. Get your behind to dance class as much as possible! (High school students: I hate to tell you this, but being in the school musical or the show choir is *far less valuable* than spending your time in ballet and jazz classes to prepare you for entrance auditions!)

Now let's take a look at the dance portion as it pertains to a callback, which is the primary focus of this chapter. If you have auditioned for a musical and have received a callback to dance, there are a few things you should think about, whether or not dancing is one of your strengths. First of all, you need to consider what the purpose of the dance call is for the particular show they are casting. Are they looking at you as a possible featured dancer, as a principal character who may need to execute some choreography, as an ensemble member who may cover one or several primary roles? Normally, you will have an idea of how they are looking at you when you go back in to dance. Is it a heavy dance show or does it contain some simple movement as musical staging? Is it "serious dance" (as in *On the Town*) or more character/comical dance (as in *Young Frankenstein*)? Have you worked with the choreographer and the creative team before so that you know their vocabulary and style? The more you know going in, the better your mental preparation will be, considering that you really can't "prepare" for a dance call, since they will be throwing choreography at you on the fly and you are expected just to pick it up.

The real key to the whole thing is to sell yourself and your energy and passion. Dance doesn't happen in a vacuum for dance's sake in Broadway musicals. If you know the show and the characters, you should make bold *acting choices* through the dance call and help them imagine you executing their choreography as part of the world of that musical. Musical theatre dance is storytelling, and the director in the room is seeking dancing *actors* who will not distract from the primary purpose of dance in the show, which is to *tell the story in a heightened way*. To that end, don't get hung up on perfect technique (I've seen flawless dancers get eliminated from auditions countless times because they weren't *alive* or because, in spite of their great technique, they couldn't embody the style of the piece); don't sweat it if you can't deliver the choreography exactly as it was taught—obviously do your best to pick up steps quickly, but it's not truly a test of your memorization skills.

When you get into the dance call, try your best to be one of the people who moves to the front of the room—not because you're trying to call attention to yourself (those people are really annoying!), but because first, you will learn the dance better if you're not trying to see over or through a large crowd of people; and second, you won't be tempted to fade into the background and disappear. Whether you are excited or scared out of your mind about the dance call, you have to project the ethos of enthusiasm for the project, and being in or near the front will help you to do that.

Don't be afraid to raise your hand and ask the choreographer or associate choreographer questions if you miss something. Again, do not be one of those obnoxious people who asks obvious questions to which he already knows the answers, just to get the attention of the creative team (we can tell when dancers do that, and it's unappealing), but if you need clarification or repetition of a step in earnest, it's better to ask than to flounder. It is also a much better choice to ask the person leading the dance call rather than your neighbor in the room. Starting up side conversations with other dancers distracts everyone around you, it drives choreographers crazy, and it will often force you to miss some other instruction that comes while you're reviewing with the other dancer.

Once you've done your utmost to learn and repeat what has been taught to the group, you have only to execute the combination to the best of your ability, remembering to make acting choices in line with the musical and its characters. Strong choices will almost always distract from or make up for weaker dance technique or missed choreographic steps. In chapter 3, I admonished you for ever apologizing in an audition; this goes just as much in a dance call. So many actors—especially those for whom dance is not a primary or even secondary strength—feel the need to communicate their "badness" to the artistic team. They do this by making comments, by laughing at themselves, by rolling their eyes, all of which needs to be *eliminated* from your work. No director wants to hire someone who is going to comment on the work they are being asked to do; we want actors who will *do the work*. You are your product, so sell yourself at every moment in the audition. Besides, when you fall out of a turn or fail to properly execute a moment of choreography, there is always a chance that no one was looking at you. By commenting on your error after the fact, you *literally* double the chances of drawing attention to your mistake! So just shut up and dance.

When it comes to large combined calls (the aforementioned SETC, etc.) or college entrance auditions, the dance portion of the day is not character and show specific. However, we are still looking for people who can act and tell stories through their dance. Colleges don't need to see great technique, per se (it's our job to *train you* for four years), but we need to see potential at the very least. Your investment, before you go to college auditions, in ballet class will help familiarize you with the terms and the basic positions so that you are not lost at the barre. Your conditioning will show us that you can hold your body up with strong posture and core strength and that you have flexibility. We will want to see you jump without the fear of you injuring yourself and cross the floor with *grace and joy*. And your work in jazz class will teach your body the difference between turned-out and parallel positions. It will also help you be more adept at picking up combinations and style (including isolation) quickly.

While dance is not generally the *primary* factor in deciding who gets accepted into a musical theatre training program, it is often the deal breaker between two similar candidates. And once again, we are making those determinations based only partially on actual technique but more on delivery and style. So when you are in a general dance call, create a logical character for yourself that fits the particular choreography you've been taught. Who is that character? Where is she? What does she want? What has happened just before she started to dance? How is she using the choreography to get what she wants? If you put your focus on answering these questions, you will worry less about being "right" or being perfect, and you'll demonstrate an ability to personalize the movement and express yourself through dance. *That* is so incredibly appealing!

One final piece of advice about the dance aspect of the audition process: I suggest you invest in some professional attire. If you are going in for a show such as *West Side Story*, it is completely appropriate to wear jeans and sneakers in the dance call, since that's what you'd be expected to dance in if cast; however, generally speaking, you should have form-fitting dance clothing that allows the choreographer to see the line of your body and allows for the greatest flexibility. Ladies need to own leotards, tights, jazz pants, and dance skirts. Men need to own dance belts, tights, jazz pants, and form-fitted athletic shirts. Don't attend the dance call in street clothes or even gym attire. Everyone needs proper shoes, including ballet slippers, character heels (for women), jazz flats or jazz sneakers (dance-specific, not tennis shoes), and taps. I do not recommend showing up to dance calls in sweatpants and street footwear, nor should you dance in your socks—it just makes you look less professional. Make the choice to go in like a professional, even if we're talking about a college audition or an actors-who-move call. And you may want to consider color when you choose your dance attire as well. If your audition outfit is green, for instance, why not wear dance clothing in the same or a similar color family? It will only help the creative team to remember you easier through association.

Some Words of Wisdom from
Lynne Kurdziel Formato, Director/Choreographer

Jonathan has covered this topic quite thoroughly, so my comments will likely highlight the most salient points for me. If you attend a professional dance call for any show, in addition to being a highly skilled, well-trained artist, please bring an open heart and mind with a willingness to play. It is *more* than true, that sometimes the best technical dancer in the room does not make the cut, because the team is hiring storytellers who sometimes utilize the language of dance. True confidence and a sincerely positive attitude will stand out at *any* call—dancer or mover. The ability to infuse the given combination with inner life and a point of view, or deliver an interesting improvisation can indeed earn you a role. Just be careful not to do anything (for example, acrobatic passes) that you are not willing to do eight shows a week. Certainly show off any skills you are asked to perform, as long as they are solidly in your repertoire and able to be executed on a regular basis over an extended period of time. Remember that even your entrance into the room, and your behavior while watching other groups dance can impact your casting.

As far as quick pick up, try to think in concepts/chunks of material (choreographers often "name" sections—you can do the same) and utilize imagery. Attempt to access the style and specificity of port de bras, and note the high points of technically based movement—that battement, jete, and pirouette are there for a reason. Identify musical cues and accents that are utilized by the combo being taught—even played on just a piano, you will hear them. For future preparation, many dancers keep notation of every dance audition combination they experience, including a video of themselves performing it when they get home.

Yes, please wear the appropriate shoes to a dance call—unless you are auditioning for a show such as *The Lion King* or *Hair* there are rarely bare feet seen on the Broadway stage. *Learn to dance well in heels*, ladies—take every opportunity to rehearse in and make those shoes your friends. Gentlemen, please own a nice pair of jazz oxfords in addition to those ubiquitous jazz sneakers, also a pair of men's character or ballroom shoes. As far as other dance attire, lululemon still appears to be king/queen, and yes, we need to see your body lines. Other than that, rules have definitely loosened up, and I have been in rooms where nary a leotard was seen.

As Jonathan has mentioned, it is an eclectic dance world on the stage these days; the more versatile you are, the better. Ballet is, and probably always will be, the foundation for a well-trained technical dancer. In addition to the styles that Jonathan has mentioned, I also suggest that dancers explore somatic practices as early as possible for longevity of career. Any supplemental study from Pilates, Yoga, Gyrokinesis, Feldenkrais, Kinesiology, and beyond can help you understand your specific body, its strengths, weaknesses, and needs. *Cross train*! Ectomorphs: work on cardio and strength; mesomorphs: work on that flexibility and so on.

Above all, do not take anything personally (even when the director and/or choreographer is fighting for you, the necessary high "C" in the score or in regional theatre, local housing may trump your being hired)—try never to lose sight of why you began dancing, and continue to dance. "What I Did for Love" from *A Chorus Line* is truth: they say the dancer dies two deaths—the end of their "dancing life" and then their final death. *Fortunately*, as a musical theatre performer, we have other talents and skills to access even when we no longer kick our nose; storytelling in dance can happen in a variety of ways—and that clever choreographer will choreograph to feature our current skills, while still fulfilling the vision of the show!

Lynne Kurdziel Formato
Associate Professor Performing Arts, Elon University
SDC Director/Choreographer

Among her many credits, Lynne served as director/choreographer for the European premiere of *Disney's Aladdin* at the Fredericia Theatre in Denmark, remounting it at the Royal Opera House in Copenhagen in the summer of 2013, as well as the Scandinavian premiere of *Disney's The Little Mermaid*. Recent favorite experiences include direction and choreography for the regional premiere of *Memphis* at Arkansas Repertory Theatre in Little Rock and *In the Heights* at Elon University.

WHO COULD ASK FOR ANYTHING MORE?

I have already told you that the goal of an audition is to do your best, most authentic work. The desired outcome is, of course, a callback. We have now dissected how to properly handle a callback, but we have not paused to address the issue of what the actor's goal should be once she gets a callback. I mean, if you've come this far, you successfully achieved your initial objective, so what now?

You may say, "Duh, Flom. The goal of a callback is to get a job offer." And while I agree that being cast would be wonderful, I would also suggest that you may find that making it your objective will lead to a great deal of disappointment. I hate to be cynical, but let's face it, you're going to audition a lot more often than you'll be cast; it's just a statistical fact. And the more a person fails to achieve personal career goals, the likelier she is to give up and change careers. Thus it follows: if you set your mind on getting work every time you audition, you'll encounter disappointment with a high frequency, and eventually you will give up. If, however, you make it your goal at each and every callback you attend, first, to have fun and, second, to let them see you at your best, you will stand a much greater chance of achieving a 100 percent success rate. You will have more control. What's more, focusing on a positively attainable objective will make you more desirable to directors, and you will probably find yourself fielding more job offers this way.

It may sound as though I'm quibbling over subtle semantics, but I really believe that identifying a realistic goal over which you are capable of asserting your control is extremely empowering. You'll perform with confidence once you stop trying to please the director and start making every audition an opportunity to be the best performer you can be. You won't always get the part, but you'll be able to walk away feeling good about what you showed the artistic team.

I can't count the number of times I've heard of actors being passed over at one audition because they weren't right for the part, only to be called in later for a different project on the merit of their earlier showing. You can never know exactly what they're looking for or what roles have already been cast; you can only show them what you have to offer and then leave it in their hands. Most directors you audition for will be casting one current project with their next two future productions already in the back of their minds. Plus, other people in the audition room might be casting other shows as well. You never know what one good, yet seemingly unsuccessful, audition will yield later on.

BUT I PLAY ONE ON TV

As I stated earlier, you must offer a positive response to directorial adjustments in an audition. The reply "Yes, I can do that" is one you should practice and be ready to use when asked to approach a piece differently. That said, you must be careful not to say it if it isn't true.

For example, an actor goes in for a replacement call in *Wicked*. He sings well and impresses the casting director enough to earn a second audition. At the callback, it turns out that they are looking for someone with acrobatic and tumbling skills. The actor, eager to be considered for a big Broadway gig, nods enthusiastically when asked if he has any gymnastic abilities. Unfortunately, the only tumbling he's ever done has been somersaults in preschool. Now that actor has painted himself into a corner, and there is really no easy way for him to save face. You cannot always be what they need. You must remember to be honest about your abilities with the director and with yourself.

Also—when a director asks if you possess a certain skill that you do not possess, there is no need to offer an apology for not being able to do what they are asking. Actors always want to apologize for falling short of what they think the director needs. ("Do you tumble?" "I don't. I'm so sorry.") They usually assume that if they can't demonstrate the requested skill, they have been eliminated from possibly getting hired. This is also not necessarily true. I recently cast a production of *She Loves Me* and I asked every actor who auditioned if they played a musical instrument. I had the notion that if I could find the right group of actor-musicians I could include moments of live accompaniment on stage as part of the ensemble's work in the production. But my concept did not hinge on this convention, so not playing an instrument did not preclude someone from being cast.

On the other hand, there are times when you should allow yourself to ride on your acting skills. When I was back in my performing days, I was the least confident dancer you could have ever met. In spite of my four years of BFA training, I avoided dance calls like the plague. I hated having to learn choreography; however, if I ever went in for a singing audition and was asked if I danced, my answer was always, "Sure." Why did I do that? Because my very basic knowledge of ballet, jazz, and tap, combined with my acting abilities, made me very capable at faking my way through most dance calls. Sure, I didn't have great extension or pointed toes, nor could I always keep up with all the steps; but I always sold it. I sold it by having fun and *acting* like a dancer. If they were looking to fill a serious dance role, I obviously did not stand a chance at getting the part; but if they needed an actor who could move, that was perfectly achievable for me.

The bottom line is this: If they ask about skills that you absolutely do not possess (and cannot fake), you must be honest and tell them you can't do it. If, however, it may be possible to look good trying, then go for it, as long as you can appear confident. I have a friend who once went in for a production of *A Little Night Music* (Sondheim). He was perfect for the role of Henrik, the brooding young son, except for the fact that the musical requires Henrik to play the cello on stage. The character accompanies himself in his big Act 1 solo, "Later." But my friend had never played a cello in his life. When asked if he could play, my friend smiled and said, "You bet." He earned himself a callback, and two days later he had learned how to muddle his way through "Later" enough to get the part. I wouldn't recommend this kind of risk to everyone, but he knew that he was musical enough to show them what they needed to hear, and so he went for it. That kind of confidence alone can be worthy of a job.

AND THAT BRINGS US BACK TO . . .

The unique thing about being an actor (as if there were only one unique thing about being an actor!) is that even when you have a job, you're always looking for work. Broadway performers do most of their shows in the evening. During their daytime off-hours, they can often be found auditioning. It's even the same with acting schools—once you get in, you'll still be required to audition every time a show is being cast. Auditioning *is* the job of an actor. If you are ready to commit your life to the art of performing, you had better embrace the idea of auditioning. You had better be prepared to put yourself on display and to be judged, and you must learn not to take the judgment personally. Moreover, you had better take stock of what you can and cannot control and invest your time in learning to master factors that are within your command rather than beating yourself up over those that are not.

Continue to study voice and dance, even when you are out of school. Keep your body in optimum physical condition. Read and see plays as often as possible to discover new material for your repertoire. And when you attend auditions, be grateful for the opportunity to be seen performing. You will find your overall mental health enhanced greatly by maintaining a proper, positive outlook. You will also learn that people who truly love their jobs do better at them: Love to audition.

SECRET AGENT MAN

Many young actors ask me to explain agents and casting directors—what they do and the differences between them. So here's a very brief crash course on these all-important friends of your career.

An agent is an industry insider who has the power to open doors for actors. Producers and casting directors send out "breakdowns," or specifics about an audition, to agents; the agents then submit their clients who are appropriate for that particular call. Agents can get actors access to auditions that they would never otherwise have on their own. An agency may represent anywhere from 50 to 200 performers, depending on the size of the office and the scope of its operation. They may deal in theatre, film, and television (these are known as "legit" agencies) and they may also deal in commercial and/or voice-over work. When an agent takes an actor on as a client, he will frequently give the actor a modest amount of career management advice, including what to wear, which headshot is right, and on rare occasions, what material to use for auditions. The agent will sometimes seek out feedback for the client after an audition as well, in order to help the actor improve. And of course, the agent makes money when the actor makes money: the standard rate is 10 percent of the actor's paycheck. (Note: No legitimate agent should ever ask for a penny from you if you're not working. Anyone who says they'll represent you for a monthly or a yearly fee is not someone you should work with—most likely, they are scam artists.) So if you sign with a good agency, they will work hard for you.

Getting signed with an agent can prove to be quite enigmatic. I wish there were a simple cut-and-dry way to go about doing so, but unfortunately no formula exists. Some colleges will showcase their graduating class to agents as their first exposure, after which the actors may choose to follow up and ask for a formal audition. Some actors find representation when an agent sees them in a production or when a casting director refers them. And sometimes a friend who is signed with an agency may recommend you to them, getting you in the door. Those are really the most common ways to get yourself an agent. Unfortunately, sending an unsolicited letter of interest without having some introduction or common connection to the agency does not usually tend to pan out.

The casting director works on the other side of the table. She is hired by a producer or theatre company essentially to "weed out" actors and dig for appropriate talent to show the director of a production. When a casting director is hired, she must understand the needs of the show as seen through the director's vision. She will then either send a breakdown to agents or place a public advertisement in the trade papers and hold open auditions. Casting directors who have a previous relationship with certain actors will also call them directly and ask them to come in for a project that they feel would be a good match. Thus, it's your mission to have casting directors know you and like you.

Once you go through an initial screening with the casting director, if she is interested in you for the project, she will ask you to come back in for the artistic staff of the production, including the director, the producers, the writers, the choreographer, and so on. So while the casting director generally does not have final say in who gets hired, she can give you a free pass right to the final cut, where the director or the producer ultimately chooses who is cast.

Agents and casting directors tend to have a "you scratch my back, I'll scratch yours" relationship. The casting director needs the agent to submit good quality actors, and the agent needs the casting director to employ his clients. Needless to say, finding yourself in good standing with any of these people is to your benefit. Your reputation as a professional will mean everything in the profession, so establish and maintain a reputation for doing good, sincere work and for not being a jerk.

SUMMARY

- Be sure to ask questions and gather all the information when you receive a callback.
- Whether you memorize or not, always hold the script pages in your hand during a callback.
- Find a way to learn any music handed out for callbacks. Consider www.getonmysides.com.

- Unless otherwise instructed, wear the same clothes to the callback that you wore to the initial audition.
- Unless otherwise instructed, make the same acting and vocal choices at the callback that you made at the initial audition.
- Bring dance clothes and dance shoes to every musical audition you attend. In general, do not wear jeans or gym clothes and do not dance in socks or street sneakers.
- If you forget a step in the dance combination, keep moving and try to find your way back, always acting through the entire process.
- Don't focus on trying to get the job. Instead, concentrate on having fun and offering them your best performance at every audition.
- If asked to make an adjustment, say yes. If asked whether you possess a skill that you do not possess (and cannot fake), say no.
- Love to audition!

5

JOB OFFERS

WHAT TO DO, WHAT TO SAY

Most audition books tend to leave you on your own once you complete the callback; some don't even extend beyond the initial call. But I really believe that some discussion on what to do after you have been seen will be valuable. After all, fielding offers is as much a part of the game as answering casting calls. Realistically, you will not be able to (nor will you necessarily want to) take every job you are offered. So in this chapter, we will examine several factors to consider once the proverbial ball is in your court.

Back in the early pages of this book, I advised you to read casting notices carefully and to consider whether you would want a particular job before going in for an audition. But it is not always possible to make this determination before an offer is made. Even a thorough casting ad will lack certain details that you will only discover once you begin to negotiate with the producers.

Every professional actor has stories of being burned by bad project choices in his career. The greener you are, the more likely you'll be to accept any role just for the credit and the exposure. You will find that experience educates in these matters. But you can greatly reduce the risk of making unhappy commitments if you take the time to thoroughly consider the circumstances at hand and to be a little selective when possible.

My first advice to actors who have auditioned for a project and feel the delicious tingling of their phone vibrating with a potential offer is this: *Do not answer that call!* Let it roll to voicemail and make them leave you a message on the first call. This might seem very counterintuitive, but hear me out. When you receive a call with details of an offer, your adrenaline kicks in and you will not be thinking 100 percent clearly. Especially when you're younger, you are more likely to get caught up in the excitement of the offer and say yes without thinking things through. There is a certain element of negotiation that you must practice when it comes to deliberating over a job, and you will help your cause greatly if you have a moment to listen to their message and process the information privately before discussing the details with the producers. In the pages below, I will offer you some points to consider before accepting a gig. I suggest you keep a checklist of questions handy in your journal or digital notepad, so that when a contract is offered to you, you can be certain you cover all of your bases. To that end, if you let the call go to voicemail, you can take the time to prepare your questions and talk about the job with the producers when you are clearheaded and in control of the conversation.

Furthermore, by answering the phone when they first call, you run the risk of missing details of the offer due to external factors: Perhaps you're driving in the car or running around mid-town. Noise and poor reception can make for a very difficult phone call. You may not be able to jot down notes and therefore you may overlook something important. Your phone may even cut out as you are trying to catch pivotal points. By letting the call roll over, you can determine when and where to phone them back in order to guarantee the best conditions for such an important conversation. Get yourself seated in a quiet place and be prepared to take notes and to go through your checklist of priorities. Just remember that jobs are not generally offered with the caveat of *first come, first served*. You won't risk them calling the next person on their list if you don't answer the phone immediately. Just don't wait too long to get back to them. (Note: The exception to this rule is the world of commercials and television shoots. The turnover time is so fast in that field that they may literally need an answer from you *right now* or they will go to the next person on the list. If you get a call after a commercial audition, you'll want to go ahead and answer it right away or, at the very least, phone them back within minutes of the missed call.)

When you are ready to get on the phone with them, begin by gathering as much information as possible about the role that is offered to you. Find out exactly how much it pays, how long it runs, how often it rehearses, where you are expected to be and when and how you'll get there, and where you'll

Brittany Irish, actor, models an audition outfit. The outfit represents her brand: "Fiery Poise." www.brittanyirish.com. *Photo by Jonathan Flom*

Patrick Clealand Rosé, actor, models an audition outfit. The outfit is meant to proclaim his brand: "Unflinching. Unusual. Unmistakable." www.pat rickclealandrose.com. *Photo by dirty sugar*

Tess Marshall, a contemporary actor who crosses over between musical theatre and pop/rock. Her outfit is a little more casual, but it still represents who she is and looks professional. *Photo by Jonathan Flom*

Kelsee Sweigard represents her brand of "Steadfast, Savvy Vibrance."
www.kelseesweigard.com. *Photo by Jonathan Flom*

Debby's photo is an example of a horizontal "landscape" headshot. Note how the photo is primarily the actor's face, close to the camera. Her eyes really pop in this photo, and the background gives texture without being a distraction. *Photo courtesy of Jenna P. Photography*

Lauren Khalfayan is yet another example of the importance of eyes in the headshot. Her exoticism is clear, but she is warm and open as well. *Photo courtesy of Jenna P. Photography*

Nic is an example of a vertical "portrait" shot. Again, there's genuine warmth in the photo, but the jacket, the hair, and the background (blurred for texture only) give him a sense of urban-ness. *Photo courtesy of Jenna P. Photography*

Natalie Maria Szczerba

nmszczerba95@gmail.com
Height: 5' 5"   Eyes: Green
Hair: Blonde   Weight: 135 lbs
Voice: Soprano with Belt

Professional Theatre

THE FANTASTICKS	Luisa	Otterbein Summer Theatre
Dir. David Caldwell		
CARMEN	Ensemble	Toledo Opera

Educational Theatre

RENT	Ensemble, Mimi Marquez (U/S)	Otterbein University
INTO THE WOODS	Rapunzel	Otterbein University
Dir. Lenny Leibowitz		
SWEET CHARITY	Ensemble	Otterbein University
THE FULL MONTY	Vicki Nichols	Otterbein University
Dir. David Caldwell		
HMS PINAFORE	Ensemble , Cousin Hebe (U/S)	Interlochen Arts Camp
Dir. Sean Cooper		
RENT	Mimi Marquez	All-Ohio Show, STC
CURTAINS	Niki Harris	Otterbein University
THE SEAGULL	Sorin	Otterbein University

Education

Otterbein University Musical Theatre Candidate 2017
Interlochen Vocal Arts and Operetta Program 2011

Training

Acting
Lenny Leibowitz, Jimmy Bohr, David Caldwell, Melissa Lusher, Melinda Murphy, Christina Kirk, John Stefano

Voice
Lori Kay Harvey, Jeremy Davis, Jennifer Whitehead, Peg Cleveland Plambeck, Carolyn Redman

Dance
Ballet/ Jazz/ Tap/ Modern: Anna Elliott, Stella Kane, Maria, Maria Glimcher, Nigel Burgoine, Tammy Plaxico, Christeen Stridsberg

Movement
Feldenkrais/Alexander: Melinda Murphy

Speech
Dialect Training: Melissa Lusher (IPA: RP, Russian, Australian, German)

Masterclasses
Lindsay Nicole Chambers, Kolby Kindle, Ben Lipitz, Aaron Ramey, Dee Hoty, David Caldwell, Michael Cassara, Victoria Libertore, Nathan Gunn, Randy Skinner

Special Skills/Interest
High E, Piano, Juggling, Basic Tumbling Skills, Pottery (throwing), Rollerblading, Perry the Platypus Noise, Dog Barking.

Special Honors

Fine Arts Award in Music	Vocal Arts and Operetta	Interlochen Arts Camp
World Youth Honors Choir	Vocal Arts and Operetta	Interlochen Arts Camp

Natalie Szczerba Résumé. This is an actual actress in the Musical Theatre program at Otterbein. Her résumé includes a high-quality photo. *Photo courtesy of Afton Welch*

Christopher P. Castanho

Email: castanhoc@gmail.com
Height: 5' 9" Hair: Blonde Eyes: Hazel Voice: Tenor

Theatrical Experience

Educational

She Loves Me	Arpad Laszlo	Shenandoah Conservatory
To Kill A Mockingbird	Dill	Shenandoah Conservatory
Spelling Bee	Leaf Coneybear	Greater Hartford Academy of the Arts
Ragtime	Mother's Younger Brother	Greater Hartford Academy of the Arts
Hairspray	Brad	Greater Hartford Academy of the Arts
The Secret Garden	Ensemble (Dickon u/s)	Shenandoah Conservatory

Special Performances

Carnegie Hall: Lux Aeterna	Tenor	
To Judy With Love (John Fricke)	Soloist	Director: Eric Larivee

Training

Shenandoah Conservatory BFA Musical Theatre (2017)
Voice: David Meyer
Acting: Jonathan Flom, Larry Silverberg, Charles Goforth, J.J. Ruscella, Carolyn Coulson (Meisner Trained)
Dance: Shylo Martinez (Tap), Mary Robare (Ballet), Alan Arnett (Jazz & Tap), Robyn Schroth (Ballet)

Greater Hartford Academy of the Arts (Musical Theatre Major)
Voice: Phil Rittner, Eric Larivee, Janelle Robinson, Peter Peluso.
Acting: David McCamish, Debra Walsh, Jill Giles, Brian Jennings, Dexter J. Singleton, Michael Nowicki
Dance: Christine Simoes (Jazz & Ballet), Mary Cadorette (Luigi & Broadway Tap), Clare O'Donnell (Tap)
Playwriting and Directing: Brian Jennings

Master Classes
Kaitlin Hopkins, Joy Dewing, Jenny Ravitz, Jason Styres, John Fricke, Christopher Denny, Heather Provost, Marissa Perry, Pat McCorkle, Gary Krasny

Special Skills

Playwriting, Directing, Proficient Piano (since age 9), Reads Music, Strong Sight Singing, Funny voices

Christopher Castanho Résumé. This is an actual actor in the Musical Theatre program at Shenandoah Conservatory. His résumé includes a high-quality photo. *Photo courtesy of Jessica Osber*

stay. Don't be afraid to ask a lot of questions when you first get that call from a theatre. And once you have obtained all of the details, you simply *must* say, *"Let me think about it and call you back."*

Too many actors, excited just to receive an offer, wind up stuck in a miserable project because they said yes without looking at the big picture. You have every right to take some time to consider an offer before getting on board. Don't allow yourself to get swept away and make a rash decision. Most stage directors and producers will allow you 24 hours *at the very least* to ponder their offer. They will respect you for taking the time to be certain you can commit to the project before rushing in.

FOR YOUR CONSIDERATION

When a job opportunity comes your way, there are many factors that can aid in your decision-making process. Determining whether a job is worth the overall commitment comprises several questions, the answers to which may sway you strongly toward or away from accepting work. The following is a checklist of sorts that you should utilize when fielding an offer.

How long will the production require your dedication?
Will you be tied up in rehearsals and/or workshops for two months, followed by a nine-month run? Or the opposite: Will you be putting your life (and your day job) on hold to take a gig that rehearses for a week, runs for two weeks, then leaves you unemployed once more? There is no right answer to help you deal with this question—only what is right for you. Just be certain you understand what you are being asked to do before you agree to it.

Where is the gig?
For a New York actor, accepting a role with a small professional theatre in North Jersey is vastly different than taking the same role in Birmingham, Alabama. Can you afford to be away from the city for the length of the contract? Will anybody see your work if you travel to distant places? Be sure to examine and weigh all of the trade-offs involved in leaving your home to take a job. Is housing and travel included, or will you need to pay out of pocket in order to take the work? Many young actors look for opportunities to join nonunion national tours or even cruise lines after school to travel and save up money while living rent free. Is this something you want to do, or are you more interested in planting roots?

Conversely, some New York actors may relish the opportunity to get out into other regions. Often times the best directors and choreographers in the industry are making much or all of their livings by working in regional cities. Before you turn down a gig in Texas or Milwaukee or New Mexico, consider who will be part of the team and realize that New York is not the end-all, be-all for professional theatre work. You can make some great contacts by taking work in seemingly remote locations.

Can you afford to accept the job?

The sad truth is, much of the acting work that's out there will pay you little to no money. Community theatre, for instance, almost never pays. Frequently, taking a job must be considered an investment in your overall career, for example, the actor who does summer stock for $250 a week because it expands the résumé and keeps him in practice. Usually, the determining factors in whether you can financially justify taking a job are the above-mentioned commitments of time and location. If you feel that they are not paying enough money to get you to go, why not try negotiating for more? The worst thing they can say is no, and then you decide if you are willing to take what is on the table. But if they really want you, they may be willing to offer more money if you tell them you cannot work for their original figure.

I find that the best way to approach the issue of money is to get all the information on the initial call and ask for a few days to consider the offer. During this time, ask yourself how much money you would realistically need to take this job and still be able to pay your bills. Don't overshoot the mark (if their offer is $350 per week, don't ask for $1,200), but don't sell yourself short either ($375 isn't too much of a negotiation). When you call them back, you tell them how interested you are in working with them and how grateful you are for the offer; however, at this point in time it's a real stretch for you financially. Ask if the salary is negotiable. At this point, they may say one of three things: "No it's not" (in which case, you need to be prepared to accept or reject their offer); "How much did you have in mind?" (in which case, you tell them your figure); or "We can give you X dollars more" (after which you either continue to negotiate or you make a final decision). I see too many actors get into tough financial crunches because they don't treat themselves like a *business* and they make poor *business* choices. Remember, the name of this thing is show *business*.

If a theatre is unwilling to be flexible on salary, you might also ask for other accommodations in your contract to make it worth your while, such as transportation/airfare to the gig, a rental car, free housing, a meal stipend, your own room, and so on. Again, don't be so thankful for a job offer that you are willing to accept terrible conditions and a large financial hit to take work.

And speaking of contracts: When working in professional theatre, there will always be a contract. In amateur theatre, there is no pay involved, so everything is likely verbal. But if you are working in stock, regional, Off Broadway, touring theatre, cruise ships, or any venue that is going to pay you for your work, you must insist that you get everything in writing. It is the only protection you have as an actor, especially if you don't belong to the union. A verbal acceptance of a job with certain conditions attached is a fine agreement for starters, but if you start working on a job before getting a signed contract from the producer or company, there is no telling what might happen during the process. Most theatres will send you a contract without your having to ask for it. When you receive a contract, read it carefully and make sure you understand everything completely. Also, make sure that the wording reflects anything you negotiated or were promised. Remember: if it's not in writing, it's not binding. Protect yourself. You are a business, not a pawn. (Note: I offer a more detailed chapter on contract reading and negotiation in my other book, *Act Like It's Your Business: Branding and Marketing Strategies for Actors*.)

What will you be giving up?

So, you have a really great full-time day job with benefits. They even allow you to take an extended lunch when there is a great audition going on. You're making enough to live comfortably in the city while many of your friends are struggling or moving away. *But are you doing what you came to do?* I pose this question to you because I had to answer it for myself some years back, and I've seen almost all of my actor friends face it as well.

There comes a time (or possibly several times) when you will be required to sacrifice something—perhaps even another acting job—in order to accept a role. It can be a frightening proposition, particularly when the offer you are considering has high artistic value but low financial reward. And so I say that you must ask yourself if you are doing what you came to do. Can you possibly survive without the cushy day job so as to move in the direction of your career ambitions?

You'll need to weigh the situation carefully before you can assess whether it's worth the risk. Only you can judge in a given circumstance what is best for you. Just do your best not to burn bridges as you make these types of decisions. I'm speaking now to the actor who is already involved in one production when another, more exciting offer comes along. In such an instance, you must tread lightly and truly reflect on whether the second job is worth walking out on the current one. It may depend on how far into the first project you have gone. Just remember that this is a very small community, and you are only as good as your reputation. Will you be damaging your future if you walk away from a commitment in your present? In these situations, actors will often help find their own replacement to save the production staff time and money.

What will you gain?

The advice given to me when I was preparing to go out into the profession was to consider three factors in a job offer: Is the pay good? Is this a role that I really should have on my résumé? Is this a director or a theatre that I really should have on my résumé? If you answer yes to two out of the three, then you should take the job for sure. If you only answer yes to one or none, then you need to seriously consider if it's worth it.

Think about what kind of exposure a gig may offer as well. Being seen performing in a production is as good a way of being cast in the future as auditioning is. Sometimes you may be offered a minor role or even an understudy job, but it will be worthwhile because a star is involved in the project. Again, think about how any particular job will look on your résumé.

I'd also add that fun/enjoyment is a worthy factor to consider. You may stand to make a good deal of money or some contacts or a résumé credit, but the production may hold no inherent pleasure for you. (Maybe you've been the third spear-carrier on the left six times already and you know you'll be miserable if you accept this seventh contract.) Conversely, sometimes it's okay to accept a low-paying, "unexciting" credit because you just know that being in the particular production will be *fun* for you! As long as you can afford to take the work, why not do it—sometimes our artistic souls need to be fed and we can all use the reminder of how much we enjoy what we do.

Is it a union job?

This question is obviously meant for nonunion performers. I see a great deal of young actors jump at any opportunity for work that would entail joining Actors' Equity. I urge you to use caution when these offers come your way. An Equity membership is not a golden key that will unlock the door to a lifetime of work, contrary to popular and naïve opinion. In fact, many actors find that getting work, even work that pays, is much easier without being in the union.

Think about this: Once you join Equity, you can *only* take union jobs. You'll be shutting yourself out of more than half of the work out there, for starters. You'll be competing with people who have already made a successful career in the theatre and have built up a credible résumé. If you are fresh out of college and your only professional experience is ensemble work at the Pittsburgh CLO, you'll find it difficult to get your foot in the door just to be seen at Equity auditions. And if a theatre has the option of casting you or your equally talented, nonunion counterpart, you can bet they'll go with your unaffiliated colleague and save themselves some money!

I always advise young actors to take some time to build up a list of quality credits before going Equity. It may mean passing on some potentially exciting work along the way, but it can prove extremely wise in the long term for your career. Often, taking one union job will lock an actor out of several years of other work.

Now don't get me wrong, I'm not suggesting that it's never good to go union when you're young. If you are offered an Equity contract that will employ you for a long period of time or provide you with maximum exposure, or if it's simply a great role that will truly enhance your résumé, then I say go for it. What I am saying, however, is don't run to the Jekyll and Hyde Restaurant or Theatreworks/USA because they give out Equity cards to all of their employees. Be careful about working for the MUNY in St. Louis or Pittsburgh CLO, where you will be required to take your Equity card just to work in the chorus. Again, you just need to think ahead and try to anticipate whether it will pay off for you in the big picture. Seek counsel from your teachers and mentors when you are faced with the union decision.

Do you want to work with this company?

Moments ago, I mentioned that reputations mean a great deal in the theatre industry. This is true not only for performers but also for directors and theatre companies. *Before you agree to accept a job, it is wise to investigate the theatre for which you would be working.* Talk to your friends and see if they can offer any thoughts or opinions about the company based upon their experience. You may find that while a gig sounds appealing on paper, it's not worth facing the horror stories that your fellow actors tell you about how seedy the housing is or how the paychecks have a knack for bouncing.

If you can avoid getting entrenched in miserable theatrical endeavors, you'll save yourself a good amount of stress and heartache. When you hear bad things about a theatre or a director, don't hesitate to graciously refuse the work if it doesn't seem worth the hassle.

Sadly, you'll find a great deal of disreputable theatres in big cities such as New York and Chicago. The desperate need to work often leads actors to settle for being treated poorly. With experience, you will learn how to avoid such unhappy situations, and you'll develop a network of fellow actors with whom you can exchange feedback, both negative and positive, regarding theatres where you have worked.

One piece of wisdom I am always quick to offer on the subject is this: beware of jobs that require you to pay to work. I'm not speaking of networking organizations such as Actors' Connection, which happens to be well reputed for attracting big agencies. Rather, I am referring to those theatres, sometimes known as "membership companies," that charge actors a fee to perform with them. It's one thing to be financially involved with helping your friends start up a theatre company; it's another thing entirely to be asked to contribute to a theatre's budget just to be cast in a play.

You should *never* pay to work; even if they tell you that you are investing in a "showcase" production. (My dear friend Melissa was taken in this way and found herself swindled out of $75.) Legitimate showcases do not require any money from the actors. Companies that charge actors to work are either scams or very low forms of community theatre. Either way, you'll do well to avoid them.

HOW COULD I WALK AWAY?

Earlier on, I spoke to you about being careful not to attend auditions for jobs you can't or won't take. I advised that it might be perceived by the director that you are wasting her time. In the event, however, that you audition for a project with every intent to accept an offer, only to discover an unavoidable conflict after they cast you, you must make every effort to save face.

Let me give you an example of such a situation. I was casting a production of *Cabaret*, and a young man contacted me about his interest in the role of Cliff. We arranged an audition time for him, and he came in very prepared and professional. The musical director and I agreed that he would be a very competent choice, and I called him two days later to offer him the part.

When he returned my call later that day, he explained that he had also auditioned for a production of *City of Angels* at a prominent theatre closer to his home. (He is from New Hampshire, and my theatre was in Vermont.) The two shows ran for virtually the same dates, and he was up for the lead role of Stine in *Angels*. Could he have one day to get back to me about my offer?

I agreed to wait for his decision. He called me the next day, as promised, and told me he did receive the offer from the other theatre, and of course he needed to accept it. I agreed with his choice and I wished him well on the project. That actor played his cards well, communicated efficiently and timely between his potential employers, and never made me feel like he was blowing me off or disrespecting my production. His honesty and candor earned him my respect, which as an actor, he had hoped to maintain for future casting opportunities with me.

Furthermore, he made it a point to see a performance of *Cabaret* on one of his off nights. He found me after the show and offered his congratulations, expressing his eagerness to work with me in the future. And he invited me to attend a performance of *City of Angels*, leaving me with all the information about his show. (Remember: being seen in a production is as good as auditioning, if not better.)

In every way possible, this actor remained professional, and he ensured that he did not burn a bridge. All actors should follow his example in situations that require passing on work. The moral is this: *Deal justly with everyone. You never know where you'll see them next.*

SUMMARY

- When you receive a job offer, gather all of the details and then say, "Let me think about it and get back to you" before making a commitment.
- If you cannot afford to take the work, try negotiating before making your decision.
- Consider what is to be gained or lost by accepting a particular job.
- Seek counsel from teachers or mentors before accepting work that would require you to join Actors' Equity.
- Before accepting a job, try to find out about the theatre and the director and decide if you really want to work for them.
- Do not pay to work at a theatre.
- If you must turn down work, be tactful and do not burn bridges. The industry is too small and insular to get away with it.

6

HEADSHOTS, RÉSUMÉS, AND COVER LETTERS

WHO COULD THAT ATTRACTIVE GIRL BE?

Virtually every audition you ever attend will require a headshot and a résumé. If you are serious about your career as an actor, you must acknowledge the photograph as a vital tool of your trade and a necessary investment. A photo session with a decent studio can run from $400, if you get a really great deal, to over $1,200; it's certainly not pocket change. But it is imperative that you find the photographer who is the best match for you and that you do not settle for someone who works cheaply.

Don't get me wrong, I'm not suggesting that only studios that charge $1,000 and up are worth their salt; some of my favorite headshots were taken very affordably. I am, however, urging you to hire a professional photographer who does *theatrical headshots*; do not simply have your dad or your friend take you out back with the digital camera for some free snapshots. I assure you, homemade headshots are *always* noticeably low quality. Additionally, good wedding or landscape photographers and portrait studios are not in the business of understanding actor headshots and should also be avoided for this purpose as well.

So how do you begin to choose from among the hundreds of professional studios out there in every major city? What makes a particular photographer a good match for a given actor? My first advice is to browse a photographer's website. They all have online galleries compiling highlights

of their work. When you hear about a studio from Backstage.com, Playbill
.com, or Reproductions.com (all three are great sources for finding professional headshot photographers) or through an online search, you should
look at the style in which they shoot—each individual photographer has his
own unique approach (branding!)—and you must ask yourself if that is the
feeling that you are going for in your pictures. Find someone whose work
appeals to you, first and foremost.

Another great way of shopping for a photographer is to talk with actors
you know whose headshots you admire, and find out where they went. I've
always found my network of friends helpful in recommending both whom
to use and whom to avoid. I have even approached strangers at auditions if
I liked their picture and asked who shot them. There are many resources
available to you, so be selective.

Once again I will refer you to my second book, *Act Like It's Your Business*, for a more extended approach to the process of headshot shopping.
It begins with having a thorough understanding of your personal brand
and what it is that you are selling. When you pinpoint your product, it
makes it easier to find the right marketing tools. For example, if "edgy"
(or some variation of that quality) is part of your brand, you will want
to find specific photographers who capture edge (dirty sugar and David
Noles are two particular studios in New York City that do this well). If,
on the other hand, you embody more refined attributes, you may look
to photographers like Jenna Pinchbeck, Laura Rose, or Robert Mannis,
to name a few of my favorites. The point is, suit the photographer to the
marketing goals.

As you narrow your search for a headshot studio, you will want to arrange
to meet briefly with prospective photographers, if at all possible (or at least
schedule a phone interview). You'll be spending a good deal of money on
an afternoon with a particular individual whose job is to capture your essence on film. A certain element of compatibility is required to get you at
your best, so you'll want to be sure you "click" with a photographer (pun
intended) before you invest. The best cameramen are the ones who can effectively engage you in conversation and bring out your natural personality
as they shoot you *candidly*, rather than forcing you to pose and smile. Some
will even encourage you to bring your favorite music to the session. Their
intent is to make you feel relaxed and comfortable so that the photos do not
appear artificial. In general, a photo shoot that is fun for you will tend to be
successful. So do yourself a service by finding a professional with whom you
can have a good time and be your natural self.

Some Words of Wisdom from
Jenna Pinchbeck, Professional Photographer

Choosing your headshot photographer is an exciting challenge. Finding the best fit for you can truly enhance your career and take your bookings to the next level. I like to compare it to your favorite clothing store. Some people look amazing in JCrew. Others look phenomenal in Banana Republic. Just like you as an actor have a brand, so do the headshot photographers of the world. When it comes to your headshot, your audition outfit, and your repertoire, you have to find what works best for *you*.

Do your research. Communicate with the photographers. See if you get along. As a headshot photographer, it is my job to get to know the client as well as I can in a pretty short amount of time. Therefore, it is important for you as the client to open up and be ready to share the intricacies of your personality and brand with your photographer. Prepare for your shoot—mentally and physically. These shots have to show who YOU are at your BEST.

There is something magical that happens when an actor walks into the audition room and his headshot is the perfect representation of his brand and personality. Casting directors remember that.

Jenna Pinchbeck
Jenna P. Photography

Jenna Pinchbeck of Jenna P. Photography is an actress and headshot photographer living in Philadelphia. She is immensely proud to have clients booking work on and Off Broadway, at regional theatres, and on television. For more information, please visit www.jennapphotography.com.

PICTURE YOURSELF

So what should a headshot actually say about you? Over the years, trends in the industry have shifted: color versus black and white, smiling or serious, vertical or horizontal, head or full body, and so on. But one rule remains fast: the headshot *must look like you*, first and foremost. Second, it must make a statement. As a director, I must be able to assess a great deal about you from your picture and then have my expectations met when you walk in the door.

Let me repeat that *your headshot must look like you*. This sounds trite and perhaps even silly, but you'd be surprised how many actors, taken with the wonders of Photoshop, wind up with a picture that barely resembles their true likeness. Most photographers offer touch-ups as part of a package when you purchase a session with them. These corrections should be limited to color and contrast issues, flyaway hairs, and minor blemishes that are not part of your everyday look. Be careful not to let them touch you up to look like someone other than you!

I will never forget an experience I had when I was casting a production in New York some years back and I received perhaps the best looking headshot I've ever seen. She wasn't the most beautiful girl for certain, but the picture captured such a free-spirited, affable, and fun young woman that I almost wanted to cast her right out of the photograph. She was laughing, and one of her hands floated up to her chest, as if we had just shared the most amusing joke or story together. I couldn't wait to meet her and encounter that effervescent personality firsthand. And would you believe it—at her appointed time, a girl walked in the door, whom I was certain had shown up in the wrong room. I asked her who she was, and when she responded with the name that was on the headshot, I didn't believe her. I held the picture up to examine its likeness side by side with the subject, and I felt utter disappointment in being misled by a photograph.

Mind you, this girl was not unattractive, nor would she have been turned away under normal circumstances; only, her headshot looked nothing like her! The hair was a different length and style, the skin tone was different in the picture, and the overall body type was greatly misrepresented in the picture. Needless to say, I didn't call her back. I can't even remember if her audition was any good. Be sure that the image you settle on captures *you* and not some idealized version of who you'd like to be.

Remember, these are *not glamour shots*. Unless you are going into the fashion magazine industry, your photo should not emulate a supermodel. To that end, you may want to be careful when studio packages include professional makeup and hair styling. It is very common in the industry, but you need to be sure they don't present you in an artificial way. They may help you to look beautiful, stylish, and glamorous, but they don't dress you and make you up before you leave your house each day; thus, it may be difficult for them to help you look natural in your pictures. Just be sure that how they style you doesn't take you away from who you really are, since you know how you present yourself to the world. Be certain that whatever they do to prep you on the day of your photo shoot can be replicated whenever you have to get up at 5 a.m. for an open call!

Your photographer will usually offer some clothing advice before you go to your shoot, but generally you'll be choosing your own outfits from your personal wardrobe. Whether you plan to include some of your body in the picture or simply to shoot from the neck up, you should select a variety of clothes in which you feel and look sensational. In particular, if you have specific features you consider assets (bust, hair, arms, eyes, etc.), be sure to bring attire that helps you accent these attributes. Observe yourself in the mirror wearing each possible ensemble option before you commit to any. What does the outfit accentuate or hide? What statement does it make about you? (Again, refer to *Act Like It's Your Business* for a more detailed approach to picking out the actor's *branded* wardrobe.)

You obviously want to avoid wearing ragged clothes, shirts with prominent logos, extreme white (it washes out on film), or distracting patterns. But beyond that, you want to be sure that you feel comfortable and confident in whatever articles you decide to bring with you. I would also avoid distracting jewelry, such as dangly earrings or necklaces that draw attention away from your eyes and mouth.

During your session, you should be able to trust most of the work to the professional photographer. She will offer opinions on what looks or attitudes may work for you. She will ideally bring out the most in you, personality-wise. But you must never lose sight of the fact that you are the consumer. You are investing a small fortune in headshots that will serve as the calling card of your profession. You should have an idea of what you are going for when you arrive, and do not be afraid to speak up if you don't feel you are getting what you need. Tell the photographer up front: "This is my brand, and I want my photos to make that statement." Photographers are all shooting on digital cameras now, which allow the client to view previews of her photos before the session is over. It is imperative that you determine whether you have some viable options of images before you leave the shoot. Demand your money's worth and don't settle for mediocrity. It's always a good idea to discuss a photographer's policy on satisfaction guarantees before you make an appointment.

Once you do have your proofs (which will normally be sent to you on a private web link), you have an important decision to make regarding which images you wish to have touched up and reproduced. This is not a decision you should make on your own, nor is it a decision for your mother or your boyfriend or anyone else not involved in the theatre industry to determine. You should circulate your proofs among fellow artistic colleagues, mentors, teachers, and directors you know: people who know you well and who also understand the business. These are the individuals who will help you narrow down the most appropriate photos for your purpose. (Not that your family's opinion isn't important, but parents usually tend to have a very different set of criteria on which they assess pictures of you. They usually gravitate toward the shots in which you look most handsome or beautiful.) Furthermore, you should begin your search for feedback by providing your advisors with a clear understanding of your personal brand and what you are looking for the headshot to say about you, so that they have clear criteria by which to judge the efficacy of the photos. For example, "I'm looking for something that really says 'Composed, charming, girl-next-door,'" or "Fun-loving, free-spirited, generous."

Fifteen years ago, there was a more rigid set of rules guiding the practice of headshot photography. Everyone used black-and-white film. Most were shot vertically for ease of flipping the page over to view the attached résumé. Lots of actors preferred to present a full body shot as opposed to a close-up of the face. And the standard procedure was to have one smiling and one serious shot reproduced so that an actor could submit either, depending on the nature of the particular audition.

But, as trends have shifted, we have all but done away with these outmoded theories of actor photos. Now, color is the *only* acceptable mode of headshots. The decision to shoot vertically or horizontally is being guided by the specific needs of the actor being photographed, rather than by any industry standard. As more acting work (even for musical theatre performers) is trending toward film and television, many actors are gravitating toward the landscape (horizontal) shot that closely crops the head, off center in the frame—just like we see faces on the small or the big screen. Some people want to show a little body in their shot (no full body shots, please!), while others prefer a very close-up face. Keep in mind that in our digital age, most of your headshot distribution will happen online, and casting offices will often be looking at your picture in thumbnail format, so consider how much your eyes will be diminished the further the camera is from your face. Again, these are the types of choices you will make for yourself with your trusted counsel to guide you.

As far as the look you present in your headshot—serious or smiling—I offer this food for thought: directors are imaginative. Although you aren't beaming from ear to ear in your picture, I will assume you should be able to play a comical role. Likewise, if your submission captures you in a big, toothy grin, I will not disqualify you from consideration for a dramatic part. In short, you don't need a different headshot for every emotion in your range. (You certainly wouldn't submit a photo of yourself in rage for the part of an abusive husband, I hope!) Just bring the decision back to branding. Let the photograph announce your brand. And ask yourself what statement the photo is making about you. "Hi, I'm nice" is common and very boring. Unfortunately, too many headshots say nothing more than that. But something that says, "I've got a secret," or "Hey, come here and take a closer look," is far more interesting.

Finally, once you've selected your 8 x 10 image (and do be sure the headshot is not 8.5 x 11 if you are in the United States), it is important to choose a contemporary, stylish border and font for your reproductions. This is yet another expense that you mustn't scrimp on. Cheap reproductions are usually visibly low in quality, often overexposed, and always a surefire way to ensure that your photo session investment is wasted. It drives me crazy when my students invest in professional photography only to have it printed locally at Walgreens or Target, on low-quality, glossy paper. Get a sense of what is current and popular in styles of borders—usually you can't go wrong with a medium black line against a white frame, but trends are ever changing, so ask the studio for input if you aren't certain. Don't go with a borderless picture, where your name is obscured somewhere in the lower part of the photo. Be sure to have your name printed in the white border of the photo in a clean, elegant font. Branding 101 would even suggest that you match the font on your picture to the one on your résumé for consistency. Some people opt not to include their name on their picture, and this can make a director's job more difficult when weeding through actors and putting names with faces. The name you use when you work should be the name on your headshot. And the name on your headshot should match the name on your résumé. Many actors feel as though using a full first name (i.e., Jonathan, when you really go by Jon) or including their middle name will sound more formal and impressive, but this is unnecessary; it's okay to just give us the name you would like to be called if we hire you.

Figures 6.1 through 6.6 offer you examples of both landscape (horizontal) and portrait (vertical) configured shots. These are the work of New York/Philadelphia–based photographer Jenna Pinchbeck of Jenna P. Photography. She's a modestly priced professional who has been in the business for several years and is building up quite the portfolio in two major market towns. Spend some time looking at these photos and try to determine what they are saying about the subjects. What are the statements the actors are making? What is the brand they are each selling? (Note: the images are printed in black and white below, but you will find them in full color in the center spread. All headshots *must* be in full color for the industry today. No exceptions!)

Figure 6.1. Debby's photo is an example of a horizontal "landscape" head-shot. Note how the photo is primarily the actor's face, close to the camera. Her eyes really pop in this photo, and the background gives texture without being a distraction. *Photo courtesy of Jenna P. Photography*

Figure 6.2. Muslima's photo offers the possibility of a more neutral background. For her skin tone, the white or beige wall really helps to frame her and make her the focal point. Her personal warmth radiates from the shot. *Photo courtesy of Jenna P. Photography*

Figure 6.3. Michael's photograph shows a little more intensity. The eyes are piercing, and there is an air of mystery. *Photo courtesy of Jenna P. Photography*

Figure 6.4. Lauren Khalfayan is yet another example of the importance of eyes in the headshot. Her exoticism is clear, but she is warm and open as well. *Photo courtesy of Jenna P. Photography*

Figure 6.5. Nic is an example of a vertical "portrait" shot. Again, there's genuine warmth in the photo, but the jacket, the hair, and the background (blurred for texture only) give him a sense of urban-ness. *Photo courtesy of Jenna P. Photography*

Figure 6.6. Tripp's photo is another portrait layout, and his shows a little more body than the others. This is as much body as one would want to have in a headshot. *Photo courtesy of Jenna P. Photography*

The Actor with Many Faces

It's an industry myth that every actor needs to have a smiling headshot for comedic and light auditions and a serious headshot for dramatic and heavy castings. I would much prefer an actor choose one great shot that tells me who he is and sends a branding message (e.g., "My brand is Fearless Energy," or "My brand is Youthful, Sensitive Honesty"). Trust me to imagine you smiling or looking dramatic even if your headshot doesn't capture that.

As far as choosing multiple shots, you want to be careful about putting out too many different messages into the industry. Part of marketing a brand includes being repetitive and memorable. By submitting a different headshot each time you audition, you're making it harder for any one of your photos to be remembered by casting teams. I think it's okay to have one picture that you use primarily for musical theatre and another that is more for film and television or commercials. But within one facet of the business, I recommend choosing one good shot and sticking with it until you decide to rebrand.

As an actor, you will *not* want to consider using composite shots: These are 8 x 10 or postcard-size photos that contain two or more different poses of you on a single card. Composites are used in the world of print modeling, but they are not considered industry standard for actors. Likewise, you probably want to avoid full body shots for theatre or film. We want to see a close-up of your face so that we really get the eyes and the lips without much other distraction.

WHO AM I ANYWAY?

The companion to your fantastically intriguing headshot is the clean, professional résumé, which will be stapled in all four corners to the backside of the picture and trimmed to match the 8 x 10 size. Just as your photos require an investment of money, the résumé demands an investment of time and energy to produce an eye-catching list of credentials. It doesn't matter how much or how little experience you have; formatting your résumé well can impress a director by demonstrating your organization and professionalism.

Contrary to popular opinion, a résumé does not simply offer a laundry list of the roles you've played. It's much more informative. From your résumé, directors can get a sense of where and with whom you've trained and worked, what special skills you possess, even which jobs you regard highest in your personal history—an indication of your artistic values and a further opportunity to state your brand. In this unit, I will offer you some guidelines for creating a sleek, polished résumé that will impress, whether you are a high school student or a seasoned veteran. We'll also look at some examples in the pages ahead.

Any discussion on creating a good résumé must begin and end with formatting. I cannot stress enough the importance of proper spacing, handsome fonts, and clean lines. When a director receives your submission, he will glance at your photograph for a first impression, and then he will flip it over to read about your experience. Since time is always of the essence and yours is likely one of hundreds of résumés piled before him, he will want to be able to scan quickly down the page and learn as much as possible about you with minimal effort. You can help the director by making sure to choose a font that can be read without the aid of a magnifying glass. So many actors, insecure and desperate to show us *everything* they've done since birth, cram their résumés and choose a minuscule font size to fit it all in. Rule #1: Don't do this!

You will also want to become an expert on margins and the Tab key. As you add rows of information, it should fall into organized columns down the page. The spacebar will make you crazy, as it never lines everything up properly. Take your time and experiment with different fonts in order to get everything to fit the way you want directors to see it. You will notice that a 10-point Arial is a different size than a 10-point Garamond or a 10-point Times New Roman. So find the typeface that can be striking as well as functional for the amount of information you need to fit on the paper. It is also important to note that an acting résumé should *never* exceed one side of one page.

The choosing of a font and its size will likely not be finalized until you lay out the information and get a sense of how much space it requires. Be sure to save your work continuously as you go, so that you can experiment and not lose what you've already input. You'll also want to be able to access the résumé to make changes from time to time.

We'll step away from formatting now to talk about layout. The easiest way to discuss the proper organization of a résumé is to start at the top and work our way down. The résumé can be divided into several basic sections. While the specific information contained in each part will be dictated by level of experience, the headings and general ideas of each section should be fairly standard. Here are your general résumé subject areas, from the top down:

- Name and personal information
- Related experience

- Training
- Special skills

As I indicated, these general topics are standard across the board for actors from high school to Broadway. As we go through each heading, it's up to you to make it meet your personal specifications.

Name and Personal Information

The name on the résumé bears similar importance to the introduction at the top of an audition: It must state firmly, "This is who I am." Therefore, choose a larger, bold-faced font that will really jump out and catch the eye. I suggest utilizing the same font as you used for the name on your headshot, for consistency. You may want to center your name at the top of the page so everything below it will be spaced in accordance with the name. The other option that many actors choose is to put the name and personal information over to the left side of the page, leaving room for a small version of a second-look headshot to be printed in the upper-right corner of the résumé. If you go with the thumbnail headshot on the back, be sure that you are able to print it in full color, high quality. It doesn't serve you to have a grainy, black-and-white photo taking up real estate on your résumé.

"Personal information" is a catchall term for whatever details immediately follow your name and precede your experience. It includes an actor's contact information and vital statistics, but usually not much more than this. It generally begins, however, with any union affiliations you may have (AEA; SAG-AFTRA; EMC) if applicable. This information should be in a smaller point than your name, usually about half the size. If you are not yet a member of one of the actor unions, just move on to the next section; do not write "Non-Union" on your résumé.

Next, list your contact information. Again, you'll want to keep this simple; the director doesn't need four phone numbers, three e-mails, and two mailing addresses. In fact, you shouldn't list a home address at all, unless there is a specific call for it with a particular submission. You will usually be sending your materials out to strangers, and sometimes it may be best if they did not have your residential location. Unfortunately, you may encounter people whose intentions are less than respectable. It's better to protect yourself and divulge that information only when you feel comfortable doing so. It's best to list only information that will remain permanent, so that a director can contact you a year after receiving your résumé if a role should come up; trust me, I do it all the time. A cell phone number and an e-mail address will be sufficient. You should create an e-mail account that will be used solely for business, separate from your friendly, chatting e-mail or your college e-mail address. It won't cost you anything to start up an address with Hotmail, Yahoo, or Gmail, and it will help you distinguish career-related mail from everything else. I recommend the business e-mail be some form of your name, rather than a cute, catchy address that obnoxiously tells us how much you love Broadway.

Also, if you have a personal website that lists up-to-date performing credits, advertises upcoming projects, and displays headshots and production photos, you should list the web address here as well. Just be sure you're not providing a personal or untended site. A director might choose to look at it any time, and you'll want to be sure to maintain a current, professional appearance. (Once again, I shamelessly direct you to my chapter on websites in *Act Like It's Your Business*.)

One note to college students about contact information: As you begin to send out submissions for professional work and attend auditions, it is so important to establish a permanent phone and e-mail contact. Do not list a college e-mail address, which will both expire upon graduation and also label you as a student. Use an address from one of the servers I mentioned above.

After your contact details, you may leave a bit of space and provide some of your vital statistics. There's great contention in the industry over this section and what it should or should not include. Historically, actors would list height, weight, hair color, eye color, and voice part. When headshots went to full color, the necessity for hair and eye color became obsolete. You can choose to have it if you want, but it's really not integral. As for height and weight, I personally don't mind it being on there. It gives me a better picture of what you look like beyond what I can glean from a close-up headshot. However, many agents will ask their clients not to list weight on the résumé to avoid having the actor be "typed out" before they even get in the room. It becomes a personal choice, but there is no longer a specific industry standard. I would, however, encourage you to list your voice type (i.e., tenor; baritone; soprano; lyric soprano; soprano w/ belt; mezzo; rock tenor; etc.). Some people choose to be even more specific by notating their exact range, but I think this is unnecessary. For starters, what if you list your range, designating the highest and lowest notes you can sing, but you don't have those notes the morning of an audition? Second, if you only list the vocal range, many directors will not know what the letters and their corresponding numbers (i.e., A4) actually mean. I think you must give us one of the above descriptions of your vocal category, and if you want to *also* include your optimum range, that's up to you.

You will notice that I did not include age, date of birth, or age range in this section. You automatically limit yourself when you offer your age to directors. Who cares how old you are? If you are 18 but can play 35, or vice versa, then your actual age is irrelevant. Don't get typed out before they see if you read right for a part. And as far as listing an age range, it is not for you to tell a director how old or young *you think* you can play. You'll almost always view yourself differently than others, so you're better served leaving that determination to the people casting the production.

Related Experience

This is the meat of the actor's résumé. In this section, or group of subsections, you will tell the director what shows and roles you have done, where you've performed, which significant artists you have worked with, and any other artistic projects you have done that may be germane to the particular audition for which you are submitting yourself.

I want to first offer you a few general suggestions about this section before we get into specific details. First, be sure to list your credits in *priority order* rather than *chronologically*. If you have worked with a well-known director or played a lead role or performed at a major theatrical venue, these credits should be listed prominently for more immediate notice. Next, *do not try to use four columns across the page to include the directors of every production you've done*. You run into small-font cramming, and the résumé becomes cluttered and hard to read. In the pages to come, I will address when and how to appropriately mention those great directors you want people to know you've worked with; in the meantime, just plan on a three-column format that will list show, role, and venue. Third, while it is imperative that you do not lie on your résumé, it's not a bad idea to remove taboo phrases such as "community theatre" and "high school." If you can find a way of listing a credit without drawing attention to the fact that it was amateur, it will serve you better. Community theatre experience can usually be manipulated by using the word "Players," as in "Williamsport Players" in lieu of "Williamsport Community Theatre." You can use the same trick for high school credits, but truly, you'll want to wipe high school and amateur performances off the résumé as soon as possible if you plan on being a professional artist.

Which leads me to the fourth general guideline: *Purge your credits now and then*. Many actors, hoping to impress with the exhaustive number of roles they have played, wind up with an excessively long (small-print) list of experience. Many of the roles—particularly those performed in educational theatre, where you rarely find age-appropriate casting—are no current indication of that actor's castability or type. And quite frankly, too many listings diminish the value of the few important ones. Show us what you've done, but don't overload us; quality over quantity, as the old cliché states. You may even alter your experience list depending on the nature of a particular audition. For example, list more musicals if you are going in for *The Full Monty*; more classical and nonmusical theatre if it's a Shaw or a Chekhov piece.

The organization of your experience section will depend on the actual variety of experience you have had. It may be divided into subheadings to distinguish between different levels of working venues, but you should create a subheading only if you have two or more credits to list under it. If you are a beginner, you need only use one heading: "Theatre Experience" and "Representative Experience" are typically common titles for this section. If you wish to divide the unit into subgroupings to accentuate more of a range of work, you may consider the following captions to be used *when applicable*:

- Broadway (and/or) Off Broadway
- Off-Off Broadway
- National (or International) Tours
- Regional/Stock Theatre
- New York Theatre (or Chicago, Los Angeles, etc.)
- Professional Theatre
- Educational Theatre

Again, you do not want a section called "Community Theatre." It's an amateur red flag. If your experience is all or mostly in community venues, do not create a subheading under "Theatre Experience." Also, the "Educational Theatre" should be replaced credit-for-credit with each professional job you get in your postgraduate career. The only educational theatre credits you'll want to consider keeping are those roles for which you would be equally castable in the "real world."

As far as Broadway, Off Broadway, and Off-Off Broadway are concerned, these credits are based on the contract, not on the location of the theatre. In other words, if you appear in a show at the Producers Club, the American Theatre of Actors, or any of the other commonly rented venues around Manhattan, these are not considered Off Broadway performances unless you are working under an official, union-sanctioned contract. I see a lot of actors label all their New York experience as Off or Off-Off Broadway to sound more impressive, but this miscategorization only makes an actor look ignorant, desperate, or dishonest.

However you choose to title headings and subheadings, you will want to either leave some space or indent below the heading and list each role in the three-column approach I mentioned before:

Title	Character	Theatre

The clean lines you create this way will let a director easily browse your list of credits with no confusion. In the event that a title or a theatre company exceeds the allotted space in your column, you have three options: abbreviate, change font or point size, or use two lines with an indentation. For example, *Picasso at the Lapin Agile* may be shortened as *Picasso . . . Agile*.

As long as you are neat and consistent, there is no absolutely right or wrong way to approach formatting. Note that play titles *always* go in italics, not in all capitals, not in quotes, and not underlined.

I've mentioned the notion of indicating significant directors or other artists with whom you've worked. The trouble with creating a fourth column for all of these names—besides the fact that it becomes an eyesore—is that as with listing too many acting credits, listing every director diminishes the importance of those few names you wish to stand out. A name buried in a long list may be lost, whereas being selective about the frequency with which you drop names will give those you choose more emphasis. I usually recommend dropping down to the line underneath the title, indenting, italicizing, and using a slightly smaller font. Here are some examples:

Henry V	Pistol	Theatre Under the Sun
(Darko Tresjnak, dir.)		
Smokey Joe's Café	DeeLee Lively	Phoenix Productions
(w/ Gladys Knight)		
West Side Story	Riff	Struthers Library Theatre
(Spence Ford, chor.)		

I know that adding the extra line uses more space, but remember what I said about quality versus quantity? This approach is cleaner and it helps you really set out for a director those special collaborations that you wish him to notice. If you do your homework and you know who you are auditioning for, you may choose to alter your résumé, adding certain names that may provide valuable connections in particular instances. For example, if you know that the director has a history of collaborating with a choreographer with whom you've worked, throw that name on there. This is why it's important to staple résumés to the back of headshots as opposed to gluing or printing directly, so they can easily be removed and replaced when they require updating.

I told you this segment of the résumé comprised "related experience." I used this generic term because it is up to you to understand the nature of the audition and to determine what constitutes related experience. If you have film-acting credits, you need only list them when submitting for a film role. However, for movie and television castings, you may still want to include your theatre acting work, since it's relevant to screen acting; just lead with your films since they will be of greater interest for those specific auditions. If you are answering a general talent call for a cruise line (great work for young actors fresh out of school!) and you have theme park or similar variety performance experience, list it. But your role as a "Ferengi" at Paramount Park's Summer Star Trek Street Show is irrelevant when you go in for a production of *Carousel*. I speak from experience on this matter; I played the sci-fi character at a theme park attraction back in 1998. Theme parks are great summer work for a college student, since they pay you well to perform; however, they are usually not particularly helpful on the résumé when auditioning for legit theatre. Directing work and technical or backstage work of any kind is useless on the experience section of an acting résumé. Just list performing experience. Carpentry, stitching, makeup, choreography, designing, and other such talents can fall under "Special Skills," if you wish to list them. But remember, you are going for performing work. Your technical skills should be highlighted on a separate résumé that doesn't need to include your performance experience.

Again, a smart actor will not have one résumé set in stone for all purposes. The more experience you amass, the freer you are to tailor your résumé to make you more appealing for a specific project.

Training

In this portion of your résumé, begin by listing any and all degrees and certificates you hold and the institutions from which you earned them. You should even include nonartist education, such as a bachelor of science. It says something about you and your life experience, and it can be a great conversation starter (*I see you hold a degree in electrical engineering. How in the world did you end up being an actor?*) Do not list the year of graduation (unless you're still in school and wish to list the intended graduation date): remember, you don't want your age being a factor in getting or not getting auditions. Underneath each performer-specific training program, you may choose to highlight specific courses of study you took, such as Acting for the Camera, Ballet, Voice Production, and Stage Combat, although this is not absolutely necessary. What is vital, however, is a list of the faculty members with whom you studied.

In this business, whom you know is equally as important as what you know. If I recognize the person who taught your acting class, he or she may become a reference for you, which may give you an edge when auditioning for a play. All the more reason to maintain a good working reputation, even while you're in school! This business is small, and directors will call around to get "the goods" on you.

Once you list all of your institutional programs, you can round this section off with any major workshops or private classes you've taken as a non-degree student. If you've attended master classes with well-known artists, you may choose to list a limited few standouts, but again, avoid clutter.

Special Skills

Finally, every résumé should include a *short* list of your special skills. The only absolute rule for this list is that you *must be able to do anything you include on it*, if requested. If you say you are a gymnast, be prepared to show them some flips; if you say you speak French, you'd better have a response to *"Est-ce que tu veux ce travail?"* And if you say you can catch grapes in your mouth, be ready to have some fruit tossed at your face!

This section of your résumé should list any talents you possess that are not evident from your experience (singing is not a special skill, but yodeling may be). If you have any unusual abilities, it may be advantageous to note them here. A sense of humor is usually not a bad thing in this area, as long as you don't overdo it. I have a friend who rounds his skills list off with: "And if you have a cookie, I will eat it." It doesn't get him the job, but it shows off his sense of humor and he's been known to get treats at auditions.

Typical examples of relevant skills include dialects and foreign languages, listed specifically; juggling, fire-eating, or similar clown work; in-line skating; playing instruments; sight-reading; odd quirks, such as being able to touch the bridge of your nose with your tongue; contortionism; etcetera. A lot of actors list abilities such as driving (standard or automatic) and jogging, and I have yet to understand how these qualify as special skills. But I suppose if you are auditioning to play a guy who has to leg it home after his car breaks down on stage, these "talents" do come in handy.

But Look What I've Done!

Several of my students have asked me recently if awards and organizations have a place on the résumé, for example, Alpha Psi Omega (Theatre Service Organization) or All-State Chorus. My answer is almost always no. While those sorts of accolades are helpful in the business world on a résumé, and they certainly look good on a graduate school application, they do not help a director determine whether or not you are best for a role. The only exceptions would be specific *major* awards earned for theatrical or film performances (i.e., Tony, OBIE, Jefferson, Helen Hayes Awards).

The following pages contain a few sample résumés that demonstrate the different ideas I have set forth for you. The first represents a student in his first or second year of college. The second is an actor who recently finished college and has begun a professional career. The third is a more seasoned performer who has worked for a number of years on tours as well as in the city. Each of the three samples is an amalgam of actual résumés I have in my file. I altered names and venues, but any of these could be legitimate, in theory. I also offer you several different formatting looks that can serve as templates for you to create your own résumé, whatever your level of experience. Notice that each one is formatted to fill the page handsomely, without overcrowding. All three are clean and readable, and each is a representation of where that particular actor is *currently* in his or her career. (Note: Also see the résumé samples in the center, color spread, which are actual actors' résumés with full color photos in the corner.)

TO WHOM IT MAY CONCERN

When you begin to answer casting calls in the profession, and likewise when you start applying to college programs, you will need to *include a cover letter with any headshot and résumé submission* you send out. Although in most instances its purpose is simply to say, "Hello, here's my submission," you mustn't underestimate the importance of a well-drafted letter, nor should you overlook its ability to make an impact. The cover letter can convey information not listed in the résumé, such as a current project that may be of interest to the director to whom you are submitting your materials. It

WILLIAM McNAMARA

Cell: Email: WJMcNamara12@yahoo.com

   Height: 5'9"   Weight: 172lb.   Voice: Tenor

THEATRE EXPERIENCE

Into the Woods	Jack	Downtown Players
Sweeney Todd	Tobias	Downtown Players
Anything Goes	Ensemble	John Woods Theatre
Our Town	Simon Stimson	John Woods Theatre
Godspell	"All Good Gifts"	John Woods Theatre
Pinocchio	Pinocchio	Monroe Children's' Th.
A Summer's Cabaret	Soloist	Monroe City Center

TRAINING
BFA Musical Theatre, Florida State University (2018)

   Acting: John D. Smith (Meisner); Mary Linder (Classical); Ted Jones
         (Improv/Movement)
   Private Voice: Louisa Testani
   Dance: George Mathers (Ballet); Linda Lee (Jazz/Tap)

SPECIAL SKILLS

Spanish Language (Intermediate); Dialects (British, US)

Figure 6.7.   "William McNamara" Résumé. An example of a college-age actor with very few credits.

JENNIFER PERETTI

CELL:
EMAIL: PerettiJen@Yahoo.com

VOICE: Mezzo/Belter
(w/Soprano)

Related Experience

110 In the Shade (Current)	Ens., Lizzie u/s	Elon University
Twelfth Night	Maria	Elon University
A Funny Thing...Forum	Philia	Rhode Island Summer Theatre
The Addams Family	Ancestor, Weds. u/s	RI Summer Theatre
My Fair Lady	Ensemble	RI Summer Theatre
"Rock Around the Clock"	Featured Vocalist	Cedar Point
Where is the Warmth (Premiere) (Jeff Simpson, Dir.)	Ensemble	Elon Theatre Lab
The Wild Party	Swing	Elon University
"Funny Bones" (Improv Troupe)	Ensemble Member	Elon University

Training

Elon University – BFA in Musical Theatre
  Voice: Lisa James; Eleanor Rogers (MT Styles)
  Acting: Tom Flemming; Rick Peters; Manuel Rodriguez
  Dance: Margaret Slater (Ballet/Pointe); Liz Forman (Jazz/Fosse); Patti
    Garber (Tap); Mo Tallega (Modern/Contact Improv)
Dance Machine, Greensburg, OH
  Ballet, Jazz, Pointe – 12 Years
Private Voice (6 Years), John Meyers, Greensburg, OH

Special Skills

  Pointe, Sight-reading, Tight harmonies, Impersonations (Beyoncé, Christina,
  Katy, etc.), Contortion, A million one-liner jokes for every occasion

Figure 6.8. "Jennifer Peretti" Résumé. An example of a recent college graduate with some professional credits.

JEFFREY L. MARINO
AEA – SAG/AFTRA

REPRESENTATION: The Talent Agents

www.jefflmarino.com

TR@TheTalentAgents.org

Voice: Rock Bari-Tenor

OFF-BROADWAY/TOURS

The Mystery of Irma Vep	Lady Enid	Cherry St. Theatre, NYC
Legally Blonde (1st Nat'l)	Callahan	Phoenix Productions
Peter and the Starcatcher (2nd Nat'l)	Smee	Lone Star Productions
The Fantasticks	The Mute	Snapple Theatre, NYC

REGIONAL/STOCK THEATRE

Peter and the Starcatcher *Fight Captain	Smee	Minnesota Shakespeare
Next to Normal	Dan	Minnesota Shakespeare
Rock of Ages	Dennis DuPree	So. Carolina Musical Th.
Pirates of Penzance	Pirate King	The Music Factory, NJ
Much Ado About Nothing	Balthazar	Minnesota Shakespeare
Jersey Boys in Concert	Nick Massi	Starlight Prod's, NJ
Boeing-Boeing	Robert	Newberry Playhouse
The River	Man	Newberry Playhouse
The Wedding Singer	Glenn Gulia	So. Carolina Musical Th.
The Who's Tommy	The Doctor	The Music Factory, NJ

TRAINING
BM, Musical Theatre Performance – The University of Iowa
    Jim Jefferies, William Hart, Jane Dixon, Tad Fischer, Gordon
    Summers, Ilona Carter
Certified Fight Choreographer – SAFD

SPECIAL SKILLS
Karate (Brown Belt); Movement and fight choreography; Advanced
tennis player; Languages: Spanish, French, German; Dialects & Voices

Figure 6.9. "Jeffrey L. Marino" Résumé. An example of a professional actor with an array of real-world credits.

Natalie Maria Szczerba

nmszczerba95@gmail.com

Height: 5' 5"   Eyes: Green
Hair: Blonde   Weight: 135 lbs
Voice: Soprano with Belt

Professional Theatre

THE FANTASTICKS	Luisa	Otterbein Summer Theatre
Dir. David Caldwell		
CARMEN	Ensemble	Toledo Opera

Educational Theatre

RENT	Ensemble, Mimi Marquez (U/S)	Otterbein University
INTO THE WOODS	Rapunzel	Otterbein University
Dir. Lenny Leibowitz		
SWEET CHARITY	Ensemble	Otterbein University
THE FULL MONTY	Vicki Nichols	Otterbein University
Dir. David Caldwell		
HMS PINAFORE	Ensemble , Cousin Hebe (U/S)	Interlochen Arts Camp
Dir. Sean Cooper		
RENT	Mimi Marquez	All-Ohio Show, STC
CURTAINS	Niki Harris	Otterbein University
THE SEAGULL	Sorin	Otterbein University

Education

Otterbein University Musical Theatre Candidate 2017
Interlochen Vocal Arts and Operetta Program 2011

Training

Acting
Lenny Leibowitz, Jimmy Bohr, David Caldwell, Melissa Lusher, Melinda Murphy, Christina Kirk, John Stefano
Voice
Lori Kay Harvey, Jeremy Davis, Jennifer Whitehead, Peg Cleveland Plambeck, Carolyn Redman
Dance
Ballet/ Jazz/ Tap/ Modern: Anna Elliott, Stella Kane, Maria, Maria Glimcher, Nigel Burgoine, Tammy Plaxico, Christeen Stridsberg
Movement
Feldenkrais/Alexander: Melinda Murphy
Speech
Dialect Training: Melissa Lusher (IPA: RP, Russian, Australian, German)

Masterclasses
Lindsay Nicole Chambers, Kolby Kindle, Ben Lipitz, Aaron Ramey, Dee Hoty, David Caldwell, Michael Cassara, Victoria Libertore, Nathan Gunn, Randy Skinner

Special Skills/Interest
High E, Piano, Juggling, Basic Tumbling Skills, Pottery (throwing), Rollerblading, Perry the Platypus Noise, Dog Barking.

Special Honors

Fine Arts Award in Music	Vocal Arts and Operetta	Interlochen Arts Camp
World Youth Honors Choir	Vocal Arts and Operetta	Interlochen Arts Camp

Figure 6.10. Natalie Szczerba Résumé. This is an actual actress in the Musical Theatre program at Otterbein. Her résumé includes a high-quality photo. *Photo courtesy of Afton Welch*

Christopher P. Castanho

Email: castanhoc@gmail.com
Height: 5' 9" Hair: Blonde Eyes: Hazel Voice: Tenor

Theatrical Experience

Educational

She Loves Me	Arpad Laszlo	Shenandoah Conservatory
To Kill A Mockingbird	Dill	Shenandoah Conservatory
Spelling Bee	Leaf Coneybear	Greater Hartford Academy of the Arts
Ragtime	Mother's Younger Brother	Greater Hartford Academy of the Arts
Hairspray	Brad	Greater Hartford Academy of the Arts
The Secret Garden	Ensemble (Dickon u/s)	Shenandoah Conservatory

Special Performances

Carnegie Hall: Lux Aeterna	Tenor	
To Judy With Love (John Fricke)	Soloist	Director: Eric Larivee

Training

Shenandoah Conservatory BFA Musical Theatre (2017)
Voice: David Meyer
Acting: Jonathan Flom, Larry Silverberg, Charles Goforth, J.J. Ruscella, Carolyn Coulson (Meisner Trained)
Dance: Shylo Martinez (Tap), Mary Robare (Ballet), Alan Arnett (Jazz & Tap), Robyn Schroth (Ballet)

Greater Hartford Academy of the Arts (Musical Theatre Major)
Voice: Phil Rittner, Eric Larivee, Janelle Robinson, Peter Peluso.
Acting: David McCamish, Debra Walsh, Jill Giles, Brian Jennings, Dexter J. Singleton, Michael Nowicki
Dance: Christine Simoes (Jazz & Ballet), Mary Cadorette (Luigi & Broadway Tap), Clare O'Donnell (Tap)
Playwriting and Directing: Brian Jennings

Master Classes
Kaitlin Hopkins, Joy Dewing, Jenny Ravitz, Jason Styres, John Fricke, Christopher Denny, Heather Provost, Marissa Perry, Pat McCorkle, Gary Krasny

Special Skills

Playwriting, Directing, Proficient Piano (since age 9), Reads Music, Strong Sight Singing, Funny voices

Figure 6.11. Christopher Castanho Résumé. This is an actual actor in the Musical Theatre program at Shenandoah Conservatory. His résumé includes a high-quality photo. *Photo courtesy of Jessica Osber*

may also draw attention to specific credits on your résumé that are directly related to the audition at hand. And, if nothing else, the cover letter can offer more of a sense of who you are: your personality, your intelligence, and your professionalism.

Most actors keep a basic letter saved as a file in their computer, a template that can be readdressed and modified with little effort. This framework should have a cordial greeting, perhaps a sentence or two on who you are, and some highlights of your training and experiential background. And any letter you send out should *always* directly recognize the particular audition for which you are soliciting and why you feel you should be considered.

That last part is where a lot of actors get themselves into trouble, erring on the generic side and failing to be personal. When an actor sends me a letter like this—

Dear Sir or Madam,

My name is Joe Smith. I am an actor and a singer. I saw your casting call in *Back Stage*, and I was very interested in being seen for an audition. Attached, please find my headshot and résumé and feel free to contact me by phone or e-mail if it would be possible to set up an audition time.

I look forward to meeting you soon, and I thank you for your consideration.

Sincerely,
Joe Smith

—I can't help but feel that I am one of fifty recipients of the same exact mailing that day. How do I know the actor even read my specific casting breakdown? I took the time to lay out in detail exactly what I was looking for on my project, and this actor wouldn't take the time to acknowledge whether he even knew what that project was! In cases like this, I may glance at the photo and scan the experience, but you can be sure that Joe Smith will receive considerably less consideration than the person who writes this letter:

Dear Mr. Flom:

My name is Ben Becker, and I'm a New York actor. I saw your ad today seeking a cast for your production of *Forever Plaid*, and I hope that you will consider me for an audition appointment.

As my attached résumé will reflect, I hold a degree in musical theatre from Syracuse University, and I have a wide range of musical performing experience. Although I have never done a production of *Plaid*, I am able to sight-read music, and I handle harmonies very well. My range as a bari-tenor makes me an ideal candidate for the role of either "Francis" or "Sparky."

I very much hope I will have the opportunity to come in and sing for you. Please feel free to reach me by e-mail or on my cell phone—both contacts are listed on my résumé—if it would be possible to set up a convenient time to audition. I look forward to meeting you.

Sincerely,
Benjamin Becker

Notice how much more appealing Mr. Becker becomes as a person, simply because he took the time to read the casting call and to directly address the needs of the audition in his letter. The second example is also personalized by the fact that he greets me directly. A director or producer's name is almost always included in a casting call ad. "Dear Mr. So and So" is always advisable over the old "To Whom It May Concern" or "Dear Sir or Madam." If there is no name listed on the ad, you may even begin your letter with "Greetings" or "Dear Seaside Theatre." Do anything you can do to diminish the impression that this submission is just another in your busy week of mailings.

The other thing that is striking about the last letter is the fact that the actor relates his skills and abilities directly to the production at hand. He may know the show, or he may simply be responding to what the ad called for. When I actually advertised for this show, I emphasized the importance of sight-reading and part-singing, in addition to breaking down each individual character. This actor shows me that he understands the nature of the audition and he is interested in *my* production of *Forever Plaid*, not just any audition he can get.

One final note about the Benjamin Becker letter: It is concise. He does not go into a long-winded account of every musical he has done or every teacher he has trained with. He does not turn the page into a kiss-up session, praising me as a magnificent director with whom he would be honored to collaborate (you'd be surprised, but it happens). And he doesn't tell me how it's "my lucky day to find the perfect actor" for my production (I'm not making this stuff up!). He cuts to the chase, and he says exactly what he needs to communicate to be appealing for this casting. That is the essence of a good cover letter: short and to the point, yet personalized. If you can craft a good letter, you will find it gives you a certain edge in obtaining audition appointments.

When it comes to applying for colleges or training programs, you will find a more formal approach to your cover letter effective. These institutions are more likely to be interested in your intellect and your writing skills, rather than just your talent and suitability for a particular production. Just as with a casting call, you would address your interest in the specific show, so you should understand and be able to express your desire in the specific school you are soliciting. Be sure to take the time to read any literature or websites available about a program; they are all unique, and some may be better candidates for your needs, as well as you for theirs. When you write to an institution, be sure to tell them why you are interested in their program, what appeals to you about their methods, their faculty, their reputation, and so forth. And tell them why they should be interested in you as well. What makes you an ideal student for the type of training they offer?

Unsolicited Mail

Sometimes actors will send out unsolicited mailings, usually to agents, seeking representation, or to production companies that are not casting a specific project at the moment, seeking future auditions. In these cases, it is important to really research the agency or the company to which you are submitting yourself and tailor your cover letter specifically to what it is that they do.

We already discussed agents back in chapter 4, and how sending unsolicited mail to them usually leads nowhere unless you have a connection. Sending unsolicited mail to theatre companies may be much more useful to you. If you read in *Back Stage* that a company is seeking a production staff for their season, and they list the plays, some of which interest you, why not send them a letter of interest? Similarly, if you go on a theatre company's website and find their upcoming shows, why not jump the gun and submit a competent letter of interest before they hold open auditions? Remember, this is a business, so you need to be savvy. I teach my students a phrase called "The Power of Asking" (which they have affectionately morphed into #ThePowerOfAsking for our digital age), the premise of which is this: You have nothing to lose by asking for something you want. The worst they can say is no, and then you're exactly where you started. But if you never ask, you'll never hope to get the thing you want. So if you have an idea, why not ask if it's possible?

I do suggest that rather than send out hundreds of headshots to every agent and theatre in the country for little or no response, that you be selective and find the companies that are best suited for your talents. You'll save time and money, and you'll increase your likelihood of a positive response.

The only other type of mailing you'll ever really send out will be the follow-up to a great audition/callback or the announcement of a performance. This is when having a business card with your headshot, along with some nice, simple "Thank You" cards will come in handy. You can write a little personalized note on the card and place a business card inside to thank someone for taking the time to work with you, coach you, encourage you, etc. Once again, keep this short and sweet, but it's a great way to keep your name in the mind of a director. If there is someone you are very interested in working with, simply send him a card right after a positive callback (I wouldn't send these out after every open call audition you attend), saying something like:

> Dear Mr. Jones,
>   Thank you for the opportunity to audition for *Carousel*. Your adjustment on "Soliloquy" really opened up a new direction in how I see Billy Bigelow. Please keep me in mind for this and future projects. I look forward to working with you.
>
> Sincerely,
> Alexander Arnold

If you have a current project, it would be a very smart move to invite the director, so list all of the performance information. Otherwise, just keep it to a sentence or two. The card may be slightly informal, and it is customarily handwritten, as opposed to the typed business letter format of the cover letter.

I mentioned way back in our discussion on callbacks that you should have a notebook or a journal if you are to be a serious actor. The most important reason for the journal is to keep a running list of directors and casting directors with whom you've worked or for whom you've auditioned. When you are appearing in a production, you'll want to send postcards to anyone who might be able to come see you perform and may employ you later.

In general, the cover letter is another investment of time, as important as creating a powerful résumé or memorizing a book of songs. It is another tool in your arsenal as a working artist, and you must endow it with your brand, your voice, and your personality for it to properly represent you. It is another method by which you can gain a competitive edge in this challenging industry.

SUMMARY

- Invest in professional headshots if you are serious about a career in the theatre.

- The headshot must be an accurate representation of who you are, not a glamour shot.
- Remember that you're a paying customer. Demand satisfaction from your photo session.
- Seek the opinion of theatrical colleagues, teachers, and mentors when deciding on which headshot to reproduce.
- Be sure to choose an attractive border and an elegant font in which to have your name printed on the headshot reproductions.
- Format your résumé so that all the information falls into clean, even, readable columns down the page.
- Do not choose a minuscule font in order to cram too much information on your résumé.
- Be sure to establish permanent contact information, such as a dedicated business e-mail address and a cell phone number, and list it on your résumé.
- Do not list age or age range on your résumé.
- List résumé credits in order of priority, not chronology.
- Use three columns across to list show, role, and theatre company.
- Remove the phrases "community theatre" and "high school" from your résumé.
- Select the few important, standout directors and choreographers you've worked with and list them below the credit, indented and italicized.
- Tailor your résumé for the given audition. What credits will be of particular interest to this casting? Place those credits high on your list.
- Be prepared to do anything listed under your special skills section.
- Always have your cover letters address the specific audition for which you are submitting.
- A good cover letter should be short, to the point, and personalized.
- When possible after a callback, send the director a follow-up thank you note with a business card to *briefly* thank him for his time.
- Keep a running list of contact information for directors you've worked with or auditioned for and send out postcards inviting them to any productions in which you'll be appearing.

7

AUDITIONING FOR COLLEGES

One of the most exciting and intriguing aspects of my background has been recruiting for the musical theatre programs at Penn State and Shenandoah Conservatory. Both universities offer competitive, individualized training grounds, and their reputations attract hundreds of prospective young actors from all over the country every year. Consequently, I have seen some of the best, some of the worst, and some of the most misguided high school performers present themselves as candidates. In addition, as a member of and an officer in the Musical Theatre Educators Alliance (MTEA—www.mteducators.org), I have developed a wide net of colleagues with whom I have been able to exchange ideas, methodologies, and war stories! Through that organization, I have gained a pretty clear idea of what musical theatre programs are seeking and the little things that make each of these schools different and unique.

Furthermore, I offer coaching and consulting services to hopeful teens (and their stressed-out parents) seeking guidance and mentoring through the process of entrance auditions. I advise on narrowing down a list of schools, finding appropriate repertoire, and delivering compelling performances and interviews. And through my experience, I have come to understand the college screening as a singular, unique process, similar to professional auditions, but at the same time an art in and of itself.

I therefore thought it useful to dedicate a unit of this book to the specific challenges of college auditions. I offer you, the high school junior or senior, this chapter with the assumption that you have first read the preceding sections of the book, as the information I have laid out thus far will be 100 percent applicable in a college setting.

LET'S START AT THE VERY BEGINNING

I'm going to share some daunting numbers with you. Do you know that there are now over 100 schools in the United States that are offering musical theatre degree programs? Recent data tracked somewhere in the ballpark of 2,500 students auditioning for spots in these programs, but I have to confess, I think it's even higher than that, when you consider that many of the hopeful students are now being weeded out by the video prescreen process. The bottom line is that narrowing down a list of schools is harrowing and getting into the top schools is more competitive than ever.

If you have done some serious soul-searching and decided that you want to take the plunge and pursue higher education training in the field of musical theatre, you absolutely must have a systematic approach to the entire application/audition process. It used to be so much easier when there were only 30 to 40 degree programs in the United States and far fewer applicants. But now the bar for both schools and applicants has been raised so high—programs are competing with each other to offer the most cutting-edge training, and parents are spending a fortune to have their children coached and polished to perfection in order to compete for the precious spots in these institutions. I personally do not believe that one must invest a year's worth of tuition in coaching in order to be considered by the nation's top schools, but it certainly gives you an edge to understand the landscape and to create a shrewd game plan.

You must begin by doing a great deal of research. If there are truly 100+ programs available to you, how do you possibly narrow down which ones to set your sights on? The good news is that with musical theatre programs cropping up with such great frequency, there's really a program for everyone. You don't have to compromise your values and goals in order to get great training. I recommend starting with a little self-reflection before you get on the Internet and Google the Pandora's box that is "Musical Theatre Programs." Create a document, a spreadsheet, or a journal entry for your personal contemplations. Here are the major factors to take into consideration as part of your criteria for finding the right fit for you:

1. Geography.

   Is it important to you to be close to home and family or would you like to venture far away? Are you seeking a school in a particular region of the country or with a particular climate? Is nature and landscape a factor for you? Does city versus suburb versus rural setting matter to you? Do you want that real "college" experience with a beautiful campus or are you equally happy to attend classes in a city high-rise building?

2. Economics.

   Is money a factor to consider? Do you have a college fund or are you willing to take out a student loan? (I just finished paying mine off, 15 years after graduating! And I'm one of the lucky ones.) Will talent and academic scholarship money be a deal breaker for you? Remember that the "sticker price" of tuition on college websites is rarely what one will end up paying, but you need to go in knowing what your financial means are so that you don't apply to schools that you can't possibly afford to attend.

3. Size of school.

   Do you want to attend a big university on a large campus with an athletic program, Greek life, and many other accoutrements of the "college experience" (i.e., Florida State or Michigan, with 26,000–48,000 students)? Or would you prefer a smaller institution with a more intimate campus and fewer of the big college bells and whistles (i.e., Illinois Wesleyan or Webster Conservatory, with 1,500–5,500 students)?

4. Size of program.

   Musical theatre programs come in several different sizes. Small would be 8–14 students per class; medium would be 15–22 students; and large would be over 22. Is class size an important factor for you? You may want to be certain that if the class size is on the larger end, the school has the faculty and the resources to support the numbers. Will you receive individual attention as part of a larger class? Will you be showcased effectively to help launch your career? These are good questions to ask.

5. Type of degree/training offered.

   Most American musical theatre programs either offer a BFA (Bachelor of Fine Arts) or a BA (Bachelor of Arts) degree at the end of four years. A few confer BMs (Bachelor of Music), but those are more rare. Are the letters on your degree important to you? At one time, the common wisdom was that BFA equaled preprofessional, intense training, while BA programs were more well-rounded educations with an array of coursework outside of the theatre. While this is still true to some extent, it is definitely a fallacy to believe that one cannot get outstanding training in a BA track.

Furthermore, you'll encounter two primary categories of educational models in the world of theatre: the conservatory and the liberal arts approach. A conservatory generally has few, if any, class requirements outside of the theatre; a liberal arts education might have between 30–60 credits from areas other than the arts. Again, it comes back to whether you want a broad education or narrow, specific training.

If I may offer my opinion here: While there is a distinct choice to make about the right fit for you between conservatory or liberal arts, I do not believe that the degree itself (BA/BFA/BM) matters *in the least*. Where you train, what you study, and with whom you study is far more important on your résumé than the degree you earned. We don't really care if you have a degree in macroeconomics—if you're good, you'll work.

6. Faculty.

When you look into schools, each program's home page should list their faculty along with bios. Are there particular teachers with whom you want to study? Perhaps they have impressive Broadway or film credits or they have authored plays, musicals, or books that have influenced you. Some will be renowned experts in a certain technique that might appeal to you, while others might be well connected to a certain part of the industry that could provide an important pipeline for you. I believe teachers at a school should be a tremendous factor in choosing where to get one's training. (Okay, perhaps I am a *little bit* biased!)

7. Program specialty.

I mentioned in a previous chapter that I have published a book on branding for actors since the last edition of *Get the Callback*. I am a firm believer that actors must have a specific brand for the unique product they are selling to the industry. But guess what? Musical theatre programs have brands, too. What are you looking for in a program? Is there a particular specialty you find appealing? Some examples may include:

- A specific approach to voice training (e.g., classical; contemporary; pop/rock)
- A specific approach to actor training (e.g., Meisner; Michael Chekhov; Viewpoints)

- A reputation for particularly strong dance training
- Dedication to developing new musical works
- Connection to a major regional theatre
- A slate of impressive guest teaching artists
- A strong film and television component

These are just a few of the many possible strong suits that separate musical theatre programs from one another. As you start to research, it's important that you know what is appealing to you.

Once you have spent some time deeply considering all of the above factors, you will be ready to begin crafting a list of schools that meet your particular criteria. The right fit is *everything* when choosing a musical theatre program. Let me repeat that:

The right fit is everything when choosing a musical theatre program.

If you are reading this book, you have probably been barraged already with more information about training programs than your brain can possibly sort. You have friends, family, and/or teachers telling you where to go; you have read the playbills of every musical you've seen and examined the actors' bios to see where they went to school; you have been assaulted by brochures and pop-up ads touting the rich and storied histories of many different institutions. As you delve into the abyss of the application process and campus visits, you will be inundated with even more facts and figures. But just keep a clear head through all of this and focus on trusting your intuition to guide you toward the place where you belong. If you know what you're looking for from the outset, it will be so much easier to recognize it when you find it, don't you think?

You may notice that I did not list reputation or famous alumni in my suggested criteria. Let me explain why that is. First of all, every musical theatre program will find something about which to brag. You are comparing apples to apples, and even though every week it seems like there is a new "official" rankings list of the "best" musical theatre programs in the country (ranked by whom and on what basis???) on social media, the fact of the matter is you can get great training at any of the schools you will research. Sometimes those best-of lists are based solely on the ratio of applicants to accepted students; however, just because admission to a program is competitive doesn't guarantee you'll get the best training. As far as alumni, while I think that people graduating and going on to successful careers might logically draw your attention to a particular school, it's not necessarily an indicator of how good the program is *right now*. It's far better to sit in on classes and look at rehearsals or productions to see what is currently happening in the program, rather than basing your decision on how they trained someone 5–20 years prior, before that person became a Broadway star. (Maybe the curriculum has changed or there has been faculty turnover. Some schools even boast of famous alumni who dropped out and never even graduated from their program!)

When I auditioned for colleges many years ago, I had my sights set on a well-reputed school with a rich history in the industry. I wanted to brag that I attended that program. I *knew* I was going there. All my plans were made, and I had but to audition and get accepted. As a back-up plan, I scheduled an audition at a great, storied university with a brand-spanking-new musical theatre program. They had no reputation of which to speak; they had no famous alumni since the program was only a year old; there was no way I would choose them over some of the vaunted establishments to which I was applying.

Well, long story short, I began by auditioning at my dream school and I left with a feeling of emptiness and discomfort. I did not care for the way they treated me in the audition, and I did not feel like I was even remotely important to them. My gut said that in spite of my long-term dream of attending the school (and I was accepted), I would ultimately be very unhappy there. Bookend that with my visit to Penn State, where I was welcomed by a warm and caring faculty who made me feel safe and comfortable. It was the best audition experience of my entire college circuit. I took a big risk choosing a start-up program with no reputation, but I knew in my heart that it was the right fit for me: It felt like home. That, my friends, was the best decision I ever made. (And the program hasn't done too badly for itself since I left!)

The right fit is everything.

WHAT MUST I DO?

Once you have established your personal criteria and identified what you are seeking in a college, you'll begin to seek out schools that offer some or all of those elements. It's going to make your life much easier in the long run if you create a spreadsheet to track the details of each school (audition requirements, deadlines, tuition costs, etc.), since most future musical theatre majors generally audition for between 10–18 schools. I urge you to stay organized. And I highly recommend that you apply only to schools that fit most or all of your specifications. I tell my coaching clients that they must have a solid reason why they want to attend *every* school on their list (even the "safety" schools). If you only got into one school, could you genuinely say you'd be happy with it being any of the ones on your list? The process is too expensive and time consuming to waste on schools where you would be unhappy.

The first trick to solving college auditions is to understand their purpose. Unlike professional casting, which seeks performers with developed technique who fit certain character types suited to the roles of the particular production, institutions are seeking talented, eager, young, and up-and-coming artists to mold. Some technique is certainly required to be competitive, but *potential* is the goldmine for college program recruitment. And while we want an array of "types" in each incoming class, we are certainly not casting specific characters. (Despite rumors among parents to the contrary, I've not heard of any school that chooses their incoming class based on a particular show or shows they are casting for the following years.)

The idea that a student must be a polished "triple threat" to earn consideration from a decent school is false. A good program seeks trainable candidates: young men and women who possess the potential to grow and blossom into successful artists under four years of tutelage. What would a teacher have to offer the complete, accomplished performer? How can that student truly be a *student*? I tell kids that if they are really that good at 18 years old, they should skip school and move to New York now. (Don't worry, parents; most students are aware that they still have much to learn.)

What you must present to college instructors is an enthusiastic, pliable piece of high-quality clay that they can sculpt—a sapling that, under their care and tending, will bear glorious fruit. In short, to dispense with lofty metaphors, you need to display the basic fundamentals of a performer, the capability of tremendous growth, and the unquestionable desire to achieve that growth. A great personality is also a must, since we will be spending four years getting to know each other very closely and personally in a college theatre program.

Don't get me wrong, if you can't carry a tune or speak coherently, there might not be a program in the country that will accept you, but you certainly do not have to be a teenage Sutton Foster. Generally, if you are proficient in at least one area (acting, singing, dancing), strong or capable in a second, and teachable in the third, you should have options available to you. (If you only feel confident in one of the three areas, there are also dance, acting, and vocal performance majors that you might wish to consider as an alternative to the rigors of musical theatre.) It's not a bad idea to inquire as to whether the programs that interest you lean heavily on any one of the areas of performance more than others, either in the training process or in the entrance auditions. For instance, if you've never taken a dance class in your life, it may be a disadvantage to audition for a program that is reputed for seeking advanced dancer skills.

When you have a solid list of programs that you've identified as potential fits for you, you must begin the process of preparing the best audition presentations possible. It's imperative that you read *very carefully* the specific and individual requirements for each school—and track them all on your spreadsheet. While most musical theatre schools will have similar audition criteria, there will be variations and outliers, and it is absolutely necessary that you follow each school's audition guidelines to the letter. Some schools may ask for one of your songs to be Golden Age, while others will just request two contrasting cuts. Sometimes they will want to hear 16 or 32 bars, while others may use time restrictions. Monologues may be desired as one-minute, two-minute, or three-minute cuts—contemporary or classical. Do not make the mistake of so many young hopefuls who create their "package" and use it for every school regardless of the stipulations of each program. That is a lazy way to ensure that you won't be invited to some of your target institutions. Take the time to cater your material specifically to the requirements of each individual school, even though it will mean more work for you.

Refer back to the earlier chapter on repertoire and keep in mind that schools are seeking authenticity above all. I don't think high school students are ready to launch a *brand*, but I certainly believe that doing some basic adjective work and having a clear perspective about who you are *essentially* should be your primary guide when selecting material. Do not fall into the trap of making your audition about showing off tricks and tremendous range. Nine times out of ten, we'll wind up asking you to simplify your choices and "act less." (This doesn't mean we don't want you to act through your material; rather, it usually means that you aren't projecting honesty in the room—you're likely pretending or overdoing it—and we want to give you permission to connect more truthfully to your pieces. Simplicity can be magical.) Every song and monologue in your audition repertoire should reveal something about *you* as a person. That does not mean that every character you play must be exactly like you. However, it does mean that you have chosen your material based on some connection to the role (i.e., one piece shows off your vulnerability and sensitivity; one piece shows off your intellect, charm, and humor; one piece shows off your strength and poise; etc.), as opposed to cuts chosen on the basis of high notes, low notes, or dramatic intensity, for example. Don't get me wrong; if your voice is a great strength, it's certainly good to show it off, but the power and range of the voice should be a secondary consideration to the authentic human aspect.

Once more, I will advise you to steer clear of monologue books as your source for material. So many high school actors use them because those books offer pieces that are uber-dramatic or comedic, but that material is rarely effective in auditions. You'll make a much better impression by choosing material from a good published play with a full context, as opposed to a stand-alone speech with made-up circumstances.

AUDITIONING BEFORE YOU AUDITION

As I mentioned at the beginning of this chapter, the number of musical theatre schools and students auditioning for spots in those programs has become staggering over the last decade. Many programs have begun instituting a video prescreen process, which requires students to upload recorded material before they may be invited for a live audition. The benefit of the prescreen is that schools can often save a student and his or her parents the time and expense of traveling across the country for an audition if they do not believe the student is suitable for admission to the program. Furthermore, when you are invited to audition live, you can treat it like a callback and have the confidence that they already believe you have the talent and potential to be a viable candidate.

Do not panic about the prescreen. If you have done all the preparatory work I have suggested in the preceding pages and chapters, this should be a cakewalk for you. Just pay attention to the guidelines and try to deliver a quality product, and then it's out of your hands. When I say "quality product" I do not mean to imply that you should go spend a fortune on studio recording and high-end camerawork and editing. Rather, I mean that you should choose material that really makes you pop and sparkle, just as you would for an in-person audition. While it does not serve you to stare into your laptop camera and sing a cappella in your bedroom, the prescreen really just needs to give them an idea of who you are and what you do well. We can get more than enough information from a video shot on an iPhone (no selfies, please!) or a DSLR camera, so there's no need to buy or hire fancy equipment. You should experiment with lighting and audio and find the best location to shoot and the proper distance to stand from your recorder to ensure the optimum video. The great advantage to auditioning on tape is that you can utilize trial and error to come up with a really solid final product that looks and sounds great. (I'm always surprised by how many of these prescreens are slapped together with no indication that the student actually *watched* it before uploading it! Take your time and do it well.) Make sure that your high notes aren't distorted in the playback. Be sure the clothing you choose looks good on camera. And give us a shot that allows us to see your face as well as some of your body (in other words, not too close, but not too far away). Those are really the most intricate instructions I can offer you about prescreen videos. The rest is up to you to demonstrate good taste and judgment.

I recommend that you learn to use basic editing software, such as the iMovie program that comes free on Mac products. If you know how to use more advanced products such as Final Cut Pro or Adobe Premiere, all the better, but knowing how to do basic cuts and title overlays will really make your submission professional grade, and you don't need a rocket science degree to do the basics.

Finally, I suggest that you get your prescreen videos uploaded and your applications in well ahead of any posted deadlines. Schools only have a finite number of audition slots each year, and even when a deadline is met, you run the risk of all the spaces on your chosen audition day being taken by the early birds who submitted their materials ahead of you. Do not record and send unpolished or underprepared footage, but just be aware of the due dates and work hard to ensure that you are ready to deliver some quality audition cuts as early as possible once they open their application process.

EVERY LITTLE STEP

After you have submitted your prescreens, you'll be playing the waiting game as schools deliberate over whom to invite to their live auditions. In the interim, you should prioritize your list of programs and keep track of when they hold their on-campus auditions, because once they start getting back in touch with you, you will need to organize your schedule to accommodate being seen by as many as you possibly can, considering time and money as factors. And prioritizing your preferences in advance will help you if you have to make a choice between two auditions that conflict with one another.

Some schools participate in an organization called National Unified Auditions (www.unifiedauditions.com), through which they gather en masse in four cities across the United States—New York, Chicago, Los Angeles, and Las Vegas—for several days each and offer students the chance to audition for multiple schools in one single visit. The upside is that you can generally expect to knock out four to six different programs in one weekend. There are downsides: not all schools participate in Unifieds; you must schedule individual auditions for each program, rather than being seen by many schools in one shot; you miss out on seeing the campus and experiencing the environment of the programs; and most of the schools do not provide piano accompaniment at these regional auditions—they require you to audition with prerecorded music. That being said, the convenience is undeniable, especially when you are trying to cast a wide net. So if attending one of the Unified audition weekends is a possibility for you, then make sure to note which schools on your list participate, and consider that as you start scheduling your visits. However, if you do audition for and get accepted by a school at Unifieds, I suggest you pay the campus a visit before making your final decision—but we'll cover that more in a little while.

AN INVITATION TO THE DANCE

Now that you've navigated the process of setting up all of your auditions, you need to wow these programs and open yourself up to the widest array of possibilities. It's very unlikely that you will get accepted by every school to which you apply (even if you are terrific, there are factors beyond your control, so don't take this personally), but having at least a few choices will empower you to make an informed decision and feel some degree of control over your future. You do so by preparing fully and displaying professionalism beyond your years, as I have detailed throughout this book.

The girl who comes in with two random cuttings from *The Ordinary Soprano's Anthology* and a gut-wrenching tale of anorexia, bulimia, or suicide from *The Book of Pointless Monologues for Young People* is quickly forgotten; but the girl who has chosen contrasting, well-considered songs that make a statement of who she is while displaying acting range *and* vocal ability, along with an *age-appropriate* monologue from a play for which she would be suitable, distinguishes herself.

Although it is understood that you have not yet been taught all of the ins and outs of auditioning well, you can really stand out and impress college panels by exceeding expectations with your preparedness. Having a book of well-rehearsed songs—however small the selection—organized neatly in a binder; dealing appropriately with the accompanist; presenting yourself confidently and delivering a poised, if imperfect, performance; and conveying a sincere love for what you do—these aspects will win you as much interest and respect as a terrific belt voice or a triple pirouette. Remember the key word: authenticity.

Outside of the Unified audition process, few colleges will require your music to be tape-recorded—most will provide an accompanist. Unless otherwise specified, be prepared to work with the school's pianist. Do not bring a parent to play for your audition. Colleges are often turned off by overinvolved stage parents who wish to walk their child through everything and micromanage. A parent should be supportive . . . outside of the audition room. To that end, I also emphasize to my young clients that they must take responsibility for communicating with the faculty when questions arise—do not let your parents be the primary go-betweens. Since we will be dealing with *you*, the student, over the next four years if we accept you and you choose to study with us, we want to know that you have the maturity and professionalism to communicate with us directly throughout the application process. So don't let your parents make all the phone calls and send all the e-mails when there are questions.

On your audition days, dress in clothes that make you look and feel your best and represent the same essences of your authentic self that you used to guide you to repertoire. Most young people don't tend to feel at home in jackets and ties, so there's no need to bring that sort of formality to your college auditions. Nice casual is usually preferable to overly dressy. But do not allow yourself to go as casual as sweatpants and sweatshirts or hoodies, shorts, T-shirts with logos or print, or street sneakers. Also, please do not come into the room with a lanyard of keys hanging out of your pocket. Make some effort to combine professional with genuine. Wear shoes you can walk in. And girls should also be careful about how revealing their clothing is—it can make for a very uncomfortable experience when a 17-year-old shows too much skin.

Make strong acting choices, just as I suggested in dealing with professional castings. And likewise, be flexible and open to adjustments. My colleagues and I almost always offer some direction to students who interest us. For example, an actor might be asked to try the song again with a live scene partner to work off of, or he might be told to try operating from a different point of view or emotional state. Again, we are looking to discover whether a prospective trainee will accept instruction and take risks. Occasionally, you may also be asked if you have an alternative song selection, just like in a professional audition.

Staying the Course

The decision to attend a professional training program for acting or for musical theatre is a serious matter and should be reflected upon before making a commitment. I say this to you because I have noticed more and more often that students seem to get distracted during their school years. If they are in close enough proximity to a city—particularly New York— they will go off to attend open casting calls for shows that are in their age and type range, such as *Spring Awakening*, which requires a particularly youthful cast. One such student of mine was once offered a contract in the first national tour of that very production.

While it is wonderful for someone so young and fresh to walk off with a national tour contract before even moving to New York and "paying his dues," as it were, it is also a risky move. Once that tour is over, if the student does not move directly to the Broadway company of that show, he will be left without a degree and, more important, without being completely trained. Although his rawness was ideal for *Spring Awakening*, he may not be suited for the majority of professional work that is available when he finishes his tour. Furthermore, he is now stuck with his Equity union card, and he can only audition for union productions for which he'll be competing with older, more seasoned performers.

That young actor also finds himself without agent representation, since he was cast out of an open cattle call. Although some would argue that having an agent is not an essential, it certainly would be a big help to a young, inexperienced actor with no real knowledge of how to navigate his way through the business. That young man has made a decision to abandon his training and take advantage of a wonderfully exciting opportunity that will likely employ him for one year; however, he is not considering the long-term big picture.

Don't get me wrong—I'm not saying his career will be over the minute he returns from his tour. I have another former student who took a Broadway gig after his sophomore year. When that show closed, he returned to school for two years and now is back in New York and back on Broadway. But I must emphasize how exceedingly rare such instances are. You need to remember why you chose to go to school in the first place, and you need to trust that there will be just as many exciting audition opportunities available to you after you finish school as there are now. New York will always be there!

Some schools will not allow students to attend outside auditions, period. If you feel as though the draw to get out and work will be too strong for you, then consider attending a two-year certificate program in the city, such as AMDA or the Neighborhood Playhouse. But realize that if you commit to a four-year institution, it will take all your concentration and dedication to get the most out of your training experience.

TELL US ABOUT YOURSELF . . .

Since we have already discussed handling the dance call in chapter 4 (my advice for college auditions is the same as professional ones), we'll move on to the last segment of a college entrance audition: the interview. Some colleges will talk with every candidate, while others, in the interest of time, will only sit down with those whom they are seriously interested in recruiting. When I auditioned as an incoming student for Penn State, everyone had an interview; however, now that they attract the overwhelming numbers of a top-tier training school, they tend to release a good deal of the young men and women after their performance portion is complete, in order to dedicate more time to becoming acquainted with their top prospects.

And that is exactly the purpose behind the interview: getting to know you as a person, outside of your performance. *It is essential, then, that you not try to put on any sort of artificial display when you meet with the panel.* You've already shown them your acting abilities; now you need to share your humanity. The successful candidate is one who can be serious and personable, tenacious and levelheaded, confident and humble. Before you attend a college audition, ask yourself why you want to study musical theatre and why you'd like to do it at that particular institution. (Aren't you glad I already encouraged you to do some of that reflecting when you began your process? Now you already have a list of reasons why you love each school on your list!) These are likely the first questions they'll ask you. You don't want to sound too rehearsed and robotic, but you don't want to be caught off guard stammering, either.

When I first began recruiting for Penn State, I asked the head of the program why we even bothered with interviews. They all seemed exactly the same to me. Nine out of ten went just like this:

"Well, I started performing when I was five. I've *always* wanted to be an actor. I live for the thrill of applause. I know someday I'll make it on Broadway. I just *have* to do it . . ."

So what is it that we glean from the same tired story over and over? His answer: It's the one in ten who tells a different story. It didn't take me long to see what he meant.

My friend Morgan was a nontraditional candidate for the program at Penn State. She was several years older than the incoming class, as she had taken some time off to work after high school. She knew that musicals were her one true passion—that's prerequisite for a life in this business—and she researched all of her options for training. At a particular convention in New Mexico, where she lived, she met Mary Saunders, the Penn State voice instructor. Something drew Morgan to her and they just clicked as teacher and student.

Morgan began to read about the rest of the program at Penn State, and she decided that it was the perfect match for her. She visited, attended classes, and confirmed her belief that "Happy Valley" was where she belonged. She also discovered that an out-of-state school was unaffordable, an impossible dream (pardon the musical theatre reference) without scholarships and financial aid, for which she might not qualify.

But she was undeterred by economic obstacles. Morgan moved in with her sister in Philadelphia and waited tables for a year while she earned legal residency status to qualify for in-state tuition rates. She just *had* to go to Penn State, and she would go to any lengths to get there.

When she finally came to audition for us, she was not the best, most exciting performer in the pack. She had raw vocal abilities and little dance training, and she was aware of her shortcomings. In her interview, she related her story of determination, and she told us she wanted Penn State to make her a better dancer, a better singer, a better actor. She said she had chosen this school because she felt she could find her full potential with the individualized training being offered, and she asserted her absolute commitment to work hard to achieve the best results possible.

I don't need to tell you that the interview secured Morgan's place in the incoming BFA class. In two minutes, this girl showed more grit, more candor, and more personality than anyone else I had ever seen in a college interview. And it really paid off for her.

Now, that's not to say that you need to have a tale of uphill, against-all-odds battles to have a successful interview. And it certainly doesn't mean that taking a year off to earn residency in the school's state will get you in; Morgan took a huge risk with that move. But you do need to find your unique voice and show them that you are special and worthy of their attention. Spending some time reflecting on these "why" questions will help you to better know yourself, and self-awareness will get you far in life. Not to mention, a keen sense of self is both very appealing and fairly unusual in prospective college students.

There are other common questions they may ask in an interview: Why do you want to study musical theatre here? (Remember I told you earlier to have a good reason why you want to attend every school on your list? Now you get to share that.) What are some dream roles for you? (Here's a chance to demonstrate more self-awareness. We want to be sure you have a realistic view of how you fit into the industry.) What do you like to do outside of performing? (Your other "unrelated" hobbies are of great interest to us. Don't assume that we only want theatre machines; we want well-rounded human beings.) Where do you see yourself in five years? What are *you* looking for in a program? (It helps me to know if a student's interests are in line with what my program can actually offer.) And what area(s) of musical theatre would you consider your greatest strength(s) and where do you need the most work?

Assuming you've done your research and read up on a program before going to your audition, you may find that you have some questions for them as well. The interviewers will usually ask if you have any questions, and you should not be shy to speak up if you do. In fact, I am a firm believer that you should always ask one or two questions in an interview. Consider the following questions:

- How many general education credits will I need to graduate?
- What merit-based scholarships might be available to me?
- What is the first-year campus living experience like?
- Will I be allowed to audition for and be cast in productions in the first year?
- Does this school have a network of alumni in New York, Chicago, and Los Angeles?
- Is there a culminating industry showcase?

You will need this information when making your final choice of schools, plus it's an opportunity to continue conversing with the auditors. Don't overlook the fact that you are interviewing them just as much as they are you. They are shopping for students, but you are shopping for a suitable training program all the same. When you begin to receive acceptance letters and you must decide where your tuition dollars are to go, you'll want to make the most informed decision possible. So why not engage the professors in a little Q and A yourself and see how well they respond to your queries? Just be careful to choose two or three questions, as opposed to overstaying your welcome with a laundry list.

One of my favorite questions that we get every so often from prospective students is, "What do you like most about working here?" It gives each of us behind the table the opportunity to share our enthusiasm about our school from a very personal perspective, and it gives the student the chance to hear several points of view from their possible future teachers.

WHERE AM I GOING?

The selection of a college training program is a highly personal, life-shaping decision that should not be taken lightly. As I said earlier, you must do your own research and try to learn what all the different schools have to offer before you even begin applying and auditioning. Although all of your friends may tell you that school A is the place to go if you want to make it as an actor, you may find that school B speaks more to your own individual interests. Furthermore, you may find that what you thought you loved about a school on paper wasn't the reality when you visited the campus. (That was certainly my experience when I was 18.)

I encouraged you to get a sense of what you were looking for before you began auditioning. Now, be sure to visit all of your possible schools throughout the audition/decision process. I suggest that unless time and money are not factors for you and your family, you do not try to visit every school on your long list before you even apply. With as many as 18 to 20 schools, that can really add up fast and deplete your resources. Rather, use audition appointments as the first opportunity to visit and tour campuses; then once you start to receive acceptance letters, take a trip to the colleges that interest you the most. Sit in on classes and attend departmental productions when possible to get a sense of the kind of work they do. Schedule a meeting with the head of the program and spend some time with him or her to see if you really gel. Talk to current students and find out what they like and dislike about their program. They're usually more than willing to give you the inside scoop. Remember, once you've been accepted, the ball is in your court. You are the consumer and you are about to commit to four years (and a lot of money) to pursue your dream.

I've said it before and I'll repeat myself: You need to get out there and experience these campuses firsthand and find the one that feels like *home* to *you*. Forget all of the other noise and focus on discovering the place where you'll feel safe to be vulnerable and to fail on a daily basis. For this is what you will need to do in order to grow as an artist: fail. (I love the

O'Neill Center/National Theatre Institute's motto: "Risk. Fail. Risk again.")
Which teachers and fellow students do you trust to pick you up and help
you get stronger? The importance of selecting the overall environment for
your training must not be underestimated. Only then will you be making
the best possible decision for your college years.

Along the way, I want to offer you a few further resources that may help
you prepare for and choose your degree program. Matt Edwards maintains
a brilliant blog at www.auditioningforcollege.com, where he posts articles,
FAQs, and guest interviews, all dedicated to demystifying the process for
students and their parents. College Confidential (www.collegeconfidential
.com) is an online forum for parents and their students to seek advice and
to post anonymously about experiences, good and bad, related to the application process.

I briefly mentioned some coaching services earlier in this chapter.
While I told you that they are not a necessary expense (and they are
expensive, believe me), and while some people out there have no credentials (but will take your money just the same), I want to point you toward
a few sources that I have personally found to be consistently reliable
and legitimate, in case you really feel like you need hands-on guidance
through the process. MTCA (www.mtcollegeauditions.com) and Arts-
Bridge (www.artsbridge.com) are both audition and consulting services in
the northeast that will work with students all over the country. I generally
find that their counsel leads to strong auditions. Dave Clemmons, a former Broadway casting director, has also moved into the world of college
prep with Dave Clemmons College Advisory Program (www.dccapcoach
ing.com). Dave is obviously extremely knowledgeable and he makes it a
constant point to stay connected to all of the major university programs
so that he's current on what each is seeking and what they are offering to
students. Finally, as I mentioned, I also do a good deal of consulting and
coaching, so you may feel free to contact me through my website (www
.jonathanflom.com) or by direct e-mail to actorcoach@hotmail.com. I'm
always happy to help young artists find the best fit for them and prepare
a great audition package.

As for creating a list of schools to research, the following index may be
helpful to you if you are starting from scratch with no information. These
are just some of the many schools that offer training programs in musical theatre. This is by no means a complete list—it is simply a collection
of some of the more well-known schools regionally. It may help you get
started on your search.

Auburn University (Auburn, Alabama)
Baldwin Wallace University (Berea, Ohio)
Boston Conservatory (Boston, Massachusetts)
Brigham Young University (Provo, Utah)
Carnegie Mellon University (Pittsburgh, Pennsylvania)
Cincinnati College and Conservatory of Music (Cincinnati, Ohio)
Coastal Carolina University (Conway, South Carolina)
Columbia College (Chicago, Illinois)
East Carolina University (Greenville, North Carolina)
Elon University (Elon, North Carolina)
Emerson College (Boston, Massachusetts)
Florida State University (Tallahassee, Florida)
The Hartt School, University of Hartford (Hartford, Connecticut)
Illinois Wesleyan University (Bloomington, Illinois)
Indiana University (Bloomington, Indiana)
Ithaca College (Ithaca, New York)
James Madison University (Harrisonburg, Virginia)
Montclair State University (Montclair, New Jersey)
New York University—Tisch and Steinhardt Schools (New York, New York)
Northwestern University (Evanston, Illinois)
Oklahoma City University (Oklahoma City, Oklahoma)
Pace University (New York, New York)
Penn State University (State College, Pennsylvania)
Point Park University (Pittsburgh, Pennsylvania)
Rider University (Lawrenceville, New Jersey)
Roosevelt University (Chicago, Illinois)
Shenandoah Conservatory (Winchester, Virginia)
SUNY Fredonia (Fredonia, New York)
Syracuse University (Syracuse, New York)
Texas Christian University (Ft. Worth, Texas)
Texas State University (San Marcos, Texas)
University of Alabama (Tuscaloosa, Alabama)
University of the Arts (Philadelphia, Pennsylvania)
University of Central Florida (Orlando, Florida)
University of Miami (Miami, Florida)
University of Michigan (Ann Arbor, Michigan)
University of Northern Colorado (Greeley, Colorado)
University of Oklahoma (Norman, Oklahoma)

Webster Conservatory (St. Louis, Missouri)
Western Carolina University (Cullowhee, North Carolina)
Western Connecticut State University (Danbury, Connecticut)
Wright State University (Dayton, Ohio)

SUMMARY

- Begin your process by preparing a personalized list of criteria of what you are seeking in a school.
- Be organized and make a spreadsheet to track all pertinent audition information about all of your schools.
- Be prepared to apply to between 10–18 schools, and include a range from "reach" to "safety," but make sure that you'd be happy with any school on your list.
- Colleges are looking for trainable candidates, not polished triple threats.
- You can set yourself apart from the multitudes of average students by being thoroughly prepared, choosing age-appropriate pieces, and making solid acting choices for each audition piece.
- Do not bring a parent to accompany your audition.
- Be yourself in the interview—don't try to "act" your way through it.
- Avoid cliché responses, such as "I've always wanted to be on Broadway," or "I do it because I love the rush of applause."
- Research the schools you are auditioning for, and ask questions of them in your interview, so that you have all the information needed to make an informed decision.
- Visit colleges and sit in on classes and productions to determine the best fit for your individual training needs.

CONCLUSION:
SOME DOS AND DON'TS

You've undoubtedly heard the odds stacked against a successful career in show business. You know that it's an industry of jaded cynics who must learn to deal with rejection as daily routine. And despite the enormous challenges that lie before you, you're determined to take a shot at it. To you I say: You can do it.

It's true that your audition-to-job ratio is likely to be easily 50 to 1 or even 100 to 1. But you know better than to accept it as judgment of your self-worth and to fall apart. You know that auditioning is your daily chance to perform, and that brings you joy. You understand that auditioning is not simply a means to an end; it *is* your career. And to you I say again: You can do it.

You will never know what the people behind the table are thinking—that they were looking for someone a little taller, a little blonder, a little less attractive. You can't know and you can't control it either. All you can do is commit absolutely to maintaining your vocal and physical instrument in top condition, studying and practicing the tools of your craft regularly, and being thoroughly prepared for any eventualities that may lie on your path to a career in the theatre.

Taking advantage of networking opportunities is never a bad idea either. While I believe that the saying "It's not what you know, it's who you know" is a bit overstated, it's certainly not without truth. This is why a good actor surrounds himself with other artists: playwrights, directors, producers, stage managers, and so on. It's an industry of friends, and people get work through word of mouth almost as much as by auditioning cold. I would suggest, however, that knowing the right people is only worth so much before you have to rely on what you know to carry you through.

In the preceding chapters, I offered you pages of practical advice designed to empower you to deliver your most potent, most authentic audition every time out. I warned you that doing this right would require a great deal of work; however, the process can still be simple. You just have to be willing to put in the effort and preparation in order to maximize your results. No book or method of training can *guarantee* getting you cast or even getting you callbacks. That being said, following the recommendations I have set forth will make you feel like you have at least some control over your artistic fate. Just to recap, here is a summary of Dos and Don'ts to remember for the work that lies ahead of you:

DO:

- explore adjectives and branding ideas to pinpoint how you want to be perceived
- choose audition attire that represents your authentic self
- build a well-varied repertoire of songs and monologues that represent you in many different genres and styles
- cut and mark your music appropriately for ease of communication with the pianist
- secure professional-grade actor headshots that make a statement of who you are
- design a clean, professional résumé
- use trade publications to find auditions and get yourself in the room as much as possible
- review the "anatomy" of an audition, from warm entrance to graceful exit
- treat the accompanist in an audition like a friend and communicate effectively
- prepare for callbacks and be open for anything that may happen in the room
- remember that you are a professional, so you may negotiate and ask for what you need
- learn to read contracts carefully and protect yourself
- be the kind of person you would want to work with on an important project

DON'T:

- worry, stress, or focus on the things that are not within your control
- try to be all things to all people
- go into any audition underprepared to show you at your very best
- choose material that is overly "show-off-y" and keeps you from being your authentic self
- bring bound vocal books or loose sheets to a pianist in an audition
- go to any audition without having a varied selection of monologues as well as songs
- overstay your welcome in the audition room
- shake their hands when you walk in or leave the audition
- take the results of any audition as a judgment of your personal worth

If you make sure to apply this system, you are likely to note a more positive reaction from the artistic teams who see you. They will respond to your professional delivery. And though you will not always be cast in the end, you will find yourself attending a lot more callbacks. And, after all, that's the best result an actor can hope to achieve in an audition: the callback.

Ⓐ

REPERTOIRE GENRE LISTS

The following is a checklist of genres that make up a well-rounded repertoire. Here I also offer you a few select titles to get you started on your search, but don't limit yourself to the short list that I provide. Use these as a jumping-off point to discover some songs you may not know. Then choose material that suits your individual, authentic self. Consider "chasing the carrot" to find more repertoire! This means beginning with an actor you admire and relate to, researching what roles he/she has played, finding material from those shows, then looking into who else has played the role and following what *that* actor has done, etc. You can also start with the song, research the role, see who played the role, then look into the actors from there. Enjoy the hunt. And remember to make your *primary* criterion for choosing repertoire your essence or *brand*, not your vocal technique or acting chops.

As you continue in your training and your career, you should make sure to have at least one piece that covers each of the following genres. This way, you'll be prepared for any audition on short notice.

MUSICAL THEATRE REPERTOIRE GENRES

Standard Ballad

"At Last" by Mack Gordon and Harry Warren

"But Not for Me" (by George Gershwin and Ira Gershwin) from *Girl Crazy*

"Come Rain or Come Shine" (by Harold Arlen and Johnny Mercer) from *St. Louis Woman*

"Embraceable You" (by George Gershwin and Ira Gershwin) from *Girl Crazy*

"Far from the Home I Love" (by Jerry Bock and Sheldon Harnick) from *Fiddler on the Roof*

"Goodnight, My Someone" (by Meredith Willson) from *The Music Man*

"I Could Write a Book" (by Richard Rodgers and Lorenz Hart) from *Pal Joey*

"If I Loved You" (by Richard Rodgers and Oscar Hammerstein II) from *Carousel*

"I'm a Stranger Here Myself" (by Kurt Weill and Ogden Nash) from *One Touch of Venus*

"It Might as Well Be Spring" (by Richard Rodgers and Oscar Hammerstein II) from *State Fair*

"Just in Time" (by Jule Styne, Betty Comden, and Adolph Green) from *Bells Are Ringing*

"A Little Bit in Love" (by Leonard Bernstein, Betty Comden, and Adolph Green) from *Wonderful Town*

"Lonely Town" (by Leonard Bernstein, Betty Comden, and Adolph Green) from *On the Town*

"The Man That Got Away" by Harold Arlen

"Melisande" (by Harvey Schmidt and Tom Jones) from *110 in the Shade*

"Mira" (by Bob Merrill) from *Carnival*

"Mr. Snow" (by Richard Rodgers and Oscar Hammerstein II) from *Carousel*

"My Best Girl" (by Jerry Herman) from *Mame*

"My Funny Valentine" (by Richard Rodgers and Lorenz Hart) from *Babes in Arms*

"Night and Day" (by Cole Porter) from *Gay Divorce*

"No Other Love" (by Richard Rodgers and Oscar Hammerstein II) from *Me and Juliet*

"Our Love Is Here to Stay" (by George Gershwin and Ira Gershwin) from *An American in Paris*

"Ribbons Down My Back" (by Jerry Herman) from *Hello, Dolly!*

"Simple Little Things" (by Harvey Schmidt and Tom Jones) from *110 in the Shade*

"Stormy Weather" by Harold Arlen

"They Can't Take That Away from Me" (by George Gershwin and Ira Gershwin) from *Shall We Dance*

"What Good Would the Moon Be" (by Kurt Weill) from *Street Scene*

"Will He Like Me" (by Jerry Bock and Sheldon Harnick) from *She Loves Me*

Standard Up-Tempo

"Almost Like Being in Love" (by Frederick Loewe and Alan Jay Lerner) from *Brigadoon*

"A Cockeyed Optimist" (by Richard Rodgers and Oscar Hammerstein II) from *South Pacific*

"Falling in Love with Love" (by Richard Rodgers and Lorenz Hart) from *The Boys from Syracuse*

"From This Moment On" (by Cole Porter) from *Out of This World*

"I Get a Kick Out of You" (by Cole Porter) from *Anything Goes*

"I Met a Girl" (by Jule Styne, Betty Comden, and Adolph Green) from *Bells Are Ringing*

"I Wanna Be Bad" (by B. G. DeSylva, Lew Brown, and Ray Henderson) from *Good News*

"I Wish I Were in Love Again" (by Richard Rodgers and Lorenz Hart) from *Babes in Arms*

"If I Were a Bell" (by Frank Loesser) from *Guys and Dolls*

"I'm Beginning to See the Light" by Duke Ellington, Don George, Johnny Hodges, and Harry James

"It's Only a Paper Moon" by Harold Arlen, E. Y. Harburg, and Billy Rose

"Let's Do It, Let's Fall in Love" (by Cole Porter) from *Paris*

"Now I Have Everything" (by Jerry Bock and Sheldon Harnick) from *Fiddler on the Roof*

"Old Devil Moon" (by Burton Lane and E. Y. Harburg) from *Finian's Rainbow*

"Orange Colored Sky" by Milton DeLugg and Willie Stein

"She Loves Me" (by Jerry Bock and Sheldon Harnick) from *She Loves Me*

"The Surrey with the Fringe on Top" (by Richard Rodgers and Oscar Hammerstein II) from *Oklahoma*

"This Can't Be Love" (by Richard Rodgers and Lorenz Hart) from *The Boys from Syracuse*

"Wonderful Guy" (by Richard Rodgers and Oscar Hammerstein II) from *South Pacific*

"Yes, My Heart" (by Bob Merrill) from *Carnival*

"You've Got to Be Carefully Taught" (by Richard Rodgers and Oscar Hammerstein II) from *South Pacific*

Contemporary Ballad

"Easy to Be Hard" (by Galt MacDermot, James Rado, and Gerome Ragni) from *Hair*

"Fly, Fly Away" (by Marc Shaiman and Scott Wittman) from *Catch Me If You Can*

"Helpless" (by Lin-Manuel Miranda) from *Hamilton*

"How 'Bout a Dance" (by Frank Wildhorn and Don Black) from *Bonnie and Clyde*

"I Chose Right" (by David Shire and Richard Maltby, Jr.) from *Baby*

"I Don't Remember You" (by John Kander and Fred Ebb) from *The Happy Time*

"I Want to Go Home" (by David Shire and Richard Maltby, Jr.) from *Big*

"Inside Your Heart" (by Lawrence O'Keefe) from *Bat Boy: The Musical*

"Ireland" (by Lawrence O'Keefe) from *Legally Blonde*

"Larger Than Life" (by Stephen Flaherty) from *My Favorite Year*

"Lost and Found" (by Cy Coleman and David Zippel) from *City of Angels*

"Love Who You Love" (by Stephen Flaherty and Lynn Ahrens) from *A Man of No Importance*

"The Mason" (by Craig Carnelia) from *Working*

"Perfect for You" (by Tom Kitt and Brian Yorkey) from *Next to Normal*

"Sailing" (by William Finn) from *A New Brain*

"Sister Act" (by Glenn Slater and Alan Menken) from *Sister Act*

"Somebody Gonna Love You" (by Brenda Russell, Allee Willis, and Stephen Bray) from *The Color Purple*

"That Would Be Enough" (by Lin-Manuel Miranda) from *Hamilton*

"Time Heals Everything" (by Jerry Herman) from *Mack and Mabel*

"Times Like This" (by Stephen Flaherty and Lynn Ahrens) from *Lucky Stiff*

"What More Can I Say" (by William Finn) from *Falsettoland*

"What Only Love Can See" (by Christopher Curtis) from *Chaplin*

"What Say You Meg?" (by Sting) from *The Last Ship*

"What Would I Do" (by William Finn) from *Falsettoland*

"With You" (by Bruce Joel Rubin, Dave Stewart, and Glen Ballard) from *Ghost: The Musical*

Contemporary Up-Tempo/Driving Dramatic

"And They're Off" (by William Finn) from *A New Brain*

"Arthur in the Afternoon" (by John Kander and Fred Ebb) from *The Act*

"Breathe" (by Lin-Manuel Miranda) from *In the Heights* (could also be considered a ballad—depending on what you contrast with it)

"Change" (by William Finn) from *A New Brain*

"Colored Lights" (by John Kander and Fred Ebb) from *The Rink*

"Goodbye" (by Marc Shaiman and Scott Wittman) from *Catch Me If You Can*

"Holding to the Ground" (by William Finn) from *Falsettoland*

"I Believe" (by Trey Parker, Robert Lopez, and Matt Stone) from *The Book of Mormon*

"I Don't Remember Christmas" (by David Shire) from *Starting Here, Starting Now*

"I Think I May Want to Remember Today" (by David Shire and Richard Maltby, Jr.) from *Starting Here, Starting Now*

"It's an Art" (by Stephen Schwartz) from *Working*

"The Life I Never Led" (by Glenn Slater and Alan Menken) from *Sister Act*

"Lost in the Wilderness" (by Stephen Schwartz) from *Children of Eden*

"Much More" (by Harvey Schmidt and Tom Jones) from *The Fantasticks*

"Night Letter" (by Galt MacDermot and John Guare) from *Two Gentlemen of Verona*

"The Night that Goldman Spoke . . ." (by Stephen Flaherty and Lynn Ahrens) from *Ragtime*

"One Perfect Moment" (by Tom Kitt, Amanda Green, and Lin-Manuel Miranda) from *Bring It On: The Musical*

"The Other Side of the Tracks" (by Cy Coleman and Carolyn Leigh) from *Little Me*

"Proud Lady" (by Stephen Schwartz) from *The Baker's Wife*

"Right Hand Man" (by Karey and Wayne Kirkpatrick) from *Something Rotten!*

"So Much Better" (by Lawrence O'Keefe) from *Legally Blonde*

"Spark of Creation" (by Stephen Schwartz) from *Children of Eden*

"The Story Goes On" (by David Shire and Richard Maltby, Jr.) from *Baby*

"Stranger to the Rain" (by Stephen Schwartz) from *Children of Eden*

"Waiting for Life" (by Stephen Flaherty and Lynn Ahrens) from *Once on This Island*

"Where Am I Going?" (by Cy Coleman and Dorothy Fields) from *Sweet Charity*

"Wherever He Ain't" (by Jerry Herman) from *Mack and Mabel*

Pop/Rock

"Ain't Too Proud to Beg" (by Norman Whitfield and Edward Holland, Jr.) performed by The Temptations

"Blue Bayou" (by Roy Orbison and Joe Melson) performed by Roy Orbison

"Breakeven" (by Andrew Frampton, Danny O'Donoghue, Mark Sheehan, and Steve Kipner) performed by The Script

"The City of New Orleans" (by Steve Goodman) performed by Willie Nelson

"Cowboy Take Me Away" (by Martie Seidel and Marcus Hummon) performed by Dixie Chicks

"Crazy" (by Willie Nelson) performed by Patsy Cline

"Desperado" (by Don Henley and Glenn Frey) performed by The Eagles

"Different Drum" (by Mike Nesmith) performed by Linda Ronstadt

"Good Golly, Miss Molly" (by John Marascalco and Robert "Bumps" Blackwell) performed by Little Richard

"The Great Escape" (by Pink and Dan Wilson) performed by Pink

"I Walk the Line" (by Johnny Cash) performed by Johnny Cash

"I Will Always Love You" (by Dolly Parton) performed by Dolly Parton

"Landslide" (by Stevie Nicks) performed by Fleetwood Mac

"Levon" (by Elton John and Bernie Taupin) performed by Elton John

"The Night They Drove Old Dixie Down" (by Robbie Robertson) performed by The Band

"Rocket Man" (by Elton John and Bernie Taupin) performed by Elton John

"Runaround Sue" (by Dion DiMucci and Ernie Maresca) performed by Dion

"Runaway" (by Del Shannon and Max Crook) performed by Del Shannon

"Shop Around" (by Smokey Robinson and Berry Gordy) performed by The Miracles featuring Smokey Robinson

"Stupid Cupid" (by Howard Greenfield and Neil Sedaka) performed by Connie Francis

"Teenage Dream" (by Katy Perry, Lukasz Gottwald, Max Martin, Benjamin Levin, and Bonnie McKee) performed by Katy Perry

"A Thousand Miles" (by Vanessa Carlton) performed by Vanessa Carlton

"Uncharted" (by Sara Bareilles) performed by Sara Bareilles

"We Belong" (by David Eric Lowden and Daniel Navarro) performed by Pat Benatar

"When Will I Be Loved" (by Phil Everly) performed by Linda Ronstadt
"Wrecking Ball" (by MoZella, Stephan Moccio, Sacha Skarbek, Lukasz
Gottwald, and Henry Russell Walter) performed by Miley Cyrus
"You Took the Words Right Out of My Mouth" (by Jim Steinman) performed by Meat Loaf

Let's be honest, the pop/rock list can go on forever, and the songs could *literally* be updated each week as new music "drops." It is your job as a contemporary musical theatre artist to stay current and continue seeking out good material that suits your voice (yes, with pop/rock, the vocal styling is the first and foremost factor in choosing appropriate material). I suggest that you get a Spotify or Apple Music account and do some active listening to find artists that would translate well to the audition room. And be sure that your "flavor" or "color" of pop audition song suits the specific audition for which you choose to sing it.

MONOLOGUE REPERTOIRE GENRES

The following is a complete list for the professional actor. For the young performer, having five monologues (classical comedic, classical dramatic, great realism, contemporary comedic, and contemporary dramatic) will be sufficient.

Classical, Greek or Roman

Medea; *Oedipus*; *Antigone*; *The Frogs*; *The Menaechmi*

Classical Verse Piece: Comedic and Dramatic

Shakespeare; Jonson; Marlowe

18th- or 19th-Century "Manner" or Restoration Piece

Molière; Sheridan; Goldsmith; Wilde; Shaw

Early Realism or Naturalism Masters

Ibsen; Chekhov; early Strindberg (e.g., *Miss Julie*)

20th-Century American or European Realism Masters

Tennessee Williams; Arthur Miller; Clifford Odets; Eugene O'Neill; Brian Friel; Edward Albee; August Wilson; Lanford Wilson

Contemporary Realism or "Style Piece": Comedic and Dramatic

David Mamet; Neil LaBute; Paula Vogel; John Guare; Richard Greenberg; Wendy Wasserstein; Tom Stoppard; Nicky Silver; Theresa Rebeck; David Auburn; David West-Read; David Lindsey-Abaire; Annie Baker

Remember: read plays! And don't be afraid to get creative—you can cut and paste a monologue together for yourself by removing the other character(s). Just be sure that it makes dramatic sense and does not require you to respond to an imaginary answer from an invisible partner.

B

SAMPLE REPERTOIRE
BY ACTOR TYPE

In appendix A, I offered you repertoire suggestions by genre. For this section of the book, I actually polled several actor friends of mine in various different stages of their career (all successful at their respective levels!) and asked them to kindly share what is in their audition books. While they all have a variety of styles and genres, you'll probably notice that some of them lean more heavily on a specific type of song (i.e., pop) when they realize that most of their auditions are calling for that specific style. Just know that all of these actors are working, so they must be doing something right!

(*Also note, I am reprinting these contents exactly as the actors have delivered them to me, with any accompanying notes or categorizations, so you can see exactly what they are thinking in organizing their books.)

BOOK 1: FEMALE, MID-20S, MEZZO/MIX-BELTER, STRONG DANCER

MT Ballad

"A Little Bit in Love" from *Wonderful Town*
"Simple Little Things" from *110 in the Shade*
"Frank Mills" from *Hair*
"Paper Doll" from *Pop!*

MT Up-Tempo

"Killer Instinct" from *Bring It On*
"Always True to You" from *Kiss Me, Kate*

Pop Up-Tempo

"Express Yourself" by Madonna
"Firework" by Katy Perry
"Valerie" by Amy Winehouse

Pop Ballad

"Clarity" by Zedd
"Wrecking Ball" by Miley Cyrus
"What about Love" by Heart

Other (In the Works/Specific Calls)

"Party Dress" by Kerrigan and Lowdermilk
"Loud" from *Matilda*
"I Know Things Now" from *Into the Woods*
"Safer" from *First Date*

BOOK 2: FEMALE, MID-20S, AFRICAN AMERICAN/ASIAN (ETHNIC) MEZZO-BELTER

"Contemporary Is What I'm Usually Asked for Nowadays in the Room"

"Gone" by Lianne La Havas
"Bang Bang (My Baby Shot Me Down)" by Nancy Sinatra
"Rolling in the Deep" by Adele
"Rumor Has It" by Adele

"I Have One Rap Song"

"Electric Lady" by Janelle Monae

"My Contemp. MT Is Usually . . ."

"You Can Be as Loud the Hell You Want" from *Avenue Q* (also a comedy song)

"Don Juan" from *Smokey Joe's Café* ("Gonna take that out soon because it's overdone.")

"Sal Tlay Ka Siti" from *The Book of Mormon*

"There Will Be a Miracle" from *See What I Wanna See*

"Basic MT"

"I Still Believe in Love" from *They're Playing Our Song*

"If They Want to Hear Jazzy/Bluesy"

"Salty Papa Blues" by Dinah Washington

"Legit"

"Bill" from *Show Boat*

"Stormy Weather" by Harold Arlen

"To Show My Comedy Chops and My Ethnic Ambiguity, I Also Sing . . ."

"The More You Ruv Someone" from *Avenue Q*

"For Motown or Jukebox Musicals"

"Dancing in the Street" by Martha and the Vandellas

BOOK 3: MALE, MID-40S, COMIC CHARACTER, BASS/BARITONE

Classic Ballads

"Begin the Beguine" by Cole Porter

"I Could Write a Book" from *Pal Joey*

"Night Song" from *Golden Boy*

"You're the Fairest Flower" from *Little Mary Sunshine*

Comedy

"Don José (of Far Rockaway)" from *Wish You Were Here*
"Lucky" from *Lucky Stiff*
"That's All" by Heisler and Goldrich
"Together Again" from *Young Frankenstein*
"What Do You Do with Your Arms?" by Carner and Gregor

Classic Up-Tempos

"You're Timeless to Me" from *Hairspray*
"Oh, Lady Be Good!" from *Lady Be Good*
"Say That We're Sweethearts Again" from the film *Meet the People*

"You Want Some Low Notes"

"You're a Mean One, Mr. Grinch" from *How the Grinch Stole Christmas*

Contemporary Ballads

"I'd Rather Be Sailing" from *A New Brain*
"Look Over There" from *La Cage aux Folles*

Contemporary Driving Ballads

"Everybody Says Don't" from *Anyone Can Whistle*
"The Pinstripes Are All That They See" from *Catch Me if You Can*
"It's Hard to Speak My Heart" from *Parade*

Country/Folk

"Unanswered Prayers" by Garth Brooks
"When You Say Nothing at All" by Paul Overstreet and Don Schlitz

Pop/Rock

"Hip to Be Square" by Huey Lewis and the News
"I Don't Want to Miss a Thing" by Aerosmith
"One Week" by Barenaked Ladies

BOOK 4: FEMALE, MID-30S, HIGH-ENERGY, BELTY LEADING LADY

(This actress experienced a string of success in a small-market US city, and for some time was not required to attend open calls. She was invited directly to callbacks and didn't really need to maintain much audition repertoire. However, she recently moved to London and began booking work with regularity. She said the following four songs were the ones that helped her book the gigs she's earned in the last year.)

"Life of the Party" from *The Wild Party*
"(I'll Marry) The Very Next Man" from *Fiorello!* (belted, not mixed, to stand out)
"Just Imagine" from *Good News*
"Astonishing" from *Little Women*

She says her current rep book contains:

Belt

"Life of the Party" from *The Wild Party*
"The Waiting" from *Relativity*
"Cornet Man" from *Funny Girl*
"Today Is the First Day of the Rest of My Life" from *Starting Here, Starting Now*
"Hit Me with a Hot Note" by Duke Ellington
"Astonishing" from *Little Women*
"A Story of My Own" from a new British musical
"Spark of Creation" from *Children of Eden*
"I Dreamed a Dream" from *Les Miserables*
"I Don't Know How to Love Him" from *Jesus Christ Superstar*
"More to the Story" from *Shrek!*

Head

"The Very Next Man" from *Fiorello!*
"Just Imagine" from *Good News*
"Someone to Watch over Me" from *Oh, Kay*
"Goodnight My Someone" from *The Music Man*
"Warm All Over" from *The Most Happy Fella*
"What Good Would the Moon Be" from *Street Scene*

(*She says the above is just from her everyday book. It covers the majority of things she will be asked to do based on her type and current castings. But it doesn't mean she doesn't pull from a huge library of other things or that she won't learn a new song if she thinks it would be perfect for a certain audition. I'd also point out that some of her songs—"Astonishing," "I Dreamed a Dream," and "I Don't Know How to Love Him"—are considered way overdone in the United States, but they are working for this actress in London; not to mention that she is of the age and the type to perform those roles in a Broadway or a West End–level production.)

BOOK 5: MALE, EARLY 20S, COMIC CHARACTER, TENOR

"Sixteen Going on Seventeen" from *The Sound of Music*
"Try Me" from *She Loves Me*
"The Kite Song" from *You're a Good Man, Charlie Brown*
"Giants in the Sky" from *Into the Woods*
"What Do I Need with Love" from *Thoroughly Modern Millie*
"Grow for Me" from *Little Shop of Horrors*
"Not While I'm Around" from *Sweeney Todd*
"They Can't Take That Away from Me" from *Shall We Dance*
"Stay with Me" by Sam Smith
"Turn It Off" from *The Book of Mormon*

BOOK 6: FEMALE, MID-20S, SOPRANO INGENUE

"Yes, My Heart" from *Carnival* ("Go-to")
"Never Fall in Love with an Elf" from *Elf the Musical* ("Go-to")
"Mister Snow" from *Carousel*
"Jolene" by Dolly Parton
"Autumn" from *Starting Here, Starting Now*
"Will He Like Me" from *She Loves Me*
"I'll Be Seeing You" by Irving Kahal and Sammy Fain
"Lying There" from *Edges*
"Je veux vivre" from *Romeo et Juliette* (for opera/operetta auditions)
"Stranger to the Rain" from *Children of Eden*

"Touch-a Touch Me" from *Rocky Horror Show*
"Screw Loose" from *Cry Baby*

"Getting Ready to Add Some Pop/Rock Rep I Did in My One-Woman Show, Like . . ."

"No One but You" by Queen
"Try" by Colbie Callet
"Marry Me" by Dolly Parton

C

RECOMMENDED READING

The following are some suggested titles for further reading. Many of these I have mentioned within the chapters of this book, but I've also added some other favorites of mine that have served me in other ways, besides as acting/ singing resources.

Audition Freedom by VP Boyle
A Practical Handbook for the Actor by Melissa Bruder
Freeing the Artistic Mind by Dr. Bill Crawford
Acting in Musical Theatre by Joe Deer and Rocco Dal Vera
So You Want to Sing Rock 'n' Roll: A Guide for Professionals by Matthew Edwards
Never Eat Alone by Keith Ferrazzi and Tahl Raz
Act Like It's Your Business: Branding and Marketing Strategies for Actors by Jonathan Flom
Blink by Malcolm Gladwell
David and Goliath by Malcolm Gladwell
Purple Cow by Seth Godin
Sanford Meisner on Acting by Sanford Meisner and Dennis Longwell
Rock the Audition by Sheri Sanders

GLOSSARY

Actors Equity Association (AEA): The stage actors and stage managers union in the United States.

agent: Someone who works with actor clients to get them seen at as many (appropriate) auditions as possible. Agents also negotiate contracts and act as a legal liaison between producers and actors. Industry standard states that agents receive 10 percent of an actor's working salary if they represent an actor under contract.

ballad: Simply put, a slow romantic or sentimental song.

belt: The common form of singing in contemporary musical theatre, often referred to as "chest voice." A woman produces this sound in the middle of her range where the bass and treble qualities can work together (starting at G above middle C). Think of it as a "calling voice" on a sustained pitch. It should feel very free, never strained. It is meant to emulate the sound of human speech more naturally than classical singing. Visit www.belcantocanbelto.com for more information.

brand: The way in which a product is identified by a particular description or image.

callback: A follow-up to an initial audition.

casting director: Someone hired by the producers to help facilitate the audition process by screening large groups of actors and presenting the director with choices for each role in the project. Contrary to their title, they do not have final say over who is chosen, although they are the gate-keepers to being seen in auditions, and their recommendations generally carry a great deal of weight.

cattle call: An open audition during which a large number of actors are seen very briefly. Sometimes they may "type out" or make decisions to hear or not to hear actors based on look, type, or special skills; for example, the director is only looking for blondes, men over six feet tall, or people with tumbling skills.

creative team (also called the **artistic team**): The collaborators who are working on a theatrical project and likely to be in the audition room. This group may typically include writer(s), director, choreographer, music director, producers, artistic director, and casting director.

cuts/cutting: The term used for creating shortened versions of songs for the purpose of auditioning. In the U.S., common cuts required are 16- and 32-bars (or measures) long. Cuts require attention to details such as musical logic, lyric phrasing, and key signatures. It's vital for American musical actors to learn how to effectively create 16- and 32-bar cuts for auditions.

Equity (or Actors' Equity Association): The professional stage actors' and stage managers' union.

Equity Membership Candidacy (EMC): The system of "points" through which actors receive credit for working weeks at participating professional union theatres and can earn admission to Actors' Equity. Fifty weeks/points makes an actor eligible to join the union.

headshot: A close-up, professional photograph of an individual actor, used as a calling card at auditions. Shot in color, from the neck or chest up. Often abbreviated as "pix."

ingenue: A naive or innocent young female character type with a soprano voice.

juvenile: The male counterpart to the ingenue; typically a young tenor.

libretto: Also known as the "book," this is the spoken words, or script, of a musical.

monitor: The person who ushers people in and out of the audition room and/or keeps the sign-up list current and accurate.

open call: An audition that does not require an advance appointment. Generally, people either sign up for times in the morning or simply show up and are seen in the order they arrived. See also **cattle call**.

pop (or popular) music: For our purposes, this is any music that comes from records and the radio, as opposed to music composed specifically for the musical theatre. Subgenres of pop include jazz, rockabilly, doo-wop, R&B, soul, rock, hard rock, alternative, folk, Top-40 pop, hip-hop, rap, country, bluegrass, etc.

pre-screen: May either refer to a private audition with a casting director that occurs before being invited to the larger audition for the creative team; or a video submitted ahead of an audition that determines if an actor is invited to attend the main audition.

repertoire: The compilation of songs and monologues that an actor has *memorized* and *practiced*, for use in auditions. The songs should be neatly organized in a binder and brought to every audition.

rote: By memory; fixed or mechanical. An actor should know his audition pieces "by rote" so that he does not need to concentrate on remembering the words and can instead focus on acting choices.

SAG-AFTRA: The merged union of Screen Actors' Guild and American Federation of Television and Radio Artists.

score: The music portion of a musical, whether sung or instrumental; written by the composer.

sides: Short cuttings from the script used for an audition or a callback.

typing out: When a casting director eliminates people from an audition before they are heard singing, simply by look or physical type (e.g., "We are only looking for girls who are 5'11" or taller. Everyone else can go home.").

up-tempo: Usually considered the opposite of a ballad, this is a song style that moves at a quicker pace, with an "up" mood to it.

vamp: A short introductory musical passage often repeated several times before a solo or between verses.

INDEX

42nd Street, 85

accompanist, 2, 7, 8, 20, 21, 26, 30, 36, 43, 47, 49, 50, 54, 56–59, 61, 62, 67, 71, 72, 74, 77, 149, 150, 160
Act Like It's Your Business, xii, 16, 22, 101, 108, 111, 121, 179
Acting in Musical Theatre, 68, 179
acting the song, 18, 40, 42, 68–69, 77
Actors Connection, 104
Actors Equity Association (Equity), 15, 102–3, 105, 120, 182
actors who move, 12, 89
Addams Family, The, 30, 38
"Adelaide's Lament," 38
Adler, Richard, 24
AEA, 120
after the audition, 75–77, 97–105
agents, 79, 94, 95, 121, 135, 151, 181
Ah! Wilderness, 45
Ahrens, Lynn, 26, 166, 167
Alan, Scott, 25
Aliens, The, 45

"All I Need Is the Girl," 71
All My Sons, 45
All Shook Up, 27–29
"All That Jazz," 38
"Almost Like Being in Love," 165
Always Patsy Cline, 29
"Always True to You," 38, 172
amateur theatre, 4, 101, 122, 123
American Idiot, 27, 29, 30, 52, 185
American Idol, 1, 3
"American Songbook," 22
American Theatre of Actors, 123
"Another Hundred People," 40
"Anthem," 25
Antigone, 45
Anything Goes, 38, 165
"Anything Goes," 38
apologizing (when not to), 61, 62, 72, 73, 77
Apple music, 27
Apple Tree, The, 38
Arlen, Harold, 23, 164, 165, 173
Ashford, Rob, 86

"Astonishing," 38, 175, 176
audition attire, 16, 83, 84, 89, 90, 96, 110, 111, 148, 150
Audition Freedom, 25, 179
audition material, xii, 5, 6, 18, 21, 24–29, 69, 83, 147
audition notices, 12, 13
authenticity (be yourself), xiii, 2, 28, 29, 30, 36, 40, 51–55, 62, 64, 66, 69, 74, 77, 79, 91, 146, 147, 150, 158, 160, 161, 163
Awake and Sing!, 45

Back Stage, 8, 9, 108, 135
Backstage.com, 9, 108
"Back to Before," 25
Baker, Annie, 45
Baker's Wife, The, 25
ballads (songs), 22–25
Beautiful: The Carol King Musical, 27, 28
Beauty and the Beast, 38
Beehive, 28
Bells Are Ringing, 51, 164, 165
belting, 27, 31–33, 35, 36, 67, 68, 121, 150, 171, 172, 175, 181
Bennett, Michael, 86
Bergasse, Joshua, 3, 86
Bernstein, Leonard, 24
Big River, 29
Blankenbuehler, Andy, 3, 85, 86
Blink, 179
Bloody, Bloody Andrew Jackson, 25, 29
Blue Surge, 45
Bock, Jerry, 24, 164, 165
Book of Mormon, The, 16, 167, 173, 176
Boyfriend, The, 46
Boyle, VP, 6, 25, 51, 66, 179
branding, xii, 16, 22, 108, 109, 111–13, 118, 119, 136, 142, 146, 160, 163, 181
Brightman, Alex, 51

Bring It On, 25, 29
"British invasion," 31
Broadway, xii, 3, 6, 9, 15, 24, 25, 26, 29, 30, 31, 51, 61, 62, 66, 67, 80, 82, 86, 87, 90, 92, 93, 101, 120, 121, 123, 142, 144, 151, 152, 156, 176
Broadway Dance Center, 86
Brooks, Mel, 36
"Brother, Can You Spare a Dime?" 36, 60
Brown, Jason, Robert, 9, 10, 26
Bruder, Melissa, 2, 68, 179
Burn This, 45
Butterflies Are Free, 46
"buttoning" (ending a song or monologue), 70, 71, 75, 77

Cabaret, 11, 36, 104, 105
callback list, 80
callback sides, 79–83, 95
Carlyle, Warren, 3, 86
Carnor, Sam, 25
"Caro Mio Ben, 35
cast recordings, 3, 7, 18, 23, 29–31; trap of, 3, 7, 40
casting (non-traditional), 14
casting call, 9–14, 18, 23, 29, 97
casting call ads, 9, 14, 18
casting directors, xii, 5, 12, 15, 24, 29, 30, 37, 38, 43, 62, 74, 79, 82, 83, 92, 94, 95, 109, 136, 156, 181, 182
Cat on a Hot Tin Roof, 45
Catch Me if You Can, 25
Champion, Gower, 3
Chancey, Joey, 61
character breakdown, 13, 14
check-in process, 66, 69
Chekhov, Anton, 45, 123, 169
Chekhov, Michael, 142
Chenoweth, Kristen, 7
Cherry Orchard, The, 45
Chess, 25
Chicago, 38

choreographer, 3, 5, 54, 55, 82, 84–87, 89–91, 95, 100, 125, 137
choreography, 3, 34, 61, 85–91, 93, 125
Chorus Line, A, 38, 61, 80, 84, 90
City of Angels, 38, 104, 105, 166
classes, 2–4, 18; acting, 4; dance, 3, 4; scene study, 2; singing, 4; voice, 8
classical theatre, 44
Clemmons, Dave, 156
coaching, vocal, 2, 8
cold reading, 82, 160
college auditions, 23, 26, 60, 88, 139–58
College Confidential, 156
combined auditions, 60, 65, 67, 81, 82, 88
comedy songs, 36, 37, 47
Company, 40
community theatre, 4, 5, 11, 100, 102, 104, 122–24, 137
confidence, auditioning with, viii, 19, 43, 46, 54, 64,71, 83, 89, 91, 93, 147
contemporary commercial music (CCM), 27, 33–35, 47
contemporary musical theatre, 24, 25, 34, 44
contracts, 100, 101, 160
country/rockabilly, 29
cover letter, 12, 127, 133–37
Crowd You're in with, The, 45
Crucible, The, 45
cruise lines, 99, 101, 125
cutting (song), 14, 25, 43
Cymbeline, 44

Dal Vera, Rocco, 68, 179
dance: auditions, 16, 84–91; ballet, 3; call, 13, 73, 84–93; tap, 3; jazz, 3; social, 3; modern, 3; salsa, 3; swing, 3
dancers who sing, 12, 84
Danny and the Deep Blue Sea, 45

Dave Clemmons College Advisory Program, 156
David and Goliath, 179
Death of a Salesman, 45
Deer, Joe, 68, 179
"Defying Gravity," 33, 38
DeLugg, Milton, 23
DeMille, Agnes, 3, 86
Dewing, Joy, vii, viii, 30
Diary of Anne Frank, The, 46
Dimond, Christopher, 25
Diner, 28
director, 44, 79, 80–83, 87–92, 95, 99, 100–105, 109, 111–13, 118–22, 124–27, 134, 136, 137, 159
dirty sugar, 108
disco, 28
"Disneyland," 38
Doll's House, A, 45
"dot" (staying off), 66, 67, 77
drama, realist, 45
Drama Bookshop, 45
driving dramatic songs, 25, 35, 47, 166, 167

Ebb, Fred, 26, 166, 167
Edwards, Matthew, 27, 30–35, 156
Ellington, Duke, 72, 165, 175
"Empty Chairs at Empty Tables," 25
Equity Membership Candidacy (EMC), 120, 182
Every Little Step, 80

"Faerie" music, 29
Fences, 45
finances, 100, 101
Finn, William, 26, 166, 167
Flaherty, Stephen, 26, 166, 167
Flick, The, 45
Floyd Collins, 29
Footloose, 71
Forever Plaid, 14, 28
Formato, Lynne Kurdziel, 89–91

Fosse, Bob, 3, 86
Freeing the Artistic Mind, 179
Freeman, Warren, 82
Friml, Rudolf, 37
Full Monty, The, 28
Funny Girl, 38, 175

Gattelli, Christopher, 86
Gealt, Jonathan Reid, 25
Gershwin, George, 21, 23, 163, 164
Gershwin, Ira, 21, 23, 163, 164
Get on My Sides, 82, 95
"Gethsemane," 38
"Getting to Know You," 38
Ghosts, 45
Gilbert, W. S., 37
Gilbert and Sullivan Players, 37
Gilman, Rebecca, 45
Girl Crazy, 38
Glass Menagerie, The, 45, 46
"Golden Age of Musical Theatre," 22, 24, 26, 35, 37, 51, 146
Golden Boy, 45
Good News, 46
Good People, 45
"Goodbye," 25
"Gorgeous," 38
Grease, 28, 46
Great White Way, 30
"Greatest Star, The" 38
Greek theatre, 45
Gregor, Derek, 25
Guettel, Adam, 26
Guys and Dolls, 38, 165
Gypsy, 71

Hair, 2, 16, 22, 26, 31, 90, 166, 171
Hairspray, 28, 174
Hamilton, 25, 29, 30, 166
Hamlet, 44
Hammerstein II, Oscar, 22, 24
Hands on a Hard Body, 30
Harburg, E. Y., 23

hard rock, 28
Harnick, Sheldon, 24, 164, 165
Hart, Lorenz, 23
headshots, 4, 5, 9, 12, 14, 16, 18, 64, 65, 94, 107–18, 136, 137, 160
Hedda Gabler, 45
Herbert, Victor, 37
High Fidelity, 25, 28
"Hit Me with a Hot Note," 71, 175
H.M.S. Pinafore, 37
Hoggett, Steven, 86
"Hold On," 25
horizontal songs, 24
"How Could I Ever Know," 25

"I Am the Very Model of a Modern Major General," 37
"I Can't Stand Still," 71
"I Dreamed a Dream," 38, 175, 176
"I Enjoy Being a Girl," 51
"I Got Rhythm," 38
"I Met a Girl," 49, 51, 165
I Think You Think I Love You, 46
Ibsen, Henrik, 45, 169
"If I Loved You," 35
"In My Own Little Corner," 33
In the Heights, 29, 30, 167
interviews, 108, 139, 152–55, 158
"It's Only a Paper Moon," 23

"Jazz Standards," 22, 23, 27
Jenna P. Photography, 109, 113, *114–17*
Jersey Boys, 27, 28
Joe Turner's Come and Gone, 45
Jonson, Ben, 45, 169
journal keeping, 5, 77, 80, 98, 136, 140
jukebox musical, 27

Kander, John, 26, 166, 167
King and I, The, 38
King Lear, 44
Kinky Boots, 28

Kiss Me, Kate, 38, 172
Kitt, Tom, 26, 166, 167
Kooman, Michael, 25
Kopit, Arthur, 26

LaChiusa, Michael John, 26
Legally Blonde, 36
Lerner, Alan Jay, 24, 165
Les Miserables, 25, 31, 38, 175
Libkin, Cary, 36
libretto, 10, 80, 182
Light Princess, The, 29
Linderman, Ed, 1, 67
Lindsay-Abaire, David, 45, 170
Lion King, The, 90
Lippa, Andrew, 26
Little Night Music, A, 93
Little Shop of Horrors, 38, 176
Little Women, 38
Lobby Hero, 45
Loesser, Frank, 24, 165
Loewe, Frederick, 24, 165
Lonergan, Kenneth, 45
Long Day's Journey into Night, 45
lyric analysis, 42
Lysistrata Jones, 29, 30

Ma Rainey's Black Bottom, 45
MacBeth, 44
Maltby Jr., Richard, 26, 166, 167
Mamma Mia, 27, 28
Mannis, Robert, 108
Marlowe, Christopher, 45, 169
Marvellous Wonderettes, The, 28
mass auditions, 65, 148
Matilda, 51, 172
Mauritius, 45
"Me," 38
Me and Juliet, 41
Measure for Measure, 44
Meisner, Sanford, 68, 75, 142, 179
Memphis, 28
Menzel, Idina, 7

Michaelson, Ingrid, 29
Mikado, The, 37
Miller, Arthur, 45, 170
Miranda, Lin-Manuel, 85, 166, 167
monologue books (value of), 5, 6, 18
monologues, 5–7, 19, 44–47, 146, 160
Moon for the Misbegotten, A, 45
Motown, 28, 173
Motown, 28
Movin' Out, 27
"Mr. Cellophane," 38
Much Ado about Nothing, 44
Music Man, The, 36
Musical Theatre College Auditions
    (MTCA), 156
musical theatre degree programs,
    140–46
Musical Theatre Educators Alliance
    (MTEA), 139
My Fair Lady, 38
"My Favorite Things," 38

national tour, 26, 52, 61, 74, 85, 99,
    101, 123, 151
National Unified Auditions, 148, 149
Never Eat Alone, 179
New England Theatre Conference
    (NETC), 65, 82
Next to Normal, 26, 30
Nicholaw, Casey, 86
"No Other Love," 41
"Nobody Does It Like Me," 38
Noles, David, 108
nonunion, 15, 99, 102, 103
"Nothing," 38

Odets, Clifford, 45
Off Broadway, 9, 101, 123, 124
Off-Off Broadway, 123, 124
O'Keefe, Lawrence, 26, 166, 167
Oklahoma!, 41
On the Town, 86
Once upon a Mattress, 38

"One Perfect Moment," 25
O'Neill, Eugene, 45
open calls, 12, 41
operetta, 47
"Orange Colored Sky," 23
Oresteia, The, 45
Osnes, Laura, 33

Palladia, 69
Pasek, Benj, 26
Paul, Justin, 26
pay, 11; negotiation, 11, 98, 102, 104, 105
"People Will Say We're in Love," 41
personalization, 40, 47, 51, 57
Phantom of the Opera, The, 31, 38
photo shoot, 108, 110
The Piano Lesson, 45
Pinchbeck, Jenna, 108, 109, 113
Pirates of Penzance, The, 37
Playbill.com, 9, 26, 85
"Poor Wand'ring One," 37
pop/rock, 26–30, 34, 35, 169, 174, 182
"Popular," 38
Porter, Cole, 23, 164, 165, 173
positive attitude, 72, 89
Practical Handbook for the Actor, A, 2, 68, 179
preparation, 17, 39, 40
preparing music: cutting and marking, 41–43; "price tag" of, 6, 24, 38
Priscilla: Queen of the Desert, 28
Pro Actors Lab, 55
Producers Club, 123
"Proud Lady," 25
"Pulled," 38
Pump Boys and Dinettes, 29
Purple Cow, 179

Rabbit Hole, 45
Ragtime, 25
Rebeck, Theresa, 45
Rent, 26, 29

repertoire, 19–47, 57, 65, 68, 89, 94, 109, 139, 146, 150, 160, 163–77
repertoire book, 5, 7, 8, 16–47, 57, 65, 68, 149; "A" book, 7, 18, 20, 21, 40, 47; "B" book (audition works in progress), 7, 20, 38, 47; online, 9, 21, 156; resources for actors, 179
résumé, 5, 8–12, 16, 18, 65, 76, 107, 118–32, 137, 160
rhythm and blues, 28
Robbins, Jerome, 3, 86
Rock of Ages, 27–30
rock songs, 25, 28–30
Rock the Audition, 179
Rock the Audition website (www.rock-the-audition.com), 28
Rodgers, Richard, 22, 23
Roman theatre, 45
Romberg, Sigmund, 37
Romeo and Juliet, 44
Rose, Billy, 23
Rose, Laura, 108
Ross, Diana, 29
Ross, Jerry, 24
Rotenberg, David, 55

Sanders, Sheri, 28–30, 58, 69, 179
Sanford Meisner on Acting, 68, 179
Saturday Night Fever, 28
Saunders, Mary, 153
scams, 9, 94, 104
School of Rock, 51
Schwartz, Stephen, 7, 26, 167
Screen Actors' Guild and American Federation of Television and Radio Artists (SAG-AFTRA), 120, 183
Seagull, The, 45
Seasaw, 38
Secret Garden, The, 25
Seminar, 45
Shakespeare, William, 44, 45
Shanley, John Patrick, 45
Shaw, George Bernard, 123, 169

"She Loves Me," 49
She Loves Me, 38, 92, 165
Shire, David, 26, 166, 167
Show Boat, 47
Show Business, 9
"Shy," 38
Simon, Neil, 46
singer call, 85
singers who move, 12, 84
Skinner, Randy, 3, 85
slating, 63–65
Smile, 38
*So You Want to Sing Rock 'n' Roll: A
    Guide for Professionals*, 27, 35, 179
Sondheim, Stephen, 26, 40, 61, 93
Sound of Music, The, 38
South Pacific, 30
Southeastern Theatre Conference
    (SETC), 60, 65, 80, 82, 88
Spamalot, 36
Spike Heels, 45
Spotify, 27
Spring Awakening, 26, 29, 30
standards (musical), 21–24, 35, 37
standing during audition, 64, 66, 67,
    71, 147
Star Spangled Girl, The, 46
Stein, Willie, 23
Steps, 86
StrawHat Auditions, 65, 80, 82
Stroman, Susan, 3, 86
style tags, 27
Styne, Jule, 24
Suddenly Last Summer, 45
Sullivan, Arthur, 37
Summer and Smoke, 45
"Sun Whose Rays, The," 37

Taffetas, The, 28
taking direction, 72
Talley's Folly, 45
Taming of the Shrew, The, 44
"Think of Me," 38

This Is Our Youth, 45
Thoroughly Modern Millie, 46, 71, 176
Three Sisters, The, 45
"Till There Was You," 36
"Tin Pan Alley," 22, 27
Toxic Avenger, 29
training, 2, 31; vocal, 2
transitions, 70, 71
transposition (of music), 21
trunk songs, 23
Twelfth Night, 44
type out, 12, 121, 122

Unified Professional Theatre Auditions
    (UPTA), 65, 80
union jobs, 15, 99, 102, 103
University Resident Theatre
    Association (URTA), 82
up-tempo songs, 22, 23

"Vanilla Ice Cream," 38
vertical songs, 23
Village Light Opera Group, 37
vocal teacher, 22, 27, 35
vocal training, 30–35
Voice, The, 1
voice pedagogy, 32–34
voice systems, 31

Waiting for Lefty, 45
Waitress, 29
warming up, 17
We Will Rock You, 28
Webber, Andrew Lloyd, 10, 31
websites (casting calls): www.
    actorsequity.org, 9; www.backstage.
    com, 9; www.performlink.com
    (Chicago), 9; www.playbill.com, 9;
    www.tcg.org (ArtSearch), 9; www.
    upta.org, 9
websites (for finding material):
    www.amazon.com, 21; www.
    dramabookshop.com, 21

websites (sheet music): www.
    musicnotes.com, 21; www.
    sheetmusicdirect.com, 21
Wedding Singer, The, 25, 28
Weill, Kurt, 23
West Side Story, 13, 21, 89
"What Do I Need with Love," 71,
    176
"What I Did for Love," 90
Who's Tommy, The, 28
Wicked, 7, 38, 51, 92
Williams, Tennessee, 45, 46
Wilson, August, 45

Wilson, Lanford, 45
Wise, Jim, 39
Wiz, The, 28
Women of Manhattan, 45
Wonder of the World, 45
"wrong song" exercise, 36, 37

X Factor, The, 1

Yeston, Maury, 26
"You Can Always Count on Me," 38
Young Frankenstein, 86
YouTube, 3, 69, 85

ABOUT THE AUTHOR

Jonathan Flom was the Musical Theatre Program Coordinator at Shenandoah Conservatory in Winchester, VA, where he taught from 2007–2016. At the end of the 2015–2016 school year, he decided to pursue his interest in international musical theatre training by relocating to Oslo, Norway. In addition to the first edition of *Get the Callback* (2009), he is also the author of *Act Like It's Your Business: Branding and Marketing Strategies for Actors* (Scarecrow Press, 2013). Flom has taught Branding for Artists, Meisner Technique, and Acting for Musical Theatre around the globe, including some of the world's top academies in Sweden, Norway, Italy, Taiwan, and Australia. He also directed the Danish language premiere of *A New Brain* in Fredericia, Denmark.

Stateside, he has directed professional productions in New York, Chicago, Pennsylvania, Vermont, New Hampshire, Iowa, and Virginia. In 2014, he directed the College/Regional Premiere of *Green Day's American Idiot* at Shenandoah Conservatory. Flom is also a proud member (and current Vice President for Conferences) of the Musical Theatre Educators' Alliance—MTEA (www.mteducators.org)—a global organization of higher education programs dedicated to the improvement of training for the musical theatre profession.

He holds a BFA in Musical Theatre as well as an MFA in Directing for the Musical Theatre Stage from Penn State University. For more information, visit www.jonathanflom.com. For private coaching or school workshops, you can email directly at Actorcoach@hotmail.com.